try

not do it till I am no more it ~~[illegible]~~ may be considered

respected, and [illegible] happ[illegible] man alone consulted.

be derived from good intentions, and from the ex-

erious stations through a period of forty years, who

who has borne a part in most of the great transac-

ry.

deepest in my convictions ~~that~~ is that the Union of the States

garded as a Pandora with her box opened; and the dis-

urks into Paradise.

JAMES MADISON

and the Search for Nationhood

James Sharples (ca. 1751–1811), *James Madison* (from life), pastel on paper, 9 in x 7 in, Philadelphia, 1796–97. Courtesy Independence National Historical Park Collection, Philadelphia, Pennsylvania.

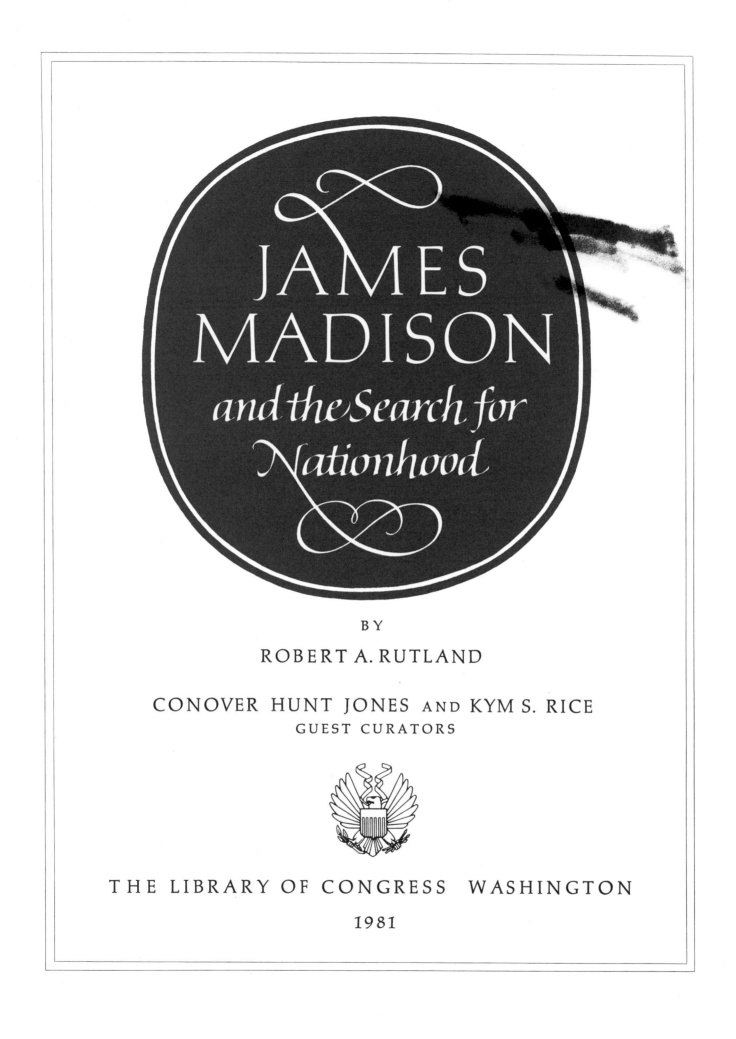

JAMES MADISON
and the Search for Nationhood

BY

ROBERT A. RUTLAND

CONOVER HUNT JONES AND KYM S. RICE
GUEST CURATORS

THE LIBRARY OF CONGRESS WASHINGTON

1981

LIBRARY OF CONGRESS CATALOGING IN PUBLICATION DATA

Rutland, Robert Allen, 1922-
James Madison and the search for nationhood.

Published in conjunction with the inaugural exhibit in the Madison galleries at the Library of Congress, Nov. 1981-May 1982.
Bibliography: p.
1. Madison, James, 1757-1836—Exhibitions. 2. United States—Politics and government—1783-1865—Exhibitions. 3. Presidents—United States—Biography—Exhibitions. I. Library of Congresses. II. Title.
E342.R87 973.5'1'0924 [B] 81-607967
ISBN 0-844-0363-6 AACR2

JAMES MADISON AND THE SEARCH FOR NATIONHOOD is published in conjunction with the inaugural exhibition held in the James Madison Memorial Building of the Library of Congress, November 17, 1981, through May 31, 1982.

For sale by the
SUPERINTENDENT OF DOCUMENTS
U.S. Government Printing Office
Washington, D.C. 20402

JACKET COVER:

Charles Willson Peale (1741–1827), *James Madison* (1757–1836) (from life), oil on canvas, 23¼ in x 19 in, Philadelphia, ca. 1792. Courtesy Thomas Gilcrease Institute of American History and Art, Tulsa, Oklahoma.

ENDPAPERS:

James Madison, *Advice to my Country*, Orange, Virginia, 1834. James Madison Papers, Library of Congress.

CONTENTS

FOREWORD

James Madison has stood so long in the shadow of Thomas Jefferson that he has become one of the most underestimated figures in our nation's history. Rich in the private virtues needed for a great public man, Madison was adept at enlisting his eminent contemporaries. He was not greedy for fame. His combination of qualities was rare even in a generation of versatile men. How many other statesmen have so brilliantly combined political effectiveness with philosophic clarity and polemic eloquence? He negotiated crucial compromises in the Constitutional Convention, and yet in *The Federalist* he bequeathed us a classic of political theory. No one was more persuasive in advocating the Constitution for a strong central government, or more effective in demanding bulwarks to the rights of citizens in its first ten amendments.

During his presidency, faced by threats of secession, he stood firm in his insistence that sectional chauvinisms be submerged in a national purpose. It was during the War of 1812 (which his enemies called "Mr. Madison's War"), the second War of Independence, that the first Library of Congress (then in the Capitol) was burned by the British invaders of Washington.

At long last, James Madison has his memorial on Capitol Hill, and in this grand Library building. As the bicentennial of the framing of our Constitution approaches, here we provide monumental evidence that our nation has not forgotten the chief architect and advocate of our still-vital Constitution. Historians will probably agree that James Madison was less effective as a politician than as a statesman, a scholar, and a political philosopher. If the politician must have his eye on the next election, and the statesman on the next generation, this Library, invigorated by the quiet scholarly spirit of Madison, can remind us of the vistas of the past, and future, generations.

DANIEL J. BOORSTIN
The Librarian of Congress

ACKNOWLEDGMENTS

When the federal government moved to Washington in 1800, the Sixth Congress created the Library of Congress for the use of its members. After British troops burned the majority of the collection in the late summer of 1814, President James Madison approved an act of Congress authorizing the purchase of the library of former president Thomas Jefferson. Madison, a noted bibliophile, must have been pleased to know his friend's great collection would now be available to the country's legislators. Indeed, as a young member of the Continenal Congress, Madison had been present when the idea of a congressional library was first proposed; a list of some three hundred books intended for that library survives today in Madison's hand. For lack of funds, the books on this list were never purchased.

In honor of James Madison, probably the most intellectual of all our presidents, ground was broken in 1971 for construction of the Library's James Madison Memorial Building. This one and a half million square foot structure was dedicated in April 1980. "James Madison and the Search for Nationhood" has been organized to inaugurate the building's large exhibition space.

This publication and the exhibition on which it is based have been prepared under the auspices of the Library of Congress and coordinated by the Exhibits Office. We wish to acknowledge the generous support and participation of Daniel J. Boorstin, the Librarian of Congress. Michael Carrigan, Exhibits Officer, Leonard Faber, Jon Freshour, and their staff have all given generously of their time and expertise to ensure the success of the project. Ingrid Maar, Curator of Exhibitions, has overseen with enthusiasm and determination the many details connected with a project of this size. We are very grateful for her contribution.

The Publishing Office of the Library directed the production of this book, and we wish to thank Dana J. Pratt, Director of Publishing, Johanna Craig, Production Manager, and James Hardin, the editor of this publication, for their assistance. Gerard Valerio of Bookmark Studio was the designer. His many suggestions and handsome design are greatly appreciated.

The project is indebted to Robert A. Rutland, Editor-in-Chief of *The Papers of James Madison*. As well as writing the essay for this publication, Dr. Rutland graciously advised us on many aspects of the project.

We wish to acknowledge the work of the late Adrienne Koch, who prepared an extensive survey of the papers of James Madison for the Library in the 1960s. Her unpublished report provided valuable guidance in the selection of manuscript materials for the publication and exhibition.

The Board of Trustees of the Dallas Historical Society and John W. Crain, its director, graciously allowed Conover Hunt Jones to participate in this project as one of the Guest Curators.

The American Institute of Architects Foundation kindly permitted access to files of their past exhibition "Dolley and the Great Little Madison" and supplied a number of photographs for the publication. Our thanks go to Jeanne Hodges, Alison MacTavish, and Jane Mutchler for their help.

In order to present the rich panorama of James Madison's life and achievements, it was necessary to reach outside the substantial collections of the Library of Congress. With gratitude we acknowledge the participation of the many institutions and private collectors who have so generously shared their holdings.

Many divisions of the Library of Congress assisted in the research for the project. In particular we would like to acknowledge the extraordinary support of Bernard C. Reilly, Jerry Kearns, and Mary Ison of the Prints and Photographs Division; Janet Chase of the Librarian's Office; Gary Kohn, Fred Coker, Charles Kelley, Ruth Nicholson, Marianne Roos, and Paul Sifton of the Manuscript Division; Margaret Brown, Norvell Jones, and George Hall of the Preservation Office; David Doyle of the Photoduplication Service; Peter Van Wingen and Clark Evans of the Rare Book and Special Collections Division; and the staffs of the Serial and Government Publications Division, the Music Division, and the Geography and Map Division.

Special thanks to the many colleagues, scholars, and private collectors who have given hospitality, advice, and assistance during the course of the project: Mr. and Mrs. Marshall Allen, Edmund Berkeley, Jr., Mary Black, Mabel H. Brandon, Georgia B. Bumgardner, Elizabeth Taylor Childs, George Chittenden, Mark Clark, Herb Collins, Clement E. Conger, S. Cooper Dawson, Jr., Mona Dearborn and the staff of the Catalog of American Portraits, Stuart Downs, Roman Drazinowsky, Ron Dwezek, Monroe Fabian, Ken Finkel, Virginius C. Hall, Jr., Richard B. Harrington, Charles M. Harris, Chester Hazard, Graham Hood, John K. Howat, Morgan Jones, John Melville Jennings, Donald Kelley, Margaret Klapthor, Robert F. Looney, Louis Manarin, Carolyn Margolis, Tom Mason, Lisa McBriety, David Meschutt, Christine Miles, John C. Milley, Betty C. Monkman, Cranwell and Sally Montgomery, Frederick D. Nichols, Lois Oglesby, Nicholas A. Pappas, Peter Parker, Paula Pumplin, Virginia Queitzsch, Rebecca T. Perrine, Joseph T. Rankin, Richard Reilly, Mark Rice, Kazuyo Sato, Ed Schamel, Karol A. Schmiegel, Mrs. Marion duPont Scott, Carroll Kem Shackelford, George Green Shackelford, Lynne A. Leopold-Sharp, Sarah Shield, Nelly Smith, Susan G. Stein, Frank Trapp, Mary Ann Thompson, Lila Tyng, and Wendy Wick.

Conover Hunt Jones
Kym Rice
Guest Curators

LENDERS TO THE EXHIBITION

Mr. and Mrs. Marshall E. Allen, Orange, Virginia
American Antiquarian Society, Worcester, Massachusetts
The American Institute of Architects Foundation, Washington, District of Columbia
Amherst College, Mead Art Museum, Amherst, Massachusetts
Brown University, Providence, Rhode Island
Century Club Association, New York, New York
Chicago Historical Society, Chicago, Illinois
George H. Chittenden, Rye, New York
The Chrysler Museum, Norfolk, Virginia
The Cleveland Museum of Art, Cleveland, Ohio
Mrs. Margaret Lee Pollock Cobb, Blacksburg, Virginia
The Colonial Williamsburg Foundation, Williamsburg, Virginia
The James S. Copley Library, La Jolla, California
The Corcoran Gallery of Art, Washington, District of Columbia
S. Cooper Dawson, Jr., Alexandria, Virginia
The Denver Art Museum, Denver, Colorado
Fraunces Tavern Museum, New York, New York
The Free Library of Philadelphia, City of Philadelphia, Pennsylvania
Greensboro Historical Museum, Inc., Greensboro, North Carolina
The Historical Society of Pennsylvania, Philadelphia, Pennsylvania
Hirschl and Adler Galleries, New York, New York
Independence National Historical Park, National Park Service, United States Department of Interior, Philadelphia, Pennsylvania
The Library Company of Philadelphia, Philadelphia, Pennsylvania
The James Madison Museum, Orange, Virginia
The Mariners Museum, Newport News, Virginia
The Maryland Historical Society, Baltimore, Maryland
Massachusetts Historical Society, Boston, Massachusetts
The Paul Mellon Collection, Upperville, Virginia

The Metropolitan Museum of Art, New York, New York
National Archives and Records Service, Washington, District of Columbia
The National Museum of American History, Smithsonian Institution, Washington, District of Columbia
The National Portrait Gallery, Smithsonian Institution, Washington, District of Columbia
The New Jersey Historical Society, Newark, New Jersey
The New-York Historical Society, New York, New York
The New York Public Library, New York, New York
Oneida Historical Society, Utica, New York
Presbyterian Historical Society, The United Presbyterian Church, Philadelphia, Pennsylvania
Princeton University, Princeton, New Jersey
Johnny Scott, Gordonsville, Virginia
Mr. and Mrs. George Green Shackelford, Blacksburg, Virginia
Louis Alan Talley, Washington, District of Columbia
The United States Naval Academy Museum, Annapolis, Maryland
United States Senate, Washington, District of Columbia
University of Virginia Library, Charlottesville, Virginia
The Valentine Museum, Richmond, Virginia
Virginia Historical Society, Richmond, Virginia
Virginia State Library, Richmond, Virginia
Washington and Lee University, Lexington, Virginia
West Point Museum, United States Military Academy, West Point, New York
The White House, Washington, District of Columbia
The Henry Francis du Pont Winterthur Museum, Winterthur, Delaware
Yale University Art Gallery, New Haven, Connecticut

John Trumbull (1756–1843), *Resignation of General Washington, December 23, 1783* (life portrait of Madison, who is to the right of the left door frame), oil on canvas, 20 in x 30 in, New York, 1816–24. Courtesy Yale University Art Gallery, New Haven, Connecticut, Trumbull Collection.

CHRONOLOGY

JAMES MADISON	AND	HIS TIMES
Born March 16, Port Conway, Virginia	1751	Colonial population estimated at one million
	1754	French and Indian War (1754-63)
Early education at Donald Robertson's school, Virginia	1762	
	1765	Reign of George III (1760-1820); Stamp Act
Tutorial studies at home with Rev. Thomas Martin	1767	Parliament passes Townshend Duties; John Dickinson's *Letters of a Farmer in Pennsylvania*
Student, College of New Jersey, Princeton	1769	First permanent missions established, California
	1770	Boston Massacre; colonial population estimated at 2,205,000
Earns bachelor's degree; returns to Virginia	1772	
Begins legal studies	1773	Boston Tea Party; Haydn's *Farewell* Symphony
	1775	Battle of Lexington and Concord; second Continental Congress, Philadephia
Delegate, Virginia Convention, Williamsburg	1776	Declaration of Independence; Thomas Paine's *Common Sense*
Defeated for seat in Virginia House of Delegates; chosen for Council of State	1777	
Delegate to Continental Congress; supports western lands motion, pressed Mississippi navigation rights and national solvency	1780	American Academy of Arts and Sciences founded, Boston
	1781	Articles of Confederation ratified
Short engagement to Kitty Floyd; retires from Congress	1783	Peace treaty signed with Great Britain
Seat in Virginia House of Delegates	1784	
Elected to American Philosophical Society; writes "Memorial and Remonstrance" anonymously	1785	
Attends Virgina Assembly and Annapolis Convention	1786	Enactment of Virginia Statute for Religious Freedom; U.S. Mint established by Congress

Returns to Continental Congress; prepares Virginia Plan; Delegate to Constitutional Convention; the *Federalist* essays published	1787	Shays's Rebellion put down
Delegate, Virginia Ratifying Convention	1788	Constitution ratified
Elected to U.S. House of Representatives; sponsors Bill of Rights	1789	George Washington inaugurated first president; French Revolution begins; William Blake's *Songs of Innocence*
	1790	Alexander Hamilton's *Report on the Public Credit*
Leads Republican opposition in Congress		Cornerstone laid, U.S. Capitol, Washington; Mary Wollstonecraft's *A Vindication of the Rights of Women*
"Helvidius" essay	1793	U.S. proclamation of neutrality; execution of Louis XVI and Marie Antoinette; Whitney's cotton gin patented
Seeks commercial restrictions against Great Britain; marries Dolley Payne Todd	1794	Jay's Treaty; Peale's Museum opens in Philadelphia
Opposes Jay's Treaty	1796	
Declines mission to France; retires to Montpelier	1797	John Adams begins term as second president; XYZ affair
Virginia and Kentucky Resolutions	1798	Alien and Sedition Acts; quasi-war with France
Elected to state House of Delegates; writes defense of Virginia and Kentucky Resolutions	1799	Washington dies; colonial population over five million; Goya's *Los Caprichos*
	1800	Government moves to Washington; establishment of the Library of Congress; Spain cedes Louisiana Territory to France
Appointed Secretary of State (1801-9)	1801	Thomas Jefferson inaugurated as third president; Tripolitan War (1801-5)
Leads in shaping foreign policy	1803	Louisiana Purchase
	1804	Lewis and Clark expedition; death of Hamilton at the hands of Aaron Burr; Napoleon's reign begins (1804-14)
	1805	Jefferson begins second term; formulation of Third Coalition Against France
	1806	Monroe-Pinkney Treaty
Embargo Act	1807	Congress prohibits African slave trade; Milan Decree; Chesapeake and Leopard incident
Elected fourth president; George Clinton, Vice President	1808	Beethoven's Fifth Symphony

Inaugurated	1809	Repeal of embargo; Nonintercourse Act signed
Resumes trade with France; annexation of West Florida	1810	
	1811	Battle of Tippecanoe; Bank of the United States refused recharter
	1812	War declared with Great Britain; surrender of Detroit; Battle of *Constitution* and *Guerriere*
Begins second term; Elbridge Gerry, Vice President	1813	British blockade of American ports; U.S. troops reoccupy Detroit; Jane Austen's *Pride and Prejudice*
Reorganization of cabinet; British invade Washington, burn public buildings	1814	End of embargo; Hartford Convention; Francis Scott Key's "Star Spangled Banner"; U.S. Mission to Ghent
	1815	U.S. defeats British at New Orleans; Treaty of Ghent ratified; Napoleon defeated at Waterloo
Presidency ends; founder, American Colonization Society, Agricultural Society of Albemarle; retires to Montpelier	1817	Founding of University of Virginia; James Monroe becomes fifth president; John Trumbull paints *Declaration of Independence*
	1819	Treaty with Spain
	1820	Missouri Compromise; Santa Fe Trail opened
Refuses to publish Federal Convention Notes	1821	U.S. population estimated at 9,700,000
	1822	Colony of Liberia founded under sponsorship of American Colonization Society
	1825	University of Virginia opens; Hudson River school of landscape painting
Rector, University of Virginia	1826	Death of Jefferson and Monroe; John Quincy Adams sixth president; first overland expedition to California
Speech, Virginia Constitutional Convention	1829	
Rebuts Hayne in *North American Review*	1830	Andrew Jackson, seventh president; Webster-Hayne debate; first issue of Godey's *Lady Book*
	1831	Nullification controversy continues; *Liberator* begins publication; invention of the McCormack reaper; formation of Democratic party
"Advice to My Country"	1834	
Madison dies, June 28; interred at Montpelier	1836	Texas Independence; Transcendentalist movement begins

JAMES MADISON

and the Search for Nationhood

Joseph Sansom (1767–1826), *James Madison Esq*^{r}. *Representative in Congress for the State of Virginia Aged 30*, black ink on paper, 4¾ in x 3¾ in, Philadelphia, ca. 1781–92. Courtesy Historical Society of Pennsylvania, Philadelphia, Perot Collection.

INTRODUCTION

James Madison was "the greatest man in the world."

This assessment came from a friendly source, but the time was 1790, when George Washington was president and the world was peopled by the likes of Goethe, Lafayette, Mozart, Napoleon, Nelson, Haydn, and Jefferson. Indeed, the remark was *made* by Jefferson. Thus we see that Madison (who was barely past his thirty-eighth birthday) had already impressed a man of sophistication and learning whose standards were high. Jefferson had only recently returned from Europe, where he met and conversed with philosophers and statesmen, rubbed elbows with fellow minister John Adams in London, and held a loose grip on some bright young Americans who were making the grand tour from his Paris base. Benjamin Rush, ever curious as to what had caused American success in the recent revolution (and a speculator as to where it would lead) had pressed Jefferson for an opinion on the Americans he had known from 1774 onward. Possibly Jefferson's response took Dr. Rush aback. Was Jefferson merely trying to shock Rush, or did he sincerely think that James Madison was the greatest man in the world?

There is every reason to believe he did, despite the rough handling Madison's reputation subsequently received after he moved into the White House in 1809 and became subject to all the invectives Americans reserve for their chief executive. Not only was Madison attacked by the newspapers and Federalist politicians generally, he was also sniped at by members of his own Democratic Republican party, almost from the day he crossed the White House threshold.

Gilbert Stuart (1755–1828), *James Madison,* oil on canvas, 40 in x 32 in, Boston?, 1822. Courtesy Mead Art Museum, Amherst College, Massachusetts, bequest of Herbert L. Pratt.

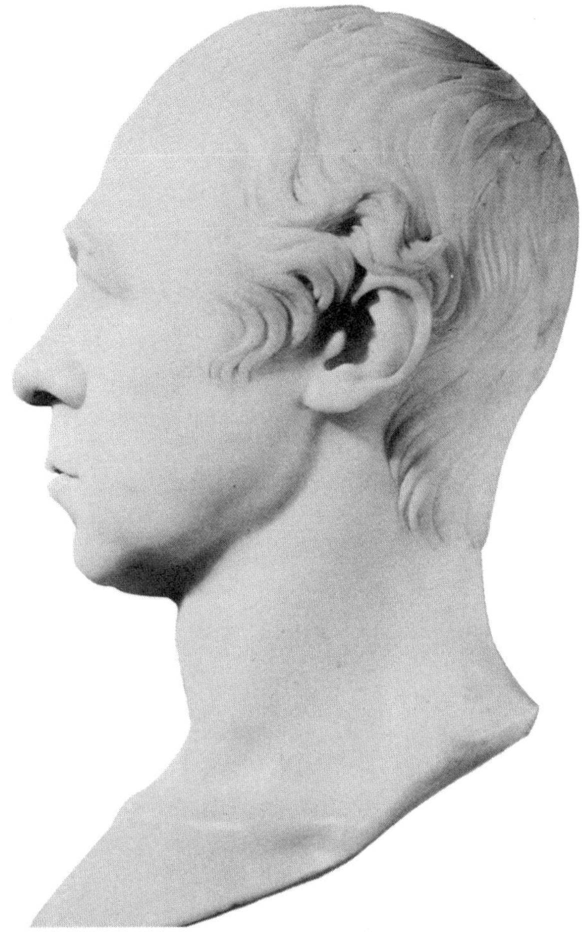

Giuseppe Ceracchi (ca. 1740–1801), *James Madison* (from life), alabaster, marble, 28½ in x 23½ in, Florence, 1794. Collection of Diplomatic Reception Rooms, Department of State, Washington, D.C. Photograph courtesy of the American Institute of Architects Foundation/the Octagon, Washington, D.C.

Most of his first four years as president were gloomy, reaching a nadir in August 1814 when he had to flee from Washington as British troops moved in from the other side of the capital. Three forces sustained Madison during all those dreary days, allowing him to finish his second term in a glow of warm appreciation from his countrymen and to retire in contentment. The three sustaining forces were his wife, Dolley, his strong intellectual powers, and his bedrock belief in the United States of America as a union of free people committed to the ideals of the American Revolution. To Jefferson's brief program of life, liberty, and the pursuit of happiness, Madison would have added only one word: Union.

Some two hundred and thirty years after Madison's birth in tidewater Virginia, Americans are still uncertain as to where Madison fits into our early history. In 1962 the late John F. Kennedy said he thought of Madison as "one of our most underrated presidents," a remark that pleased scholars who have long admired the force of *Federalist* paper no. 10 and looked with awe at Madison's record in the Federal Convention of 1787. Still, Madison's critics are quick to point out that these were accomplishments of the young Madison. What about the Madison who was Jefferson's understudy for nearly twenty

John Vanderlyn (1775–1852), *James Madison* (from life), charcoal on tinted paper, 10¾ in x 8 in, America, 1816. Courtesy Denver Art Museum, Colorado, Edward T. and Tullah Hanley Collection.

Chester Harding (1792–1866), *James Madison* (from life), oil on canvas, 30 in x 25 in, Richmond?, ca. 1829–30. Courtesy Washington and Lee University, Lexington, Virginia.

years, who served faithfully but without glory as secretary of state, and who then was awarded the presidency as a prize earned by his loyalty?

We have to remember that every president has had his critics. Even Washington was attacked by the opposition press during his second term, and his vice-president spoke of him privately as "an old mutton head." It is, perhaps, fair to say that the better presidents have had to suffer harsher criticism than the mediocre ones. Most presidential historians acknowledge that Abraham Lincoln, Franklin D. Roosevelt, Andrew Jackson, Harry Truman, Thomas Jefferson, and James Madison were mercilessly assailed by newspaper editors, political hacks, members of Congress, and disgruntled constituents. Yet with the perspective of generations we can see that the leadership these presidents offered made placid times in office impossible. Indeed, Truman himself was another admirer of Madison. The more our thirty-third president read of the fourth president's conduct and accomplishments the more he elevated Madison in his private talks and public speeches.

Thus we see that as fashions change, our views of men change, too. Madison suffered terribly at the hands of historians such as Henry Adams, who wrote with excessive rancor of the "failures" and "ruin" of Jefferson's presidency and referred to the fourth president as "the weakest of Executives . . . the dullest of men." Adams was not a friendly witness, but so powerful was his writing that generations of Americans read this assessment without blinking. Here we see illustrated the reason why history must be rewritten, and rewritten, and then written again.

Not until recent times has Madison's presidency been carefully reexamined. This gifted Virginian came out of the Piedmont country in 1776, young (twenty-five), short of breath (he spoke so low he could not be heard in some halls), and short of height (he was probably five feet two inches tall). But none of these apparent drawbacks mattered. What counted was Madison's logic, his knowledge, and the good company he kept. These, of course, are never handicaps—but Madison came onto the stage of the American Revolution when the casting was not quite finished. He started as a bit player, but through learning, conviction, and the friends he made Madison was able to work steadily higher in the emerging political drama. Before the Revolution was over, Madison came to direct the final scenes that established American nationhood. His devotion to the revolutionary cause makes him preeminent, from start to finish, in the drama of American history between 1780 and 1815. Little in the political life of the young republic escaped Madison's attention over a critical thirty-five-year span. Clearly, James Madison deserves our attention.

Joshua Fry (ca. 1700–1754) and Peter Jefferson (1708–1757), *A Map of the Most Inhabited part of Virginia* (detail), colored engraving, 31 15/16 in x 50 9/16 in, London, Thomas Jefferys, 1755. Geography and Map Division, Library of Congress.

I

THE VIRGINIA HERITAGE

An old-fashioned expression for a talented gentleman, long since abandoned but once favored by conversational America, was "a man of parts." Anyone who qualified for such a compliment deserved it by personal achievement, and certainly in 1809 as he prepared to take over the ship of state, James Madison was a man of parts. He had come a long way on the dusty road trailing from Montpelier plantation in Orange County, Virginia, to Pennsylvania Avenue in the District of Columbia. As the crow flies it is no more than eighty-five miles from Montpelier to the White House. But the career road which carried Madison from Port Conway, Virginia, to Richmond and Williamsburg and up and down the Atlantic seaboard more times than he could count was a long highway of steady achievement. Struggle? Not in the ordinary sense, for Madison was born to well-to-do parents in tidewater Virginia, the kind of people who constituted the landed gentry in the eighteenth century and who provided America with more remarkable leaders in one generation than have been provided by the people of any other region in the nation since. Historians still are overwhelmed by the circumstances which coalesced in a single decade between 1770 and 1780 to furnish the thirteen colonies and their offspring republic with George Washington, Thomas Jefferson, Patrick Henry, Richard Henry Lee, John Marshall, George Mason, James Monroe, and James Madison. All were born within a radius of 150 miles, and most of them within a few years of each other. Except for Henry, they were all "well born," which meant that none of them had to worry about where his next meal was coming from, and all of them had uncommon ability. This galaxy of talent provided America with enough leadership to win a revolution, start a new nation, develop a unique political system, and carry the idea of self-government beyond anything men had ever dreamed of before. To be sure, the Adamses and the Morrises and the Hamiltons helped. But the Virginia dynasty and the beginnings of American nationhood are inseparable.

Madison worked his way into that heady company by degrees. The oldest of eleven children born to James Madison and Nelly Conway Madison, he first drew breath at the home of his maternal grandmother on the Rappahannock River "on Tuesday Night at 12 o'Clock it being the last of the 5th. & begining of the 6th day of March 1750-1." So the family Bible, now at Princeton University, records. (The date was old style, which means we add eleven days and fix Madison's birth at March 16, 1751, new style.) While Madison was growing up, his parents bundled up their belongings and moved the family inland to an Orange County plantation some fifty-five miles westward. The land was a semi-wilderness but the region was tamed, for the Indians were already far to the west, beyond the Blue Ridge Mountains. James Madison, Sr., had plenty of worries, but Indians were not among them. Leaf wilt, stubborn stumps, pesky insects, a sudden hailstorm, a sulky slave—these were the worries besetting a Virginia tobacco planter. Add to those problems the fluctuating prices paid in England and Scotland for the annual tobacco crop and the infant mortality rate (two of *père* Madison's children died in their first year, and little Reuben when he was four), and the anxieties of Madison's time are spelled out clearly. Even so, eight of the little Madisons grew into adulthood. Nelly Conway bore children, suffered from fevers and diseases, and was constantly in her sickbed. She lived to be a hardy ninety-seven. James Madison, Jr., came from tough stock.

He needed all the help afforded by sturdy genes, for from his earliest days James Madison was what people commonly termed "sickly." Through life he suffered from a variety of ills, the worst being what he described as some persistent disease akin to epilepsy. Like other Americans of his day, Madison also knew bouts with diarrhea, influenza, and hemorrhoids—the last being a particular curse in a society where men moved about on horseback.

Yet Madison survived, sometimes to his own surprise. It is difficult to say whether he was a hypochondriac or not, for he had sickness aplenty in his youth, and as with all men he grew more infirm after he reached his seventies. We know little of the regimen of Montpelier after James Madison, Sr., built onto the opulent plantation mansion (around 1763), except that dozens of

Charles Peale Polk (1767–1822), *Nelly Conway Madison* (Mrs. James Madison Senior, 1732–1829), oil on canvas, 59½ in x 40¹⁵⁄₁₆ in, America, ca. 1798. Maryland Historical Society, Baltimore. Photograph courtesy of the American Institute of Architects Foundation/the Octagon, Washington, D.C.

Charles Peale Polk (1767–1822), *James Madison Senior* (1723–1801), oil on canvas, 63¾ in x 44½ in, America, ca. 1798. Maryland Historical Society, Baltimore. Photograph courtesy of the American Institute of Architects Foundation/the Octagon, Washington, D.C.

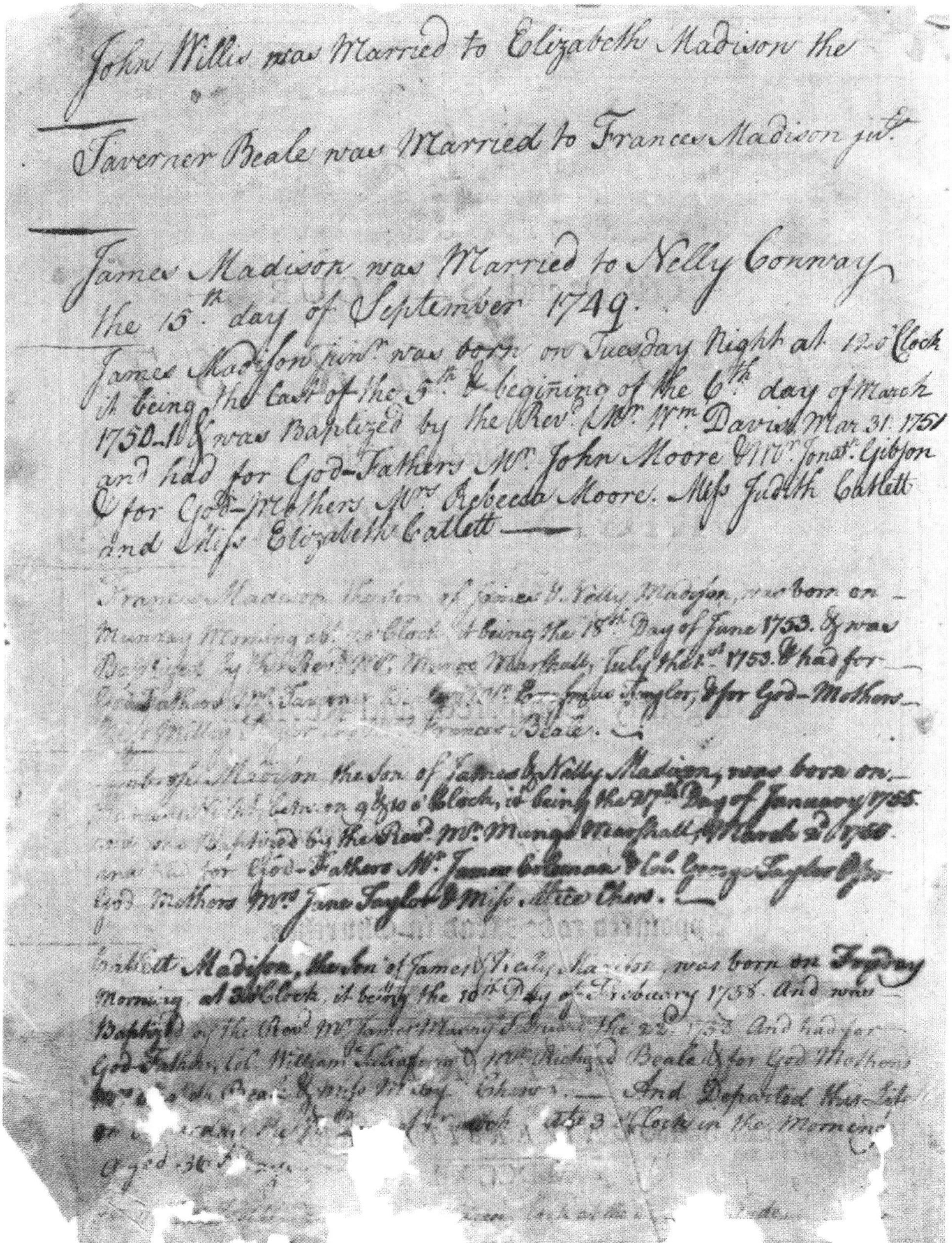
John Willis was Married to Elizabeth Madison the

Taverner Beale was Married to Frances Madison jun.r

James Madison was Married to Nelly Conway
the 15.th day of September 1749.
James Madison jun.r was born on Tuesday Night at 12 o'Clock
it being the last of the 5.th & begining of the 6.th day of March
1750-1 & was Baptized by the Rev.d M.r W.m Davis Mar 31. 1751
and had for God-Fathers M.r John Moore & M.r Jonat.n Gibson
& for God-Mothers M.rs Rebecca Moore. Miss Judith Catlett
and Miss Elizabeth Catlett —

Francis Madison the Son of James & Nelly Madison, was born on
Monday Morning at [illegible] o'Clock it being the 18.th Day of June 1753. & was
Baptized by the Rev.d M.r [illegible] Marshall, July the [illegible] 1753. & had for
God-Fathers M.r Taverner Beale [illegible] Taylor, & for God-Mothers
[illegible] Frances Beale.

[illegible] Madison the Son of James & Nelly Madison, was born on
[illegible] between 9 & 10 o'Clock, it being the [illegible] Day of January 1755
and was Baptized by the Rev.d M.r [illegible] Marshall, [illegible] March [illegible] 1755
and had for God-Fathers M.r James Coleman & Co.l George Taylor & for
God-Mothers M.rs Jane Taylor & Miss Alice Chew.

Catlett Madison, the Son of James & Nelly Madison, was born on Friday
Morning at 3 o'Clock, it being the 10.th Day of February 1758. And was
Baptized by the Rev.d M.r James Marye [illegible] the 22. 1758. And had for
God-Father, Col. William Taliaferro & M.r Richard Beale & for God Mothers
M.rs [illegible] Beale & Miss [illegible] Chew. — And Departed this Life
on [illegible] at 3 o'Clock in the Morning
Aged 30 [illegible]

Entry for the birth of James Madison, Jr., March 16, 1751 (March 5, 1751 old style) in Madison family *Holy Bible*, London, Thomas Baskett, 1759. Courtesy Princeton University Library, New Jersey. Willard Starks photograph.

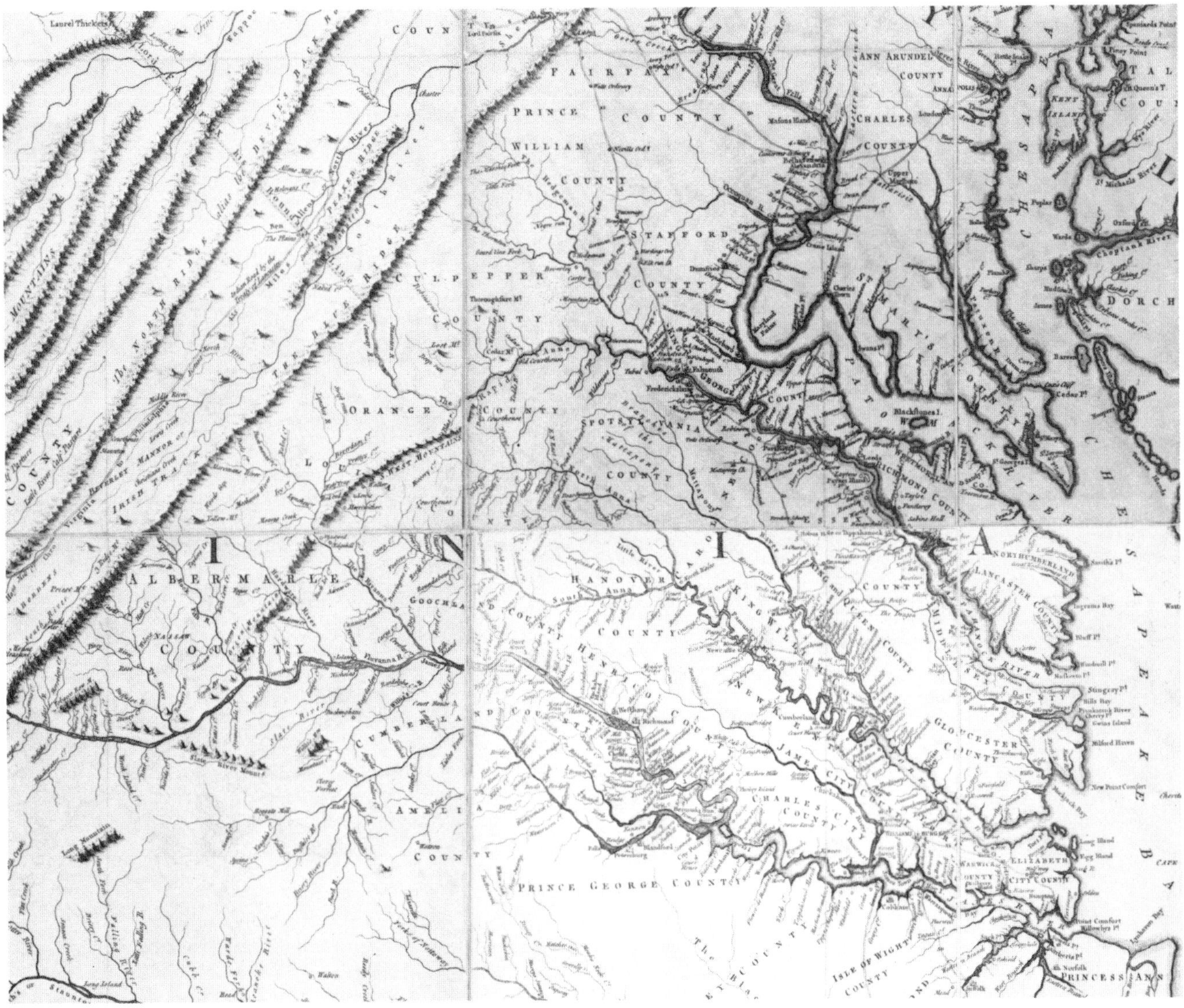

Joshua Fry (ca. 1700–1754) and Peter Jefferson (1708–1757), *A Map of the most Inhabited part of Virginia* (detail), colored engraving, $31\frac{15}{16}$ in x $50\frac{9}{16}$ in, London, Thomas Jefferys, 1755. Geography and Map Division, Library of Congress.

slaves were housed thereabouts to tend fields and carry on household chores. By 1782 Madison's overseers tended 118 blacks. Young Madison's views on slavery were shaped in those early years, and his ideas on human servitude were akin to those of others in the Virginia dynasty who thought much about it. They were disgusted with slavery but could not think of a better way to grow tobacco in a hot, humid climate.

For a time, young Madison took a slave with him when he traveled. When his servant became an embarrassment in the vicinity of Carpenters' Hall in Philadelphia, however, that ended Madison's personal indifference to the problem. He determined that Billey, a slave he brought up from Virginia, had

Benjamin Henry Latrobe (1764–1820), *"An Overseer doing his duty,"* watercolor, ink and ink wash on paper, 6⁵/₁₆ in x 10⁵/₁₆ in, near Fredericksburg, Virginia, March 13, 1798. Courtesy Papers of Benjamin Henry Latrobe, Maryland Historical Society, Baltimore.

breathed the air of freedom too deeply in the City of Brotherly Love to ever be useful again around Montpelier. He decided to let Billey gain his freedom under the seven-year contract system then prevailing in Pennsylvania, and explained: "I do not expect to get near the worth of him; but cannot think of punishing him . . . for coveting that liberty which we have paid the price of so much blood, and have proclaimed so often to be the right, & worthy the pursuit, of every human being." [1]

1. To James Madison, Sr., September 8, 1783, in James Madison, *Papers of James Madison,* ed. William T. Hutchinson and William M. E. Rachal (vols. 1–7) and Robert A. Rutland et al. (vols. 8–) (Chicago: University of Chicago Press, 1962–77; Charlottesville: University Press of Virginia, 1978–), 7:304.

Education for young Virginians came on their plantations from tutors, or with boarding at nearby academies usually run by penurious ministers who needed to supplement their incomes. Madison's training came in both ways, and we know that his father once hired a "dancing master" to teach his children the proper steps for a minuet. Serious education came into Madison's life when Scotsman Donald Robertson, "a man of extensive learning, and a distinguished teacher in the County of King & Queen," was paid one pound five shillings as an investment in the boy's upbringing. The sum proved to be well spent, for the Edinburgh-trained Robertson so instilled in young Madison a zeal for knowledge that by twelve the lad knew Latin tolerably well and had the foundations for his later skills in French, Greek, Italian, Spanish, and Hebrew. Madison's next tutor, the Rev. Thomas Martin, had graduated from the Presbyterian College of New Jersey at Princeton. Teachers who wonder about the value of their endeavors can take heart from the influence of Robertson and Martin on Madison, for the one sparked a love of learning and the other directed it to the small campus at Princeton. Unlike most of his Virginia contemporaries, who took the worn pathway to Williamsburg for study at the College of William and Mary, Madison chose to follow Martin's example. Typically, Madison chose not to take the easy way. Princeton was nearly three hundred miles away and had to be reached by vexatious inland travel, while Williamsburg was a comparatively easy 120 miles to the southeast. But Madison's appetite was whetted for the opportunity to see new territory and to encounter men like those who had trained Martin. So it was off for Princeton in 1769, with the slave Sawney at his side.

Princeton in those days was noted for its Presbyterianism, pedantry, and patriotism (in that order). Some of Madison's new college life did not

Mr James Madison Dr
£ Sh d
1767. Dec. To Master Jamie's Schooling 3 Mo. 1:5:0
1768. Jan. To Generosity - - 0:2:1
1:7:1

Donald Robertson (1717–1792), *Account with Mr. James Madison* (Sr.) (excerpt, 1767–1768), account book, 1758–1775. Courtesy Virginia Historical Society, Richmond.

James Madison's *Diploma from the College of New Jersey* (later Princeton University), engraving on parchment, silk, wax, 24 in x 20 in, October 7, 1771. James Madison Papers, Library of Congress.

agree with him, but he looked upon the Princeton library as a hungry man looks at a banquet table. Moreover, he made a few close friends and was around other students (Philip Freneau, Joel Barlow, and Aaron Burr) whose paths would cross his own more than once during the next half-century. Some of the pedantry stuck to Madison for the rest of his life. The patriotism he encountered there imbued him body and soul.

When Madison looked back on his Princeton days sixty-three years later, he did not recall the feisty doggerel he wrote or his fellow students' pranks. Instead, Madison recalled that the New Jersey climate was not good for persons reared in "a mountainous region." He also remembered that he finished his work early by day-and-night cramming, took his bachelor's degree after only two-and-a-half years of study, and also nearly had a nervous breakdown owing to "an indiscreet experiment of the minimum of sleep & the maximum of application. . . . The former was reduced for some weeks to less than five

Anonymous, *An Attempt to land a Bishop in America,* engraving, 7 in x 4½ in, London, 1768. Prints and Photographs Division, Library of Congress.

hours in the twenty four."[2] Although he nearly killed himself, Madison now had his academic credentials and was ready at twenty for whatever life held. John Witherspoon, the president of Princeton, told mutual friends that when Madison lived at Nassau Hall "he never knew him to do or say an improper thing."

Although he was wasted and pale from the self-imposed discipline at Princeton, Madison had gained academic credentials and nourished his inquiring mind in a way that left a most favorable impression on his elders. Back at Montpelier, the humdrum plantation life bored Madison, and yet he had no longing for the usual escapes from the farming routine: the lawyer's shingle or the minister's black robes.

The ministry left him absolutely cold, or perhaps it would be fairer to say that consideration of a ministerial career left him hot with unaccustomed anger. The local persecutions of Baptist and other dissenting sects in 1774 moved Madison to write a friend that in Orange County

> *Poverty and Luxury prevail among all sorts: Pride ignorance and Knavery among the Priesthood and Vice and Wickedness among the Laity. This is bad enough but It is not the worst I have to tell you. That diabolical Hell conceived principle of persecution rages among some and to their eternal Infamy the Clergy can furnish their Quota of Imps for such business. This vexes me the most of any thing whatever.*

In nearby Culpeper County there were "not less than 5 or 6 well meaning men in close Gaol for publishing their religious Sentiments which in the main are very orthodox." Madison added that he had "squabbled and scolded abused and ridiculed so long about it, to so little purpose, that [he was] without common patience." Then he struck a chord that would sound throughout his entire political career. "I leave you to pity me and pray for Liberty of Conscience to revive among us."[3]

History would catch up with Madison, but he cataloged the injustices observed during his stay in Orange County as he rode around Montpelier checking on the crops, paid an occasional call at the courthouse on family business, and generally played the role of dutiful son in his father's household. If the social life thereabouts was hardly a whirl, Madison scarcely noticed; his first love was now for books. A good portion of the cash from the Madison

2. Douglas Adair, ed., "James Madison's Autobiography," *William and Mary Quarterly*, 3d ser., 2 (1945): 197.

3. Madison to William Bradford, January 24, 1774, in Madison, *Papers*, 1:106.

Amos Doolittle (1754–1832), *The Battle of Lexington, April 19th 1775* (Plate 1), colored engraving, 11¾ in x 17⅝ in, New Haven, Connecticut, ca. 1776. Courtesy Anne S. K. Brown Military Collection, Brown University Library, Providence, Rhode Island.

tobacco crop went in remittances for books ordered from Williamsburg, Fredericksburg, or distant England. His literary diet ranged from Addison and Steele's *Spectator* to learned tomes on moral philosophy, economics, and law. He flirted with the idea of becoming a lawyer—many planters' sons took naturally to the reading-and-oral-examination route to the bar—but Madison was far more excited by some of the ideas brought forth by the Scotsmen David Hume, Francis Hutcheson, and Adam Smith. Their writings on ethics, politics, and history were part of the intellectual current, the so-called Scottish Enlightenment, that sent waves across the Atlantic to lap at the very banks of the Rapidan River. Thus, though nominally a planter, young Madison was in fact a scholar at loose ends—until the bullets whined at Concord. Thereafter, America would not be the same, and certainly James Madison's career took a different course once the news of Lexington-Concord reached the Orange County courthouse in the spring of 1775. And although Jefferson later spoke

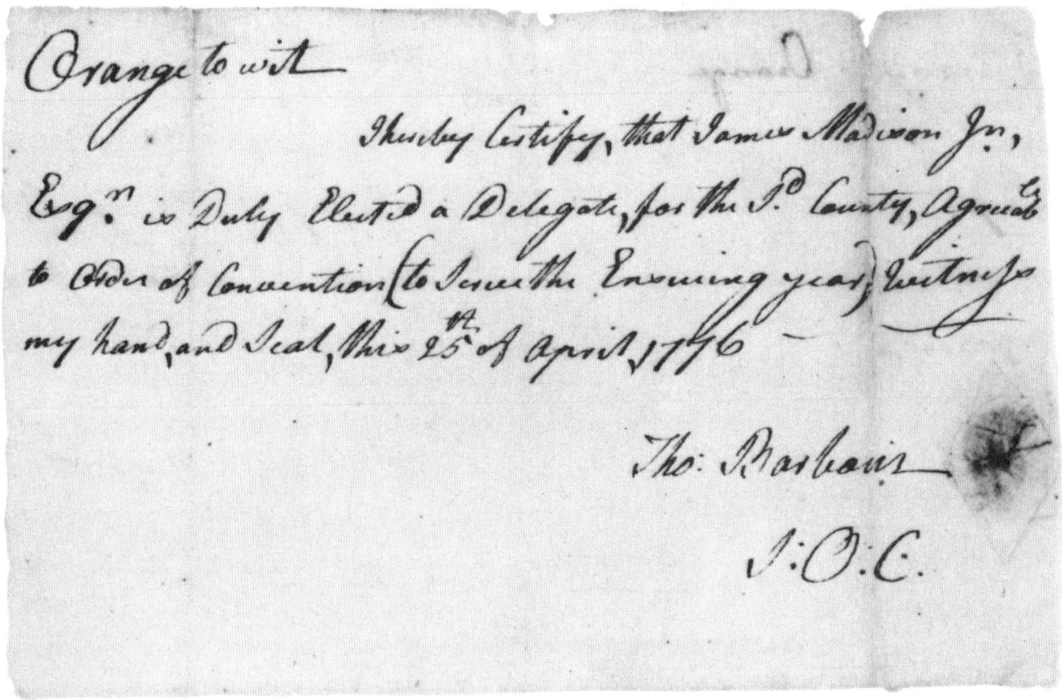

Orange to wit

I hereby Certify, that James Madison Jr, Esqr is Duly Elected a Delegate, for the sd County, Agreeable to Order of Convention (to Serve the Ensuing year) Witness my hand, and Seal, this 25th of April 1776 —

Tho: Barbour
J:O:C.

Thomas Barbour, *Certificate of election of James Madison* (to be a delegate to the Williamsburg Convention), Williamsburg, Virginia, April 25, 1776. Courtesy Archives Branch, Virginia State Library, Richmond.

of Madison as "the best farmer in America," the truth was that from 1775 onward Madison's interest in agriculture was far more theoretical than practical.

Once the American Revolution shifted from a protest movement to a real war, the lessons of self-government long practiced in the thirteen colonies began to pay off. Local committees formed to enforce economic boycotts took on new life as committees of safety, practical groups which ran county government as the neighborhood supporters of the Continental Congress. Madison's father, who had been a parish vestryman and county justice, headed the Orange County committee, and his son was chosen by the freeholders to sit beside him. Many of young Madison's friends and classmates scurried for commissions in line regiments or places with the county militia, but despite his enthusiasm and marksmanship (he told a friend that with a rifle he "should not often miss . . . the bigness of a man's face at the distance of 100 Yards") Madison was compelled to remain a civilian. "He was restrained from entering into the military service," he would recall, "by the unsettled state of his health and the discouraging feebleness of his constitution of which he was fully admonished by his experience during the exercises and movements of a minute Company which he had joined."[4] Between the lines we read of the sickly youth

4. Madison, *Papers*, 1:153; "James Madison's Autobiography," p. 199.

who might well have fainted during a hot day on the parade ground. But whatever the cause, the Virginia minutemen lost a volunteer and the Virginia Convention of 1776—one of the great legislative bodies in our history—gained a member. For after Madison's discouraging experience in the militia he turned his face toward participating in the Revolution as a legislator, a decision hastened by the Orange County voters when they elected him as a representative to the May 1776 gathering in Williamsburg.

Boys often reached manhood on the fly in early Virginia. The deaths of planter-fathers had quickly forced Jefferson, Mason, and Washington into adulthood and heavy responsibilities, and Madison was now hurried into the company of the famous Patrick Henry, the erudite Edmund Pendleton, and the solid George Mason when he took his seat in the old House of Burgesses chamber. Momentous business was at hand, as the last colonial ties with England were about to be sundered, and Madison was compelled to take his stand for both a separation from the mother country and the erection of a republican form of government. Tricky business, indeed, but Mason hobbled into the chambers with a draft of a declaration of rights and constitution that "swallowed up all the rest" and the matter was settled with a minimum of fuss. There was some argument over what it really meant to say "that all Men are born equally free and independent," for most of the delegates were slaveowners. Mason assured the worried gentlemen that he was talking about the "constituent members" of the community—white freeholders who had a stake in society—and not about black slaves. This answer smoothed things over until the delegates came to Mason's proposed article on religious toleration, and there was a query from the young Orange County delegate. Did the gentleman from Fairfax County mean "that all men should enjoy the fullest toleration" in the exercise of their religious beliefs? Madison would remember the incident two generations later and say that Mason "inadvertently adopted the word *toleration*," but when Madison intimated the need to broaden the expression, "the change suggested and accepted substituted a phraseology which declared the freedom of conscience to be a *natural* and *absolute* right."[5]

The difference was not a subtle one. Virginians already had a taste of toleration, with too much power left in the hands of petty local officials, as Madison well knew. This change of a few words entered a wedge in the Anglican church's legal support, hastened the end of any church-state tie in the Old Dominion, and would be remembered when Madison and Henry locked horns

5. "James Madison's Autobiography," p. 199.

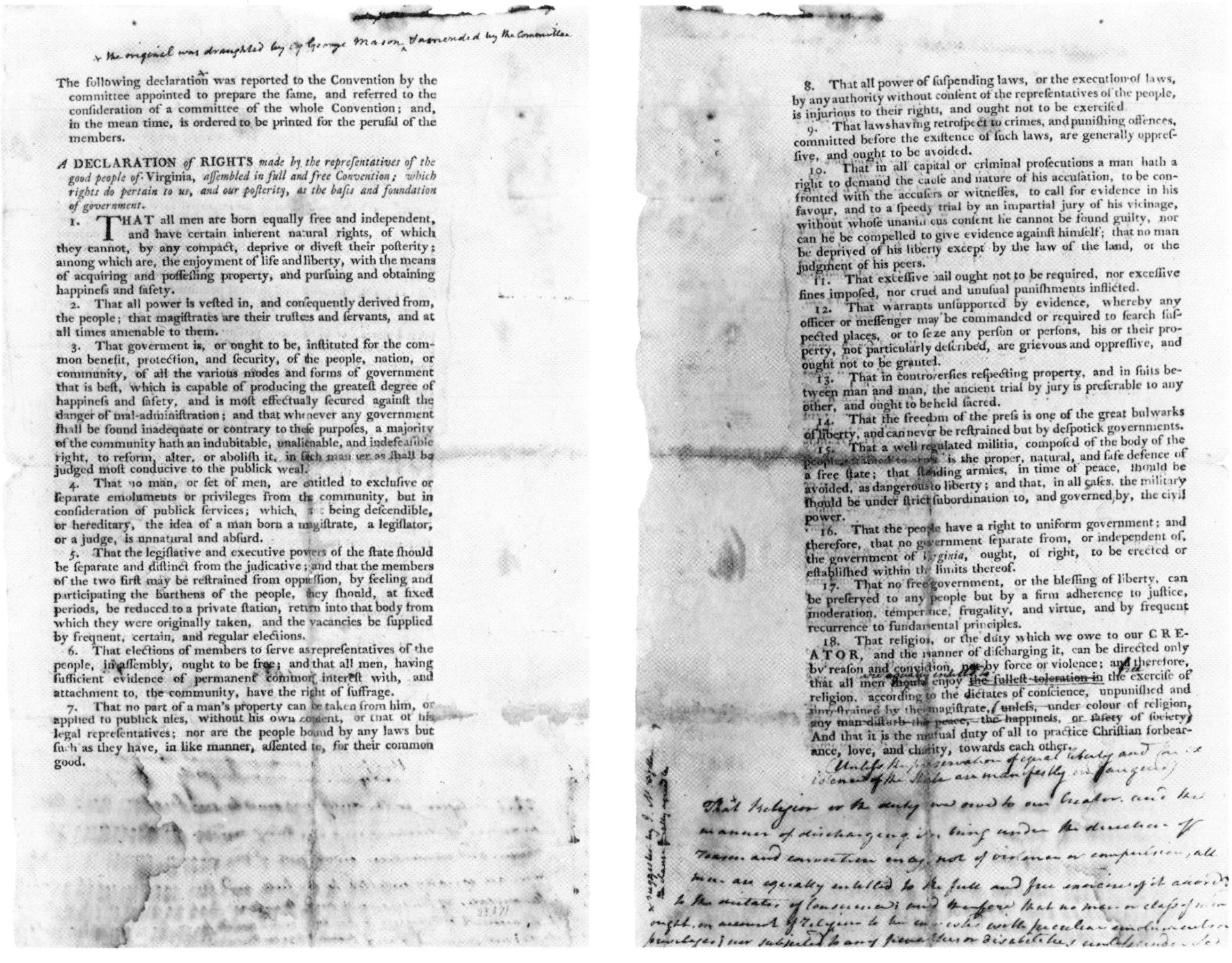

The following declaration was reported to the Convention by the committee appointed to prepare the ſame, and referred to the conſideration of a committee of the whole Convention; and, in the mean time, is ordered to be printed for the peruſal of the members.

A DECLARATION *of* RIGHTS *made by the repreſentatives of the good people of* Virginia, *aſſembled in full and free Convention; which rights do pertain to us, and our poſterity, as the baſis and foundation of government.*

1. THAT all men are born equally free and independent, and have certain inherent natural rights, of which they cannot, by any compact, deprive or diveſt their poſterity; among which are, the enjoyment of life and liberty, with the means of acquiring and poſſeſſing property, and purſuing and obtaining happineſs and ſafety.

2. That all power is veſted in, and conſequently derived from, the people; that magiſtrates are their truſtees and ſervants, and at all times amenable to them.

3. That goverment is, or ought to be, inſtituted for the common benefit, protection, and ſecurity, of the people, nation, or community, of all the various modes and forms of government that is beſt, which is capable of producing the greateſt degree of happineſs and ſafety, and is moſt effectually ſecured againſt the danger of mal-adminiſtration; and that whenever any government ſhall be found inadequate or contrary to theſe purpoſes, a majority of the community hath an indubitable, unalienable, and indefeaſible right, to reform, alter, or aboliſh it, in ſuch manner as ſhall be judged moſt conducive to the publick weal.

4. That no man, or ſet of men, are entitled to excluſive or ſeparate emoluments or privileges from the community, but in conſideration of publick ſervices; which, not being deſcendible, or hereditary, the idea of a man born a magiſtrate, a legiſlator, or a judge, is unnatural and abſurd.

5. That the legiſlative and executive powers of the ſtate ſhould be ſeparate and diſtinct from the judicative; and that the members of the two firſt may be reſtrained from oppreſſion, by feeling and participating the burthens of the people, they ſhould, at fixed periods, be reduced to a private ſtation, return into that body from which they were originally taken, and the vacancies be ſupplied by frequent, certain, and regular elections.

6. That elections of members to ſerve as repreſentatives of the people, in aſſembly, ought to be free; and that all men, having ſufficient evidence of permanent common intereſt with, and attachment to, the community, have the right of ſuffrage.

7. That no part of a man's property can be taken from him, or applied to publick uſes, without his own conſent, or that of his legal repreſentatives; nor are the people bound by any laws but ſuch as they have, in like manner, aſſented to, for their common good.

8. That all power of ſuſpending laws, or the execution of laws, by any authority without conſent of the repreſentatives of the people, is injurious to their rights, and ought not to be exerciſed.

9. That laws having retroſpect to crimes, and puniſhing offences, committed before the exiſtence of ſuch laws, are generally oppreſſive, and ought to be avoided.

10. That in all capital or criminal proſecutions a man hath a right to demand the cauſe and nature of his accuſation, to be confronted with the accuſers or witneſſes, to call for evidence in his favour, and to a ſpeedy trial by an impartial jury of his vicinage, without whoſe unanimous conſent he cannot be found guilty, nor can he be compelled to give evidence againſt himſelf; that no man be deprived of his liberty except by the law of the land, or the judgment of his peers.

11. That exceſſive bail ought not to be required, nor exceſſive fines impoſed, nor cruel and unuſual puniſhments inflicted.

12. That warrants unſupported by evidence, whereby any officer or meſſenger may be commanded or required to ſearch ſuſpected places, or to ſeize any perſon or perſons, his or their property, not particularly deſcribed, are grievous and oppreſſive, and ought not to be granted.

13. That in controverſies reſpecting property, and in ſuits between man and man, the ancient trial by jury is preferable to any other, and ought to be held ſacred.

14. That the freedom of the preſs is one of the great bulwarks of liberty, and can never be reſtrained but by deſpotick governments.

15. That a well regulated militia, compoſed of the body of the people, trained to arms, is the proper, natural, and ſafe defence of a free ſtate; that ſtanding armies, in time of peace, ſhould be avoided, as dangerous to liberty; and that, in all caſes, the military ſhould be under ſtrict ſubordination to, and governed by, the civil power.

16. That the people have a right to uniform government; and therefore, that no government ſeparate from, or independent of, the government of *Virginia*, ought, of right, to be erected or eſtabliſhed within the limits thereof.

17. That no free government, or the bleſſing of liberty, can be preſerved to any people but by a firm adherence to juſtice, moderation, temperance, frugality, and virtue, and by frequent recurrence to fundamental principles.

18. That religion, or the duty which we owe to our CREATOR, and the manner of diſcharging it, can be directed only by reaſon and conviction, not by force or violence; and therefore, that all men ſhould enjoy the fulleſt toleration in the exerciſe of religion, according to the dictates of conſcience, unpuniſhed and unreſtrained by the magiſtrate, unleſs, under colour of religion, any man diſturb the peace, the happineſs, or ſafety of ſociety. And that it is the mutual duty of all to practice Chriſtian forbearance, love, and charity, towards each other.

A Declaration of Rights, broadside completed in manuscript (hand of James Madison), 13⅜ in x 8⅞ in, Williamsburg, May 16–June 29, 1776. James Madison Papers, Library of Congress.

ten years later on the issue. At the time, however, Madison's committee service brought him to the attention of men who were running the Revolution in Virginia, and they remembered him not so much for his substitution of a few words during debate as for his overall grasp of public affairs and his clear-headed logic. Madison was hard to find in a crowd, but after the 1776 Virginia Convention his name kept bobbing up. As the delegates headed homeward, young Madison from Orange County was on nearly everybody's list as a man to be heard from.

The trouble was that the voters back in Orange County did not know about the good impression their delegate had made in Williamsburg. When the time came to elect delegates for the new state House of Delegates, the voters only knew that James Madison, Jr., was a bit too high-minded. At the

William Hogarth (1697–1764) and François Morello La Cave (?–after 1765), *An Election Entertainment* (Plate 1), etching and engraving, 17⅜ in x 22¼ in, England, 1758. Prints and Photographs Division, Library of Congress.

hustings in eighteenth-century Virginia (and in the whole country, for that matter), it was customary for the candidates to appear at the balloting with at least one large barrel of rum or hard cider. Bountiful recompense was made by grateful candidates, and a lenient view toward tipplers prevailed at election time. Madison strutted a bit too much on principle and threw his name into the race but refused to treat "by the corrupting influence of spirituous liquors."

The outcome provided a lesson Madison never forgot. He looked back on the incident and reported he was "an unsuccessful candidate" owing to his principles. Free drinks for everybody, Madison observed, was a ploy unworthy of an honest politician, "inconsistent with the purity of moral and of republican principles . . . whilst his competitors adhered to the old practice. The consequence was that the election went against him; his abstinence being represented as the effect of pride or parsimony."[6] We do not know whether Madison kept a cider barrel handy on all his future election days. We do know that he never lost again on the hustings.

The Orange County freeholders spoke, but the men running the newly independent state of Virginia were not inclined to accept the message. If Madison was not to sit in the House of Delegates, a place would be found for him in Williamsburg on the executive council created by George Mason's constitution. In November 1777 the House of Delegates remembered Madison and elected him to a vacancy on the eight-member "Privy Council, or Council of State." This board was charged with carrying on the commonwealth's executive business by working with the governor; and though in practice the council eventually became a sinecure for political hangers-on, in its early days it was a training ground for leadership. Many of the council's duties were of an emergency nature, owing to the exigencies of wartime government, and here it was that Madison first worked closely with Gov. Patrick Henry, John Blair, John Page, Thomas Walker, and other Virginians of uncommon abilities.

Madison took his duties on the council so seriously he even skipped a chance to be elected to the House of Delegates. Perhaps chagrined by their error in 1777, the Orange County freeholders attempted to undo their mistake the following year by electing Madison as their delegate *in absentia*. Too busy to campaign, Madison was also too busy to accept. He stayed on the council where the swarm of business, issuing warrants, tending to recruiting, and advising the governor on matters affecting tories went on by candlelight. Official dispatches from Philadelphia, from Washington's headquarters, and from diplomatic correspondents in the West Indies and Europe passed through the council, affording Madison a panoramic view of the war. In a typical letter to his father, written while he served on the council, Madison mentioned some books ordered from France, the news of Burgoyne's defeat at Saratoga, the price of salt, and a rumor that seven thousand sorely needed army tents were bound for "the Grand Army" from France. Weeks later, Madison reported to a friend at Valley Forge "that the French court had actually recognized Docr. Franklin as Embassador for the Independent States of America in the most public and authentic manner."[7]

6. Ibid., pp. 199-200.

Surely this news had its effect in Virginia, for we see between the lines of Madison's letter a larger message: the Revolution will succeed. Whether Madison realized it in March 1778 or not, his life's course was to be charted as a response to that implicit message, for thereafter he was never able to quit public affairs for long, not until his successor in the White House was inaugurated in March 1817. In the intervening thirty-nine years he was dominated by a slight variation of that portentous message. The American Revolution, as a military event, succeeded. Was the American Revolution, as a political event and beacon for enlightened men everywhere, to succeed? Through the remainder of his life, Madison was haunted by the question.

As one of Madison's contemporaries recalled, Virginia's leaders rushed into the Revolution and carried it on with an indescribable dedication. "We seem to have been treading upon enchanted Ground," George Mason remembered. Nonetheless, the exhilarating news of French recognition and an alliance with the great European power soon gave way to wartime fatigue and doubts.

Madison was kept too busy to turn pessimist. On June 16, 1778, he was picked by the Virginia General Assembly for a place on the Virginia delegation in the Continental Congress but declined the post to remain on the council of state. His decision to remain in Williamsburg had a fortuitous bonus, for the state legislature had chosen Thomas Jefferson to succeed Gov. Patrick Henry on June 1, thus placing Madison directly under Jefferson's notice. The arid council of state minutes are no proof that this friendship first bloomed in an official atmosphere, but a dramatic incident in mid-June 1779 indicates that both men took a lively interest when the British prisoner of war Henry Hamilton was escorted to Williamsburg and there denounced as an infamous buyer of American scalps from Indian allies. Madison and the other council members advised Governor Jefferson to place Hamilton and his two fellow prisoners "into irons, confined in the dungeon of the publick jail, debarred the use of pen, ink, and paper, and excluded all converse except with their keeper."[8]

7. Madison to James Madison, Sr., March 6, 1778, and Madison to William Bradford, March 23, 1778, in Madison, *Papers*, 1:232-33, 235.

8. Ralph Ketcham, *James Madison: A Biography* (New York: Macmillan, 1971), pp. 78-80; Order of Virginia Council, in Thomas Jefferson, *Papers of Thomas Jefferson* ed. Julian P. Boyd et al. (Princeton: Princeton University Press, 1950–), 2:292-94.

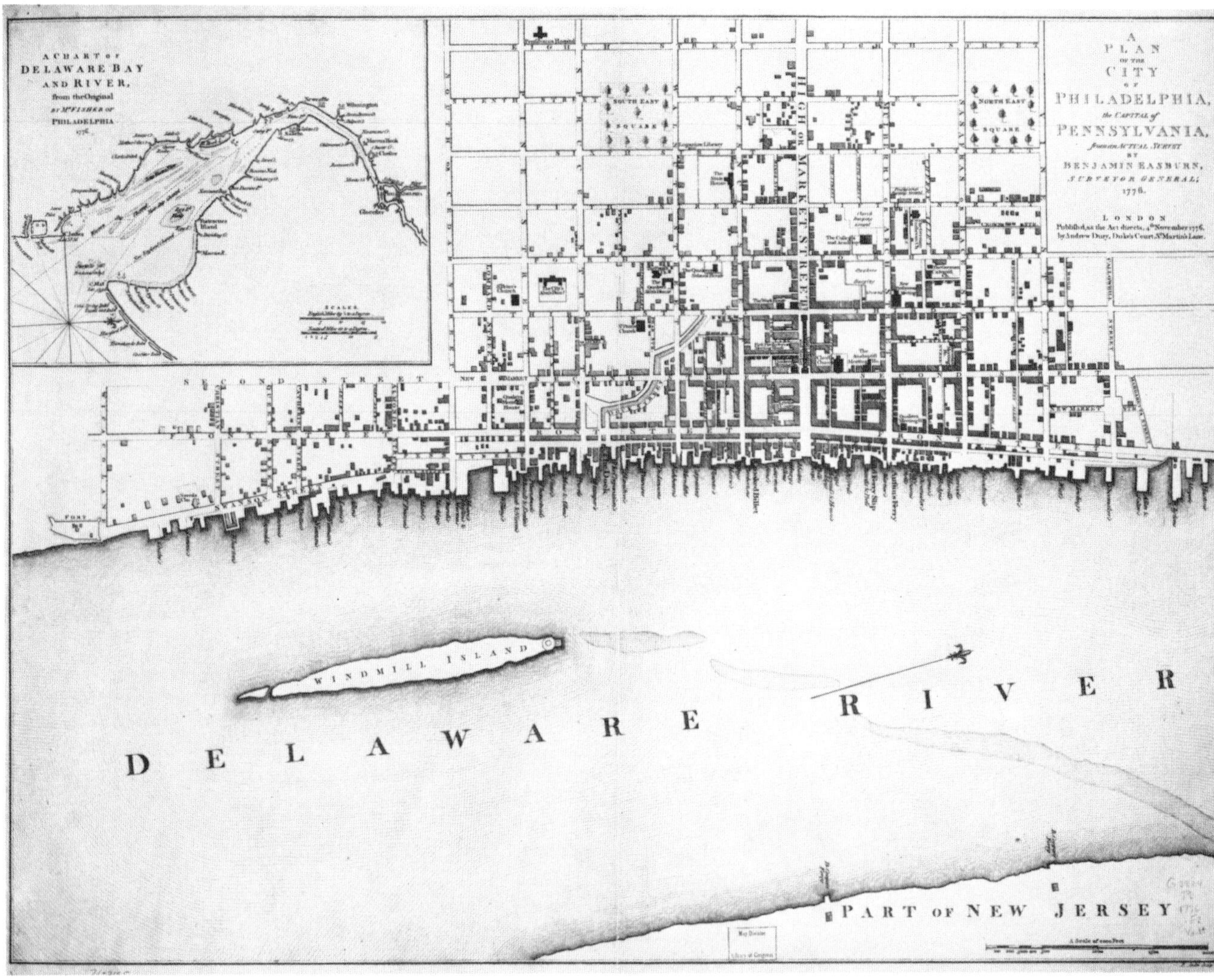

Benjamin Easburn (Surveyor General, 1733–1741), *A Plan of the City of Philadelphia,* engraving, 20½ in x 27³⁄₁₆ in, London, Andrew Dury, November 4, 1776. Geography and Map Division, Library of Congress.

Madison put the disagreeable incident out of his mind, but without a doubt he fell under the spell of Jefferson's conversation and personal charm during these summer months of 1779. Their first collaboration ended in December, when Madison decided (perhaps at Jefferson's urging) not to refuse a second effort by the legislature to send him to the Continental Congress. What was to have been a brief Christmas recess and some tidying up of personal affairs turned into a long vigil at Montpelier as the worst storm in years kept him snowbound until March. At the first thaw, Madison headed for Philadelphia and—despite the chilly halls—a new forum for his revolutionary ardor.

His enthusiasm was needed, for when Madison reached the imposing State House in March 1780 the times were gloomy. Inflation and supply

Charles Willson Peale (1741–1827), *Thomas Jefferson* (1743–1826), oil on canvas, 23⅓ in x 19 in, Philadelphia, ca. 1791. Courtesy Independence National Historical Park Collection, Philadelphia, Pennsylvania.

problems caused Washington's army to suffer far more than the British army, and Congress seemed powerless in its efforts to remedy a deteriorating situation. Thus Madison's first known letters to Jefferson were official, reportorial, and marked by despair—a poor beginning for what was to become one of the greatest exchanges in our history. "Our army has as yet been kept from starving, and public measures from a total stagnation, by draughts on the States for the unpaid requisitions," Madison wrote the governor.[9] Madison's zeal had not cooled, but the harsh fact of an empty treasury and little prospect of aid from the apathetic state legislatures were like buckets of water dashed into the Virginian's face. He awoke to some of the realities of conducting a war without money, a problem forced on Congress by the foot-dragging of state legislatures. The lesson was learned quickly and never forgotten. When Madison came back to Philadelphia in 1787 to help draft a constitution, his experiences as a congressman between 1780 and 1784 led to his preference for national (rather than state) control of finances in the new republic.

If things were bad in Philadelphia in 1780, they were worse in Virginia. Jefferson was reelected governor when the state government was moved to Richmond as a precautionary measure. Then Benedict Arnold's startling raid in December swept through the new capitol, leaving the state government paralyzed. And to make matters worse, the British destroyed mounds of irreplaceable official records before they retired. There had been little improvement by June 1781. Jefferson's second term expired amidst the confusion caused by a British raiding party that almost captured Jefferson himself and did cause an embarrassed set of state legislators to flee to Staunton for a makeshift session. An angry set of delegates demanded an inquiry into Jefferson's conduct during the fiasco, but later the lawmakers sent the offended former governor an apology, an act which pleased Madison since he yearned for the older man's company in Philadelphia. But on the day the legislature exonerated Jefferson and offered him a seat in Congress, he refused with a blunt no. Madison was grieved, for there was much that Virginia, the largest of all the states in the Union, might do if she could provide the same kind of leadership evident in 1775-76. Jefferson would not budge, however, so the main burden of leadership in the Virginia delegation fell on Madison's slight frame.

9. Madison to Jefferson, May 6, 1780, in Madison, *Papers*, 2:19.

Anonymous, *A Tobacco Plantation* (detail), engraving, 12¼ in x 8¼ in, London, Bowles and Carver, ca. 1760–80. Courtesy New York Public Library, New York City, Arents Tobacco Collection.

James Madison's family was part of the Virginia tobacco plantation gentry, with extensive acreage in Orange County overlooking the Blue Ridge mountains.

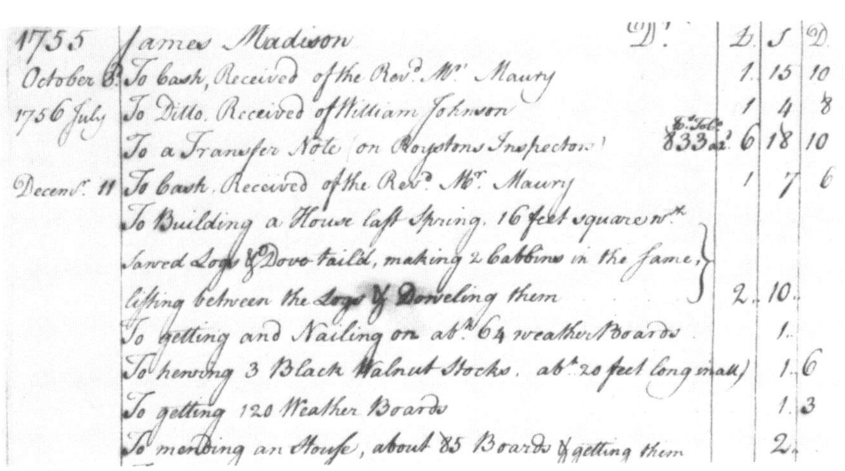

			£	s	d
1755	James Madison	D^r.			
October 3	To Cash, Received of the Rev^d. M^r. Maury		1.	15	10
1756 July	To Ditto. Received of William Johnson		1	4	8
	To a Transfer Note (on Roystons Inspection)	lb. Tob^o 833 at	6	18	10
Decem^r. 11	To Cash. Received of the Rev^d. M^r. Maury		1	7	6
	To Building a House last Spring, 16 feet square wth sawed Logs & Dove tailed, making 2 Cabbins in the same, lifting between the Logs & Doweling them		2..	10..	
	To getting and Nailing on ab^t. 64 weather Boards			1..	
	To hewing 3 Black Walnut Stocks, ab^t. 20 feet long (small)			1..	6
	To getting 120 Weather Boards			1.	3
	To mending an House, about 85 Boards & getting them			2..	

James Madison, Sr. (1723–1801), *Housebuilding Accounts* (excerpt, December 11, 1755), account book, Orange, 1755–63. Courtesy Presbyterian Historical Society, Philadelphia, Pennsylvania.

James Madison, Sr., began building a house on his Orange County land when James was still an infant; the original house was completed sometime before 1765. This 1755 account lists expenditures for the construction of temporary quarters for the family, a two-room log house with weatherboard siding.

Anonymous, *Side Chair* (one of a set of twelve), walnut, 34 in x 20¼ in x 17 in, Fredericksburg or Falmouth, Virginia, 1773. Collection of Mrs. Whitfield Cobb. Photograph courtesy American Institute of Architects Foundation/the Octagon, Washington, D.C.

James Madison grew up in an atmosphere of quiet prosperity. His parents furnished their home with an impressive array of native and imported furnishings.

Nicholas A. Pappas, FAIA, *Conjectural Plan of Montpelier, 1755–97.* Courtesy American Institute of Architects Foundation/the Octagon, Washington, D.C.

Structural remains of the original Madison house suggest that it was a tall rectangular building with four rooms per floor divided by a central transverse hallway. Only a single original window and some paneling are still visible in the house today.

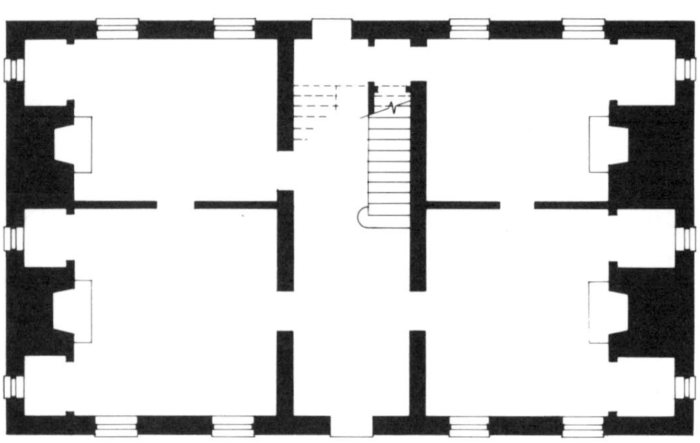

OPPOSITE:

James Madison, *Letter to Rev. Thomas Martin* (excerpt), Princeton, August 10, 1769. James Madison Papers, Library of Congress.

Thomas Martin, one of Madison's early teachers, probably urged Madison to attend his alma mater, Princeton, instead of the College of William and Mary in Williamsburg, Virginia.

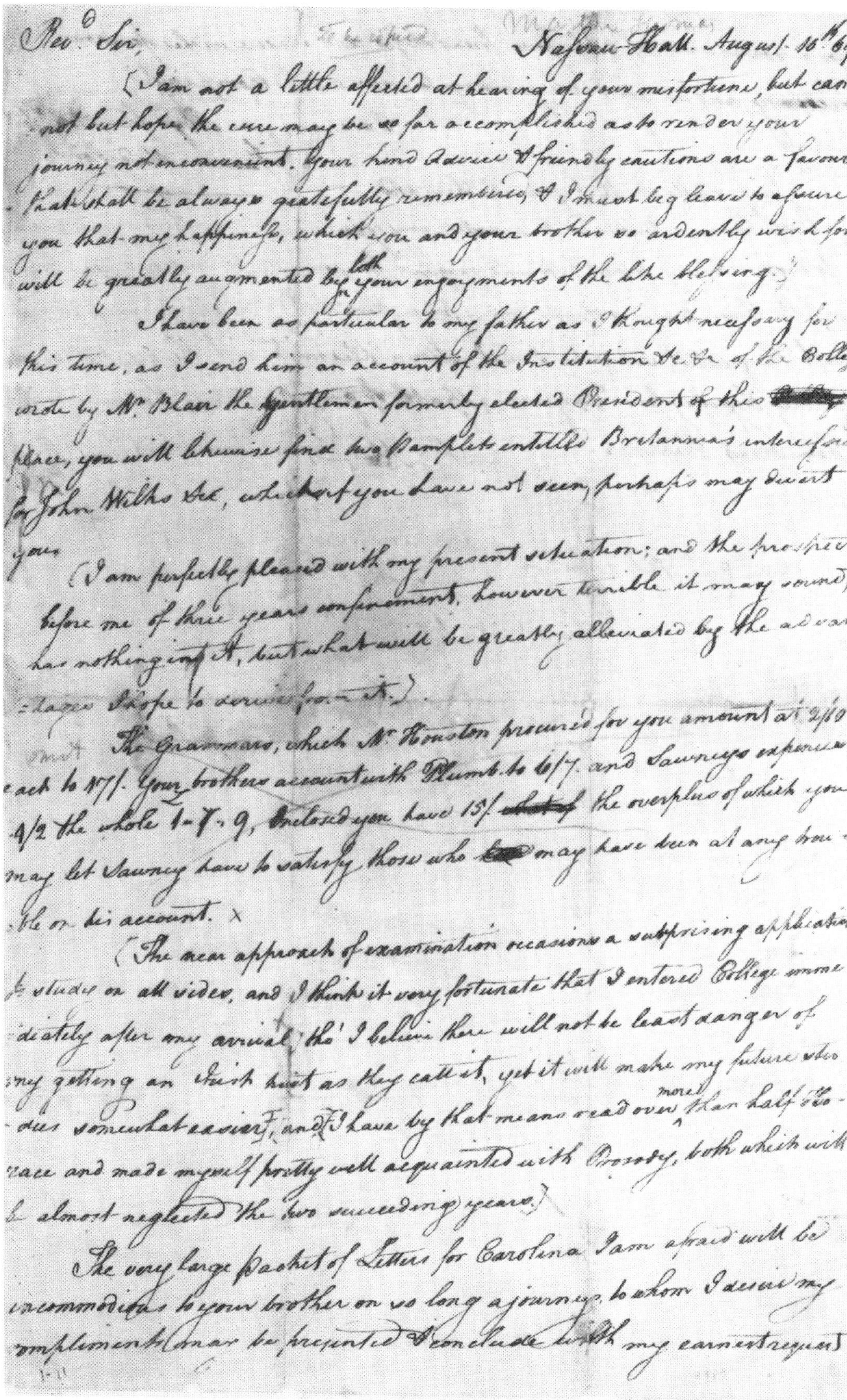

Revd. Sir, Nassau-Hall. August 10th 69

[I am not a little affected at hearing of your misfortune, but can-
-not but hope the cure may be so far accomplished as to render your
journey not inconvenient. Your kind Advice & friendly cautions are a favour
that shall be always gratefully remembered, & I must beg leave to assure
you that my happiness, which you and your brother so ardently wish for,
will be greatly augmented by both your enjoyments of the like blessing.]

I have been as particular to my father as I thought necessary for
this time, as I send him an account of the Institution &c &c of the College
wrote by Mr. Blair the Gentleman formerly elected President of this ~~place~~
place, you will likewise find two Pamphlets entitled Britannia's intercession
for John Wilks &c, which if you have not seen, perhaps may divert
you.

[I am perfectly pleased with my present situation; and the prospect
before me of three years confinement, however terrible it may sound,
has nothing in it, but what will be greatly alleviated by the advan-
-tages I hope to derive from it.]

omit The Grammars, which Mr. Houston procured for you amount at 2/10
each to 17/. Your brothers account with Plumb. to 6/7. and Sawneys expences
4/2 the whole 1-7-9, Inclosed you have 15/ ~~[illegible]~~ the overplus of which you
may let Sawney have to satisfy those who ~~[illegible]~~ may have been at any trou-
-ble on his account. x

[The near approach of examination occasions a surprising application
to study on all sides, and I think it very fortunate that I entered College imme-
-diately after my arrival, tho' I believe there will not be least danger of
my getting an Irish hint as they call it, yet it will make my future stu-
-dies somewhat easier, and I have by that means read over more than half Ho-
-race and made myself pretty well acquainted with Prosody, both which will
be almost neglected the two succeeding years.]

The very large Packet of Letters for Carolina I am afraid will be
incommodious to your brother on so long a journey, to whom I desire my
compliments may be presented & conclude with my earnest request

Henry Dawkins (fl. America, ca. 1753–1786) after W. Tennant (?–d. 1810), *A North-West Prospect of Nassau-Hall* (detail), engraving, $10\frac{1}{8}$ in x $14\frac{7}{8}$ in, Philadelphia?, 1764. Courtesy Library Company of Philadelphia, Pennsylvania.

Princeton president John Witherspoon (1723–1794) encouraged intellectual freedom among his students, who were introduced to liberal studies like natural science, contemporary literature, and modern philosophy. Madison completed his degree in just two years and remained at the college for an additional six months to study Hebrew and theology with Witherspoon.

OPPOSITE:

James Madison, *Distance of the Hour Lines . . .*, pen and ink on paper in notebook entitled *A Brief System of Logick*, ca. 1770–72. James Madison Papers, Library of Congress.

This schoolboy notebook, believed to have been kept by Madison during his junior and senior year at Princeton, includes an exposition of the fundamental principles of logic and more than a dozen scientific ink drawings.

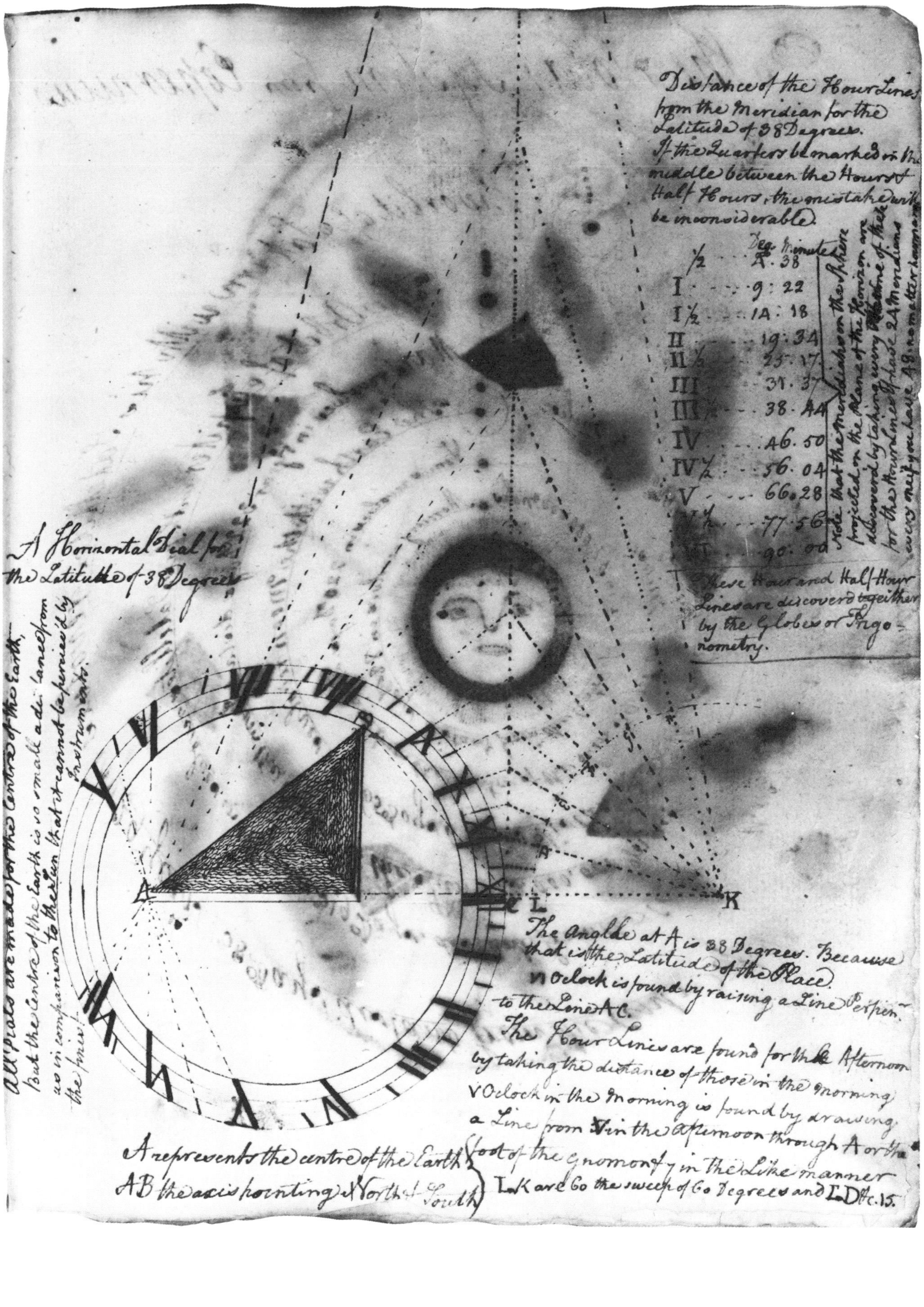

Distance of the Hour Lines from the Meridian for the Latitude of 38 Degrees.
If the Quarters be marked in the middle between the Hours & Half Hours, the mistake will be inconsiderable.
Deg. Minutes
½ 4. 38
I 9. 22
I½ 14. 18
II 19. 34
III 31. 37
III½ 38. 44
IV 46. 50
IV½ 56. 04
V 66. 28
90. 00
These Hour and Half Hour Lines are discoverd together by the Globes or Trigonometry.
A Horizontal Dial for the Latitude of 38 Degrees
The Angle at A is 38 Degrees. Because that is the Latitude of the Place.
The Hour Lines are found for the Afternoon by taking the distance of those in the morning
A represents the centre of the Earth
AB the axis pointing North & South
LK are 60 the sweep of 60 Degrees and LD &c. 15.

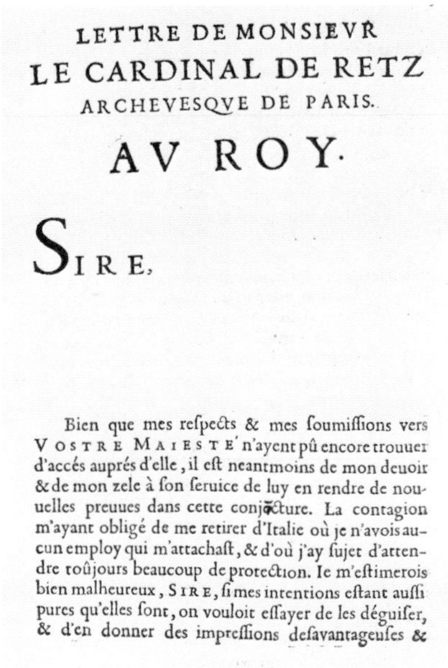

LETTRE DE MONSIEVR
LE CARDINAL DE RETZ
ARCHEVESQVE DE PARIS.

AV ROY.

SIRE,

Bien que mes reſpects & mes ſoumiſſions vers VOSTRE MAIESTE' n'ayent pû encore trouuer d'accés auprés d'elle, il eſt neantmoins de mon deuoir & de mon zele à ſon ſeruice de luy en rendre de nouuelles preuues dans cette conjecture. La contagion m'ayant obligé de me retirer d'Italie où je n'avois aucun employ qui m'attachaſt, & d'où j'ay ſujet d'attendre toûjours beaucoup de protection. Ie m'eſtimerois bien malheureux, SIRE, ſi mes intentions eſtant auſſi pures qu'elles ſont, on vouloit eſſayer de les déguiſer, & d'en donner des impreſſions deſavantageuſes &

(Jean François Paul de Gondi, Cardinal de Retz) (1614–1679), *Lettres Du Cardinal de Retz 1654–1660*, pamphlet, 8¾ in x 6 7/16 in, Paris, 1654–60. Rare Book and Special Collections Division, Library of Congress.

Madison is remembered as one of the most intellectual of our early American leaders. He was a voracious reader and eventually developed a reading proficiency in French, Greek, Italian, Spanish, and Hebrew, as well as the customary Latin. This booklet was among the many volumes that Madison studied at Princeton; he later purchased a copy for the library at Montpelier.

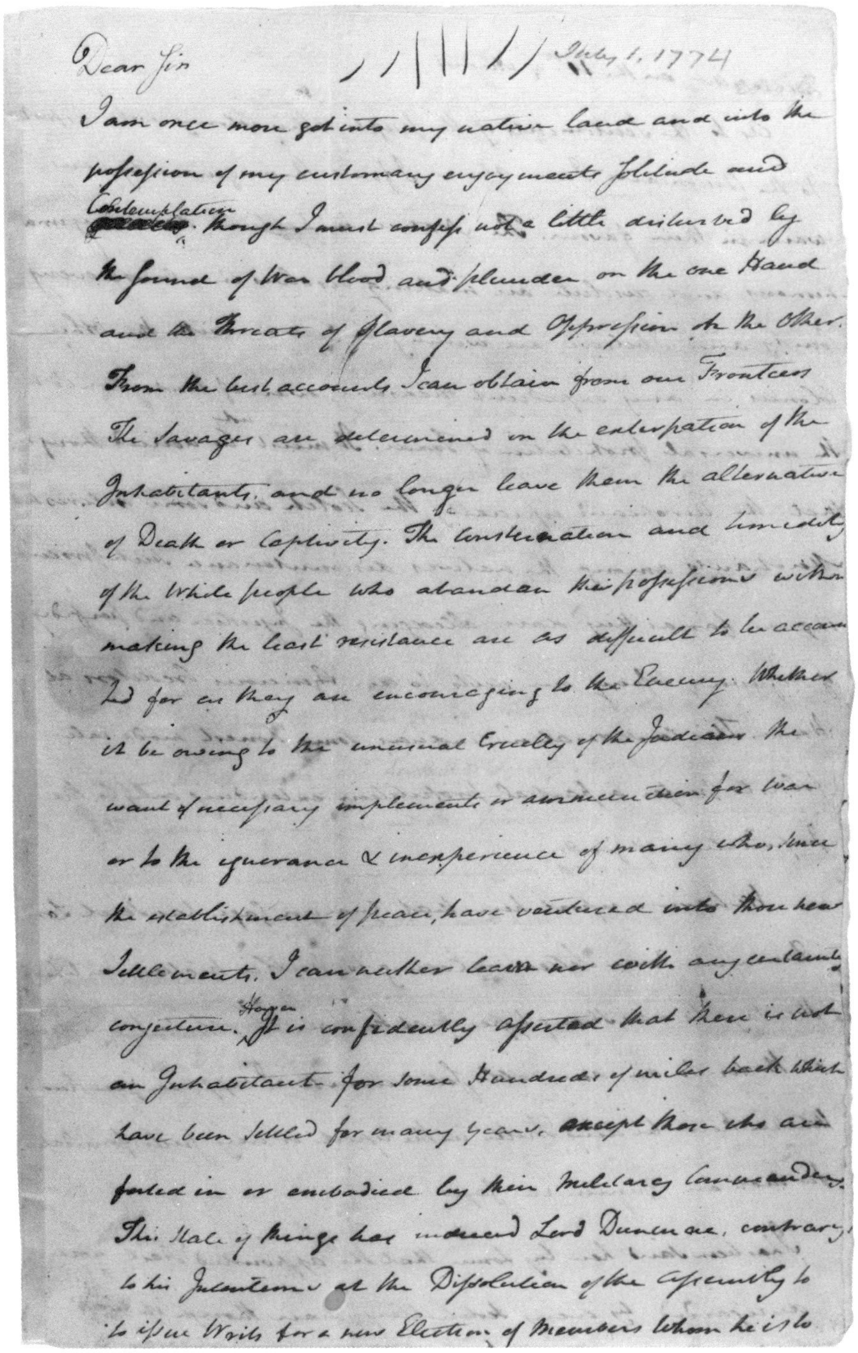

Dear Sir July 1, 1774

I am once more got into my native land and into the possession of my customary enjoyments Solitude and Contemplation, though I must confess not a little disturbed by the sound of War Blood and plunder on the one Hand and the Threats of Slavery and Oppression on the other. From the best accounts I can obtain from our Frontiers The Savages are determined on the extirpation of the Inhabitants and no longer leave them the alternative of Death or Captivity. The consternation and timidity of the White people who abandon their possessions without making the least resistance are as difficult to be accounted for as they are encouraging to the Enemy. Whether it be owing to the universal Cruelty of the Indians the want of necessary implements or ammunition for War or to the ignorance & inexperience of many who, since the establishment of peace, have crouded into those new Settlements, I can neither learn nor with any certainty conjecture. However It is confidently asserted that there is not an Inhabitant for some Hundreds of miles back which have been settled for many years, except those who are forted in or embodied by their Military Commanders. This state of things has induced Lord Dunmore, contrary to his Intentions at the Dissolution of the Assembly to issue Writs for a new Election of Members whom he is to

James Madison, *Letter to William Bradford* (excerpt), Orange, July 1, 1774. Courtesy Historical Society of Pennsylvania, Philadelphia.

After receiving his degree from the College of New Jersey, Madison spent several years at home in Orange County considering various careers. His correspondence with former Princeton classmate "Billey" Bradford (1755–1795) of Philadelphia provides valuable insights into the factors that led the young Virginian into politics.

OPPOSITE:

Jean Nicholas Desandroüins (1729–1792), *Carte des Environs de Williamsburg en Virginie*, pen and ink, watercolor on paper, 29 3/16 in x 39 9/16 in, America?, ca. 1782. Geography and Map Division, Library of Congress.

The Orange County voters elected Madison as a delegate to the Virginia Convention of 1776 in Williamsburg, an event that marked the beginning of a long political career.

Dominic W. Boudet (1745–1845) after J. Hesselius (1728–1778), *George Mason* (1725–1792), oil on ticking, 36 in x 31 in, America, ca. 1811. Courtesy collection of S. Cooper Dawson, descendant of George Mason.

George Mason, Patrick Henry, and Edmund Pendleton were among the prominant Virginia politicians who attended the 1776 convention in Williamsburg to frame a new plan of government. Mason arrived with a draft for a Declaration of Rights and a Constitution, which the delegates adopted in principle.

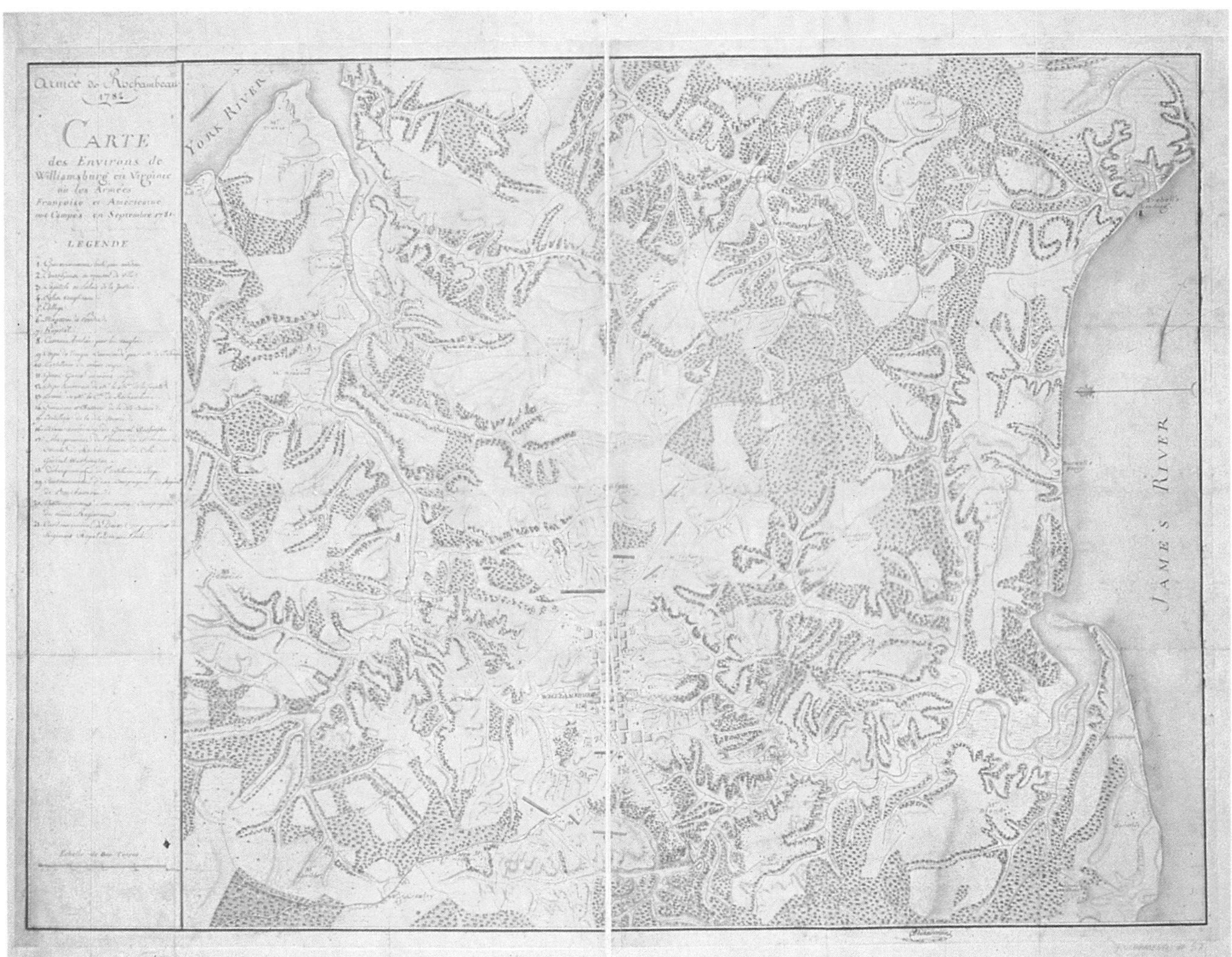

FRIDAY, July 5, 1776. SUPPLEMENT. No. 75.

IN A GENERAL CONVENTION

Begun and holden at the CAPITOL, in the city of WILLIAMSBURG, on MONDAY the ſixth day of MAY, one thouſand ſeven hundred and ſeventy ſix, and continued, by adjournment, to the day of JULY following.

The CONSTITUTION, *or* FORM *of* GOVERNMENT, *agreed to and reſolved upon by the Delegates and Repreſentatives of the ſeveral counties and corporations of* VIRGINIA.

WHEREAS *George* the third, king of *Great Britain* and *Ireland*, and elector of *Hanover*, heretofore intruſted with the exerciſe of the kingly office in this government, hath endeavoured to pervert the ſame into a deteſtable and inſupportable tyranny, by putting his negative on laws the moſt wholeſome and neceſſary for the publick good:

By denying his governours permiſſion to paſs laws of immediate and preſſing importance, unleſs ſuſpended in their operation for his aſſent, and, when ſo ſuſpended, neglecting to attend to them for many years:

By refuſing to paſs certain other laws, unleſs the perſons to be benefited by them would relinquiſh the ineſtimable right of repreſentation in the legiſlature:

By diſſolving legiſlative aſſemblies repeatedly and continually, for oppoſing with manly firmneſs his invaſions of the rights of the people:

When diſſolved, by refuſing to call others for a long ſpace of time, thereby leaving the political ſyſtem without any legiſlative head:

By endeavouring to prevent the population of our country, and, for that purpoſe, obſtructing the laws for the naturalization of foreigners:

By keeping among us, in times of peace, ſtanding armies and ſhips of war:

By affecting to render the military independent of, and ſuperiour to, the civil power:

By combining with others to ſubject us to a foreign juriſdiction, giving his aſſent to their pretended acts of legiſlation:

For quartering large bodies of armed troops among us:

For cutting off our trade with all parts of the world:

For impoſing taxes on us without our conſent:

For depriving us of the benefits of trial by jury:

For tranſporting us beyond ſeas, to be tried for pretended offences:

For ſuſpending our own legiſlatures, and declaring themſelves inveſted with power to legiſlate for us in all caſes whatſoever:

By plundering our ſeas, ravaging our coaſts, burning our towns, and deſtroying the lives of our people:

By inciting inſurrections of our fellow ſubjects, with the allurements of forfeiture and confiſcation:

By prompting our negroes to riſe in arms among us, thoſe very negroes whom, by an inhuman uſe of his negative, he hath refuſed us permiſſion to exclude by law:

By endeavouring to bring on the inhabitants of our frontiers the mercileſs *Indian* ſavages, whoſe known rule of warfare is an undiſtinguiſhed deſtruction of all ages, ſexes, and conditions of exiſtence:

By tranſporting, at this time, a large army of foreign mercenaries, to complete the works of death, deſolation, and tyranny, already begun with circumſtances of cruelty and perfidy unworthy the head of a civilized nation:

By anſwering our repeated petitions for redreſs with a repetition of injuries:

And finally, by abandoning the helm of government, and declaring us out of his allegiance and protection:

By which ſeveral acts of miſrule, the government of this country, as formerly exerciſed under the crown of *Great Britain*, is TOTALLY DISSOLVED:

We therefore, the delegates and repreſentatives of the good people of *Virginia*, having maturely conſidered the premiſes, and viewing with great concern the deplorable condition to which this once happy country muſt be reduced, unleſs ſome regular adequate mode of civil polity is ſpeedily adopted, and in compliance with a recommendation of the General Congreſs, do ordain and declare the future form of government of *Virginia* to be as followeth:

The legiſlative, executive, and judiciary departments, ſhall be ſeparate and diſtinct, ſo that neither exerciſe the powers properly belonging to the other; nor ſhall any perſon exerciſe the powers of more than one of them at the ſame time, except that the juſtices of the county courts ſhall be eligible to either Houſe of Aſſembly.

The legiſlative ſhall be formed of two diſtinct branches, who, together, ſhall be a complete legiſlature. They ſhall meet once, or oftener, every year, and ſhall be called the GENERAL ASSEMBLY OF VIRGINIA.

One of theſe ſhall be called the HOUSE OF DELEGATES, and conſiſt of two repreſentatives to be choſen for each county, and for the diſtrict of *Weſt Auguſta*, annually, of ſuch men as actually reſide in and are freeholders of the ſame, or duly qualified according to law, and alſo of one delegate or repreſentative to be choſen annually for the city of *Williamsburg*, and one for the borough of *Norfolk*, and a repreſentative for each of ſuch other cities and boroughs as may hereafter be allowed particular repreſentation by the legiſlature; but when any city or borough ſhall ſo decreaſe as that the number of perſons having right of ſuffrage therein ſhall have been for the ſpace of ſeven years ſucceſſively leſs than half the number of voters in ſome one county in *Virginia*, ſuch city or borough thenceforward ſhall ceaſe to ſend a delegate or repreſentative to the Aſſembly.

The other ſhall be called the SENATE, and conſiſt of twenty four members, of whom thirteen ſhall conſtitute a Houſe to proceed on buſineſs, for whoſe election the different counties ſhall be divided into twenty four diſtricts, and each county of the reſpective diſtrict, at the time of the election of its delegates, ſhall vote for one Senator, who is actually a reſident and freeholder within the diſtrict, or duly qualified according to law, and is upwards of twenty five years of age; and the ſheriffs of each county, within five days at fartheſt after the laſt county election in the diſtrict, ſhall meet at ſome convenient place, and from the poll ſo taken in their reſpective counties return as a Senator the man who ſhall have the greateſt number of votes in the whole diſtrict. To keep up this Aſſembly by rotation, the diſtricts ſhall be equally divided into four claſſes, and numbered by lot. At the end of one year after the general election, the ſix members elected by the firſt diviſion ſhall be diſplaced, and the vacancies thereby occaſioned ſupplied from ſuch claſs or diviſion, by new election, in the manner aforeſaid. This rotation ſhall be applied to each diviſion, according to its number, and continued in due order annually.

The right of ſuffrage in the election of members for both Houſes ſhall remain as exerciſed at preſent, and each Houſe ſhall chooſe its own ſpeaker, appoint its own officers, ſettle its own rules of proceeding, and direct writs of election for ſupplying intermediate vacancies.

All laws ſhall originate in the Houſe of Delegates, to be approved or rejected by the Senate, or to be amended with the conſent of the Houſe of Delegates; except money bills, which in no inſtance ſhall be altered by the Senate, but wholly approved or rejected.

A Governour, or chief magiſtrate, ſhall be choſen annually, by joint ballot of both Houſes, to be taken in each Houſe reſpectively, depoſited in the conference room, the boxes examined jointly by a committee of each Houſe, and the numbers ſeverally reported to them, that the appointments may be entered (which ſhall be the mode of taking the joint ballot of both Houſes in all caſes) who ſhall not continue in that office longer than three years ſucceſſively, nor be eligible until the expiration of four years after he ſhall have been out of that office. An adequate, but moderate ſalary, ſhall be ſettled on him during his continuance in office; and he ſhall, with the advice of a Council of State, exerciſe the executive powers of government according to the laws of this commonwealth; and ſhall not, under any pretence, exerciſe any power or prerogative by virtue of any law, ſtatute, or cuſtom, of *England*: But he ſhall, with the advice of the Council of State, have the power of granting reprieves or pardons, except where the proſecution ſhall have been carried on by the Houſe of Delegates, or the law ſhall otherwiſe particularly direct; in which caſes, no reprieve or pardon ſhall be granted but by reſolve of the Houſe of Delegates.

Either Houſe of the General Aſſembly may adjourn themſelves reſpectively. The Governour ſhall not prorogue or adjourn the Aſſembly during their ſitting, nor diſſolve them at any time; but he ſhall, if neceſſary, either by advice of the Council of State, or on application of a majority of the Houſe of Delegates, call them before the time to which they ſhall ſtand prorogued or adjourned.

A Privy Council, or Council of State, conſiſting of eight members, ſhall be choſen by joint ballot of both Houſes of Aſſembly, either from their own members or the people at large, to aſſiſt in the adminiſtration of government. They ſhall annually chooſe out of their own members a preſident, who, in caſe of the death, inability, or neceſſary abſence of the Governour from the government, ſhall act as Lieutenant-Governour. Four members ſhall be ſufficient to act, and their advice and proceedings ſhall be entered of record, and ſigned by the members preſent (to any part whereof any member may enter his diſſent) to be laid before the General Aſſembly, when called for by them. This Council may appoint their own clerk, who ſhall have a ſalary ſettled by law, and take an oath of ſecrecy in ſuch matters as he ſhall be directed by the board to conceal. A ſum of money appropriated to that purpoſe ſhall be divided annually among the members, in proportion to their attendance; and they ſhall be incapable, during their continuance in office, of ſitting in either Houſe of Aſſembly. Two members ſhall be removed by joint ballot of both Houſes of Aſſembly at the end of every three years, and be ineligible for the three next years. Theſe vacancies, as well as thoſe occaſioned by death or incapacity, ſhall be ſupplied by new elections, in the ſame manner.

The delegates for *Virginia* to the Continental Congreſs ſhall be choſen annually, or ſuperſeded in the mean time by joint ballot of both Houſes of Aſſembly.

The preſent militia officers ſhall be continued, and vacancies ſupplied by appointment of the Governour, with the advice of the Privy Council, on recommendations

In A General Convention, broadside supplement to the *Virginia Gazette,* Williamsburg, Alexander Purdie, July 5, 1776. Serial and Government Publications Division, Library of Congress.

Madison's work at the 1776 convention in Williamsburg impressed the seasoned Virginia leadership. Madison served on George Mason's committee to produce a Declaration of Rights and suggested that Mason's section dealing with religious toleration be reworked into a statement guaranteeing "the free exercise of religion, according to the dictates of conscience." The Virginia Declaration of Rights was introduced to the Continental Congress on June 7, 1776.

OPPOSITE:

Gilbert Stuart (1755–1828), *Thomas Jefferson* (1743–1826), oil on canvas, 30 in x 25 in, Washington, 1805. Courtesy Colonial Williamsburg Foundation, Virginia.

After Madison's defeat in a race for a seat in the Virginia House of Delegates in 1777, state leaders quickly appointed him to the Council of State, which supervised the wartime business of the government. In Williamsburg, Madison had an opportunity to work closely with the newly elected governor, Thomas Jefferson; their collaboration lasted nearly fifty years and ranks among the most productive friendships in American political history.

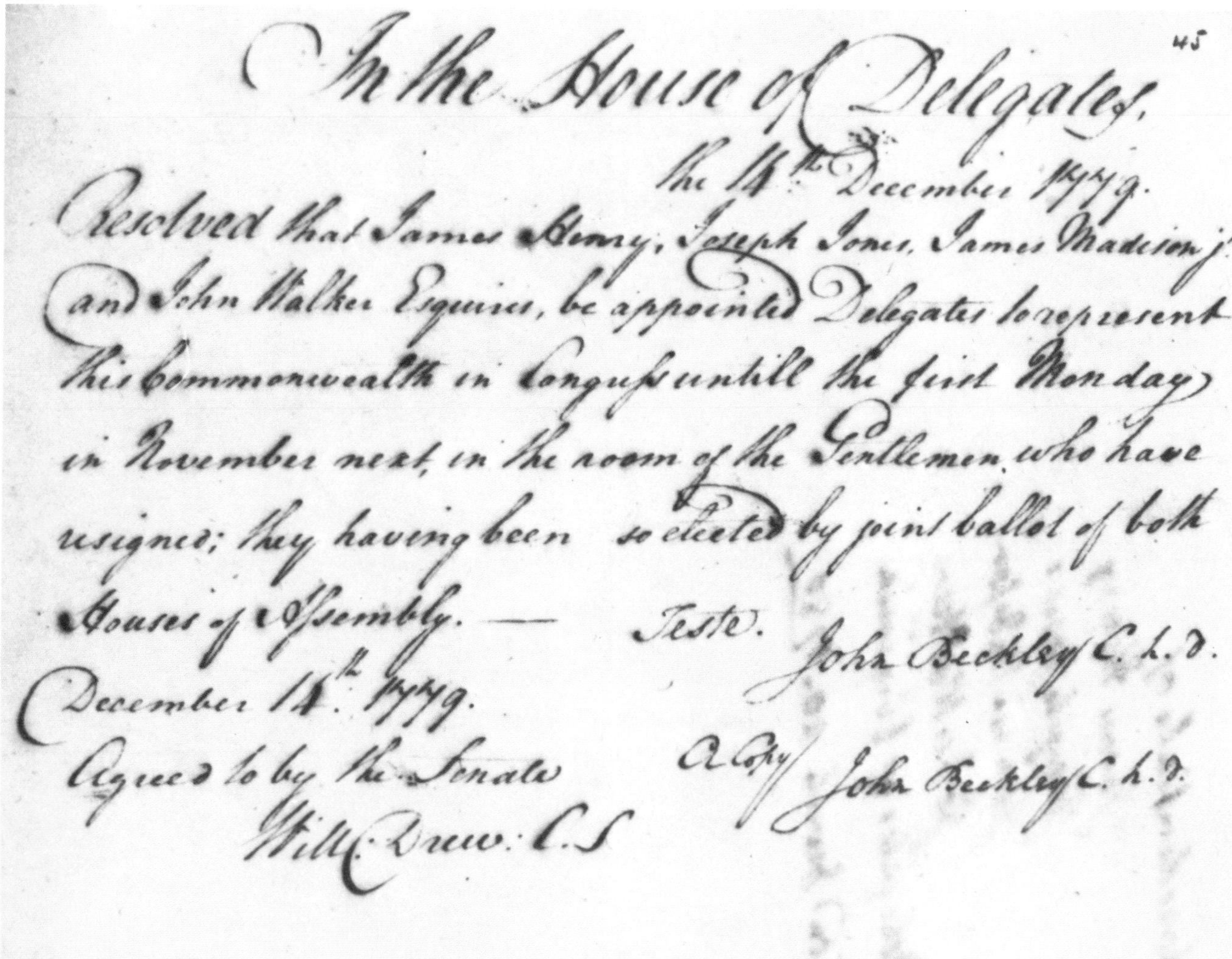

45

In the House of Delegates,
the 14th December 1779.

Resolved that James Henry, Joseph Jones, James Madison jr and John Walker Esquires, be appointed Delegates to represent this Commonwealth in Congress untill the first Monday in November next, in the room of the Gentlemen who have resigned; they having been so elected by joint ballot of both Houses of Assembly. — Teste. John Beckley C. h. D.

December 14th 1779.
Agreed to by the Senate
Will: Drew: C.S

A Copy John Beckley C. h. D.

Resolved that James Henry, Joseph Jones, James Madison jr and John Walker Esquires, be appointed Delegates . . . (excerpt), December 14, 1779. Courtesy National Archives and Records Service, Washington, D.C.

Madison's work in Virginia prepared him well for the national Congress, which he entered as a delegate in 1780. He served as a congressman in Philadelphia for three and a half years and played an important role in the final resolution of the American Revolution.

OPPOSITE:

James Madison, *Instructions to John Jay Respecting the Mississippi*, October 17, 1780. Courtesy National Archives and Records Service, Washington, D.C.

Madison asserted to Jay, then American representative in Spain, the right of America to free navigation of the Mississippi River. The American claim to the Mississippi was one of the first manifestations of this country's expansion to the West.

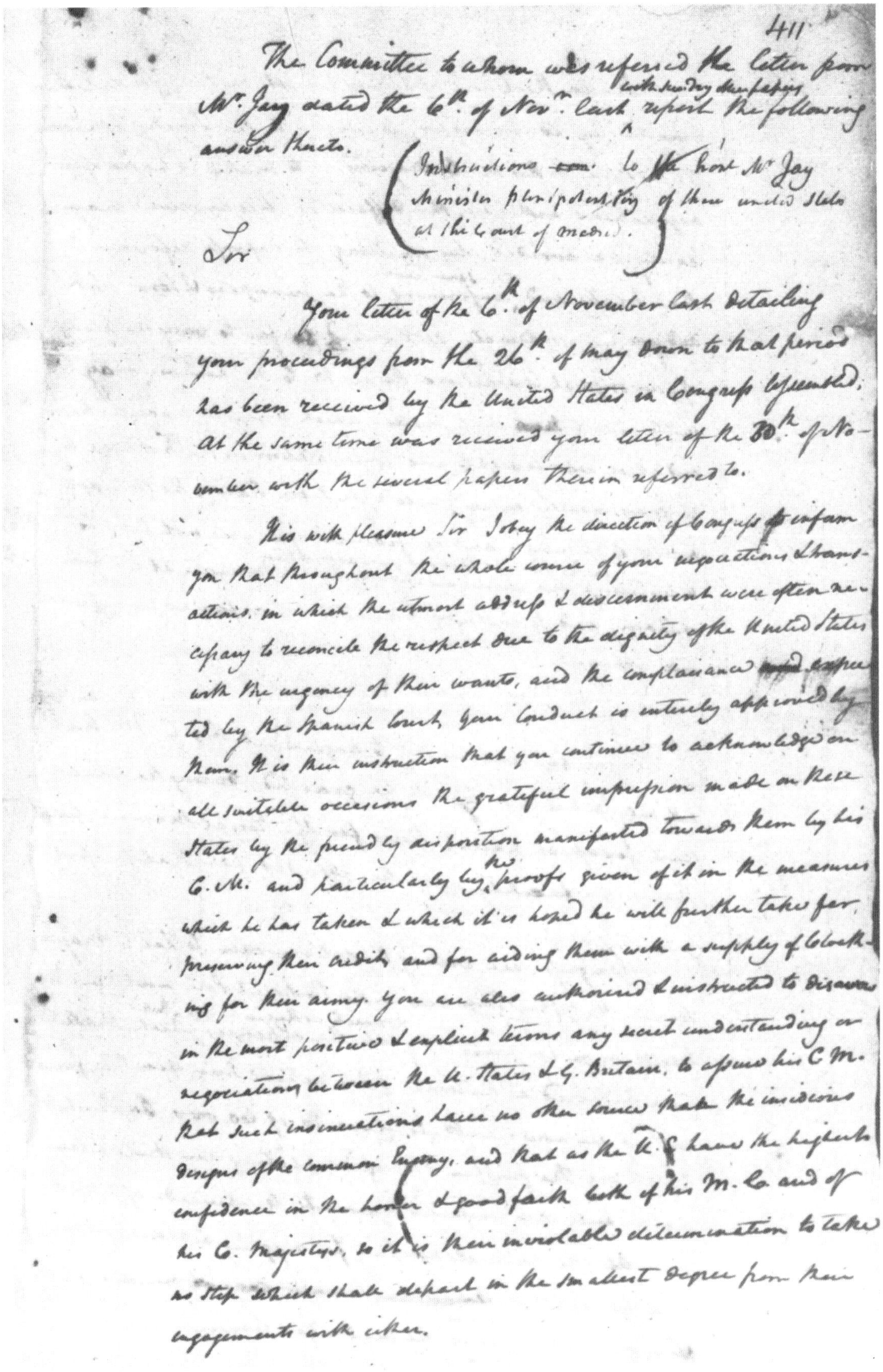

411

The Committee to whom was referred the letter from Mr. Jay dated the 6th. of Novr. last with sundry other papers report the following answer thereto.

(Instructions &c. to the honl. Mr. Jay Minister plenipotentiary of these united States at the Court of Madrid.)

Sir

Your letter of the 6th. of November last detailing your proceedings from the 26th. of May down to that period has been received by the United States in Congress assembled; At the same time was received your letter of the 30th. of November with the several papers therein referred to.

It is with pleasure Sir I obey the direction of Congress to inform you that throughout the whole course of your negociations & transactions in which the utmost address & discernment were often necessary to reconcile the respect due to the dignity of the United States with the urgency of their wants, and the complaisance expected by the Spanish Court, your Conduct is entirely approved by them. It is their instruction that you continue to acknowledge on all suitable occasions the grateful impression made on these States by the friendly disposition manifested towards them by his C. M. and particularly by the proofs given of it in the measures which he has taken & which it is hoped he will further take for preserving their credit and for aiding them with a supply of cloathing for their army. You are also authorised & instructed to disavow in the most positive & explicit terms any secret understanding or negociations between the U. States & G. Britain, to assure his C. M. that such insinuations have no other source than the insidious designs of the common Enemy, and that as the U. S. have the highest confidence in the honor & good faith both of his M. C. and of his C. Majesty, so it is their inviolable determination to take no step which shall depart in the smallest degree from their engagements with either.

John Trumbull (1756–1843), *Resignation of General Washington, December 23, 1783* (life portrait of Madison, who is to the right of the left door frame), oil on canvas, 20 in x 30 in, New York, ca. 1816–24. Courtesy Yale University Art Gallery, New Haven, Connecticut, Trumbull Collection.

Madison's political career began in 1776, when the twenty-five-year-old Virginian was elected to the Virginia Convention in Williamsburg. By the time George Washington resigned his military commission in 1783, Madison was a seasoned congressional leader.

OPPOSITE:

Gregorio Leti (1630–1701), *Li Segreti Di Stato* (with bookplate of William Byrd II of Westover and a mss. note "from the Library of James Madison"), 5½ in x 3⅛ in, Colonia, A. Turchetto, 1676. Rare Book and Special Collections Division, Library of Congress.

The young congressman began his own book collection at the sale of the large Westover library of Virginian William Byrd II in 1781. Madison's Montpelier library eventually numbered several thousand volumes; less than one-third of his collection was in English.

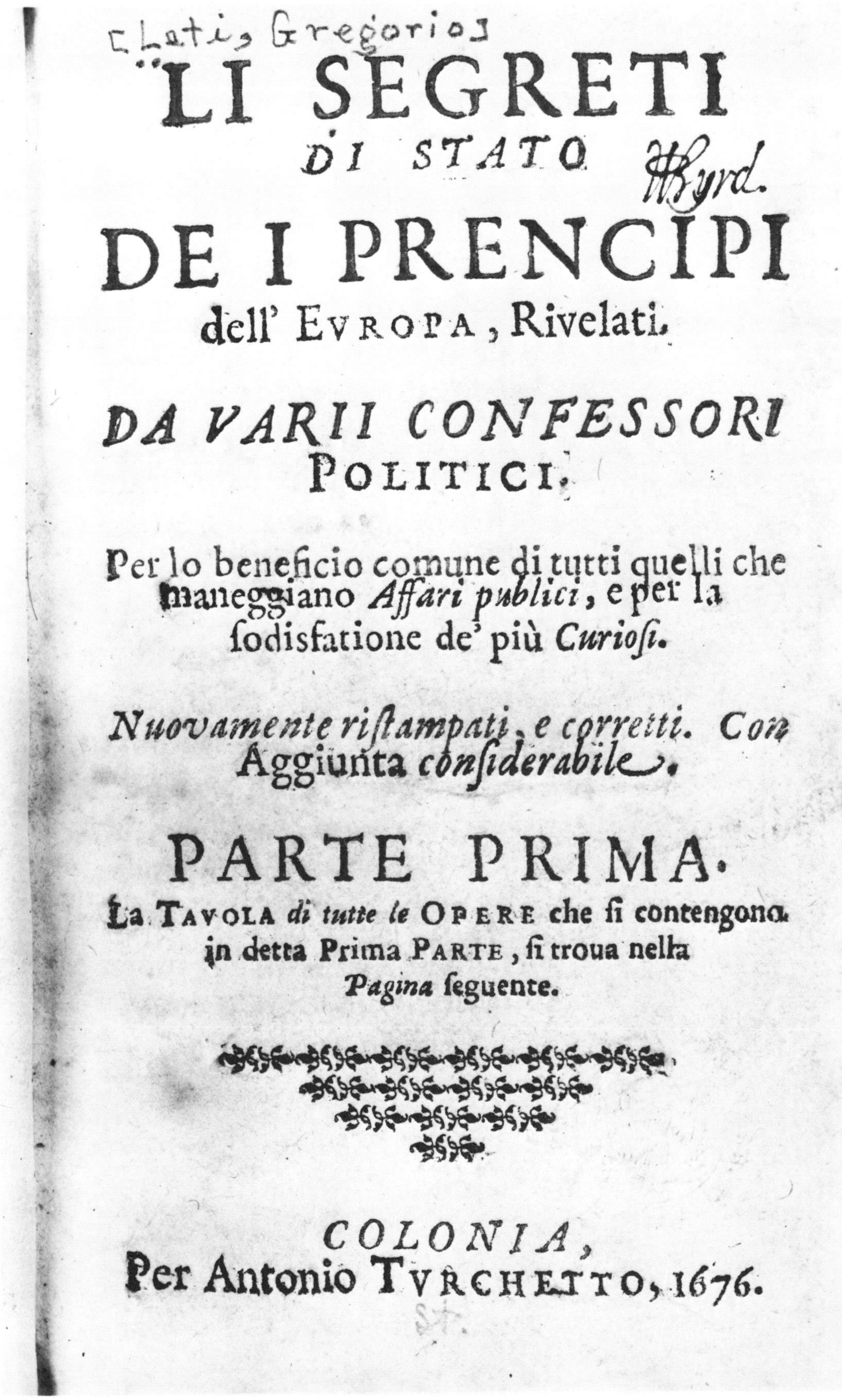

[Lati, Gregorio]

LI SEGRETI

DI STATO W Byrd.

DE I PRENCIPI

dell' EVROPA, Rivelati.

DA VARII CONFESSORI

POLITICI.

Per lo beneficio comune di tutti quelli che maneggiano *Affari publici*, e per la sodisfatione de' più *Curiosi.*

Nuovamente ristampati, e corretti. Con Aggiunta *considerabile*.

PARTE PRIMA.

La TAVOLA *di tutte le* OPERE che si contengono in detta Prima PARTE, si troua nella *Pagina* seguente.

COLONIA,

Per Antonio TVRCHETTO, 1676.

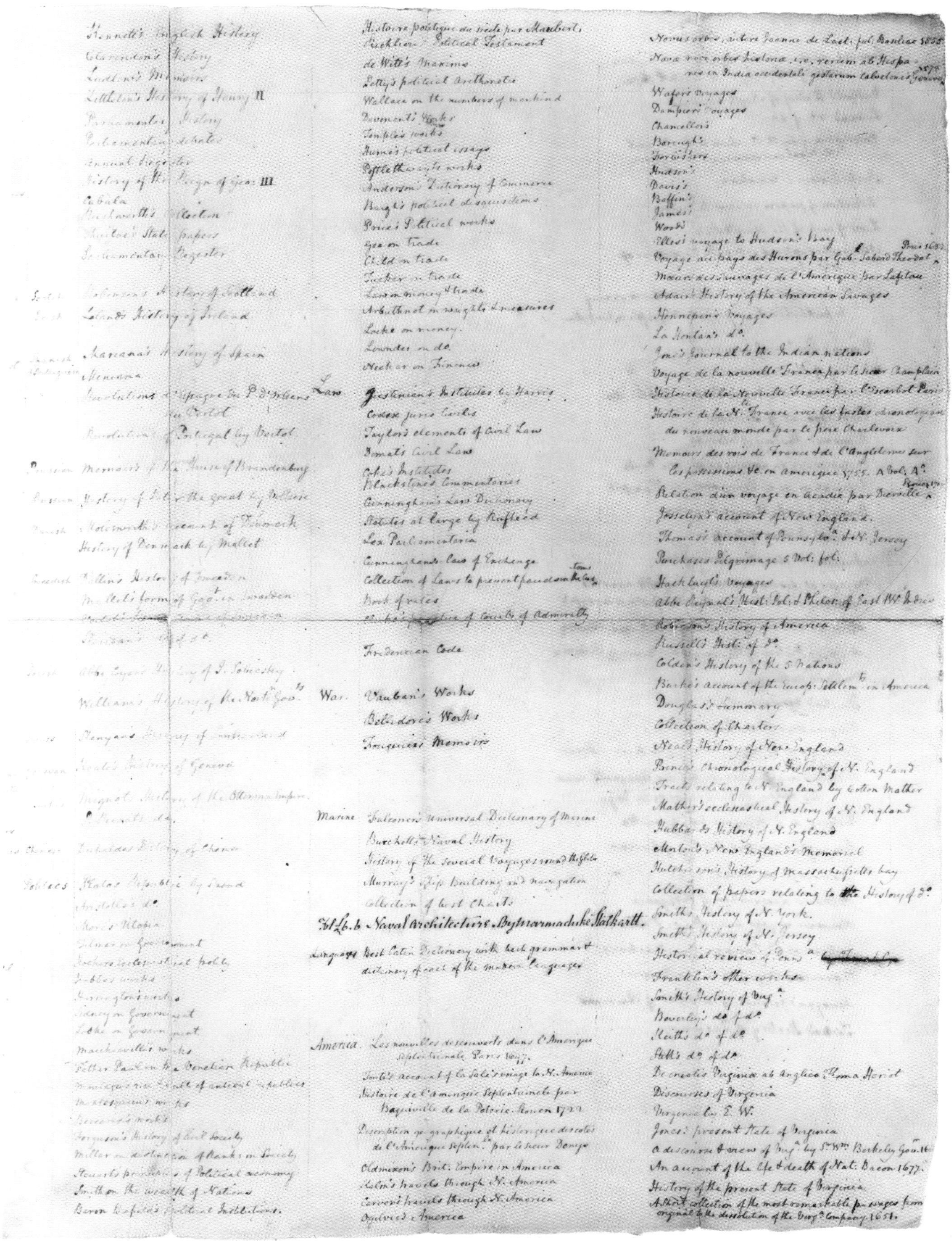

Kennett's English History
Clarendon's History
Ludlow's Memoirs
Littleton's History of Henry II
Parliamentary History
Parliamentary debates
Annual Register
History of the Reign of Geo: III
Cabala
Rushworth's Collection
Thurloe's State papers
Parliamentary Register

Scotch — Robinson's History of Scotland
Irish — Leland's History of Ireland

Spanish, Portuguese — Mariana's History of Spain
Moncana
Revolutions d'Espagne du P. D'Orleans
Revolutions of Portugal by Vertot

Prussian — Memoirs of the House of Brandenburg
Russian — History of Peter the great by Voltaire
Danish — Molesworth's account of Denmark
History of Denmark by Mallet
Swedish — Vertot's History of Sweden
Mallet's form of Gov.t of Sweden
Sheridan's d.o of d.o
Polish — Abbe Coyer's History of J. Sobieski
William's History of the North Gov.ts
Swiss — Stanyan's History of Switzerland
Geneva — History of Geneva
Turkish — Mignot's History of the Ottoman Empire
Rycaut's d.o
Chinese — Duhalde's History of China

Politics — Plato's Republic by Spend
Aristotle's d.o
More's Utopia
Filmer on Government
Hooker's ecclesiastical polity
Hobbes works
Harrington's works
Sidney on Government
Locke on Government
Machiavelli's works
Father Paul on the Venetian Republic
Montague's rise & fall of antient republics
Montesquieu's works
Beccaria's works
Ferguson's History of Civil Society
Miller on distinction of Ranks in Society
Steuart's principles of Political economy
Smith on the wealth of Nations
Baron Bielfeld's political Institutions.

Histoire politique du siecle par Maubert.
Richlieu's Political Testament
de Witt's Maxims
Petty's political Arithmetic
Wallace on the numbers of mankind
Davenant's Works
Temple's works
Hume's political essays
Postlethwayte's works
Anderson's Dictionary of Commerce
Burgh's political disquisitions
Price's Political works
Gee on trade
Child on trade
Tucker on trade
Law on money & trade
Arbuthnot on weights & measures
Locke on money.
Lowndes on d.o
Necker on Finances

Law — Justinian's Institutes by Harris
Codex juris Civilis
Taylor's elements of Civil Law
Domat's Civil Law
Coke's Institutes
Blackstone's Commentaries
Cunningham's Law Dictionary
Statutes at large by Ruffhead
Lex Parliamentaria
Cunningham's Law of Exchange
Collection of Laws to prevent frauds on the Customs
Book of rates
Clerke's practice of Courts of Admiralty
Frederician Code

War. — Vauban's Works
Belidore's Works
Feuquieres Memoirs

Marine — Falconer's Universal Dictionary of Marine
Burchett's Naval History
History of the several Voyages round the Globe
Murray's Ship Building and navigation
Collection of best Charts
Naval Architecture. By Marmaduke Stalkartt.

Languages — Best Latin Dictionary with best grammar & dictionary of each of the modern languages

America. — Les nouvelles descouvertes dans l'Amerique Septentrionale Paris 1697.
Tonti's account of La Sale's voyage to N. America
Histoire de l'Amerique Septentrionale par Baqueville de la Potterie. Rouen 1722
Description geographique et historique des cotes de l'Amerique Septen.le par le sieur Denys
Oldmixon's Brit: Empire in America
Kalm's travels through N. America
Carver's travels through N. America
Ogilvie's America

Novus orbis, autore Joanne de Laet. fol. Batavia 1633
Novæ novi orbis historia, i.e. rerum ab Hispanis in India occidentali gestarum &c. Genevæ 1578
Wafer's voyages
Dampier's voyages
Chancellor's
Borough's
Frobisher's
Hudson's
Davis's
Baffin's
James's
Wood's
Ellis's voyage to Hudson's bay
Voyage au pays des Hurons par Gab. Sabard Theodat Paris 1632
Mœurs des sauvages de l'Amerique par Lafitau
Adair's History of the American Savages
Hennepin's voyages
La Hontan's d.o
Jones's Journal to the Indian nations
Voyage de la nouvelle France par le sieur Champlain
Histoire de la Nouvelle France par l'Escarbot Paris
Histoire de la N.e France avec les fastes chronologiques du nouveau monde par le pere Charlevoix
Memoires des rois de France & de l'Angleterre sur les possessions &c. en Amerique 1755. 4 Vol. 4.o
Relation d'un voyage en Acadie par Dierville Rouen
Josselyn's account of New England
Thomas's account of Pennsylv.a & N. Jersey
Purchase's Pilgrimage 5 Vol: fol:
Hackluyt's voyages
Abbe Raynal's Hist: Pol. & Philos. of East & W. Indies
Robertson's History of America
Russell's Hist: of d.o
Colden's History of the 5 Nations
Burke's account of the Europ: Settlem.ts in America
Douglas's Summary
Collection of Charters
Neal's History of New England
Prince's Chronological History of N. England
Tracts relating to N. England by Cotton Mather
Mather's ecclesiastical History of N. England
Hubbard's History of N. England
Morton's New England's Memorial
Hutchinson's History of Massachusetts bay
Collection of papers relating to the History of d.o
Smith's History of N. York.
Smith's History of N. Jersey
Historical review of Penns.a ~~by Franklin~~
Franklin's other works
Smith's History of Virg.a
Beverley's d.o of d.o
Keith's d.o of d.o
Stith's d.o of d.o
De Insulis Virginiæ ab Anglico Thoma Heriot
Discourses of Virginia
Virginia by E. W.
Jones's present State of Virginia
A discourse & view of Virg.a by S.r W.m Berkeley Gov.r 16
An account of the life & death of Nat: Bacon 1677.
History of the present State of Virginia
A short collection of the most remarkable passages from original to the dissolution of the Virg.a Company. 1651.

Charles Willson Peale (1741–1827), *Catherine Floyd* (1767–1832), watercolor on ivory, gold, 1¼ in x 1$\frac{1}{16}$ in, Philadelphia, 1783. Rare Book and Special Collections Division, Library of Congress.

Madison's intense involvement in congressional affairs did not prevent him from the pursuit of personal interests. During 1783 the young Virginian courted Catherine "Kitty" Floyd, the young daughter of New York congressman William Floyd. The couple sealed their engagement by exchanging miniature likenesses, but Kitty later broke off the suit.

Charles Willson Peale (1741–1827), *James Madison* (from life), watercolor on ivory, gold, 1¼ in x 1½ in, Philadelphia, 1783. Rare Book and Special Collections Division, Library of Congress.

OPPOSITE:

James Madison, Thomas Mifflin, Hugh Williamson, *Report of Committee on Books for Congress* (excerpt), January 24, 1783. Continental Congress Papers, Library of Congress.

While in Congress, Madison served as a member of a committee to prepare a booklist for a proposed congressional library. The report, in Madison's handwriting, listed some three-hundred titles (approximately thirteen-hundred volumes) and included works on international law, politics, geography, history, language, war, and "American antiquities and the affairs of the United States." The Library of Congress was finally created in 1800 during the presidency of fellow bibliophile Thomas Jefferson.

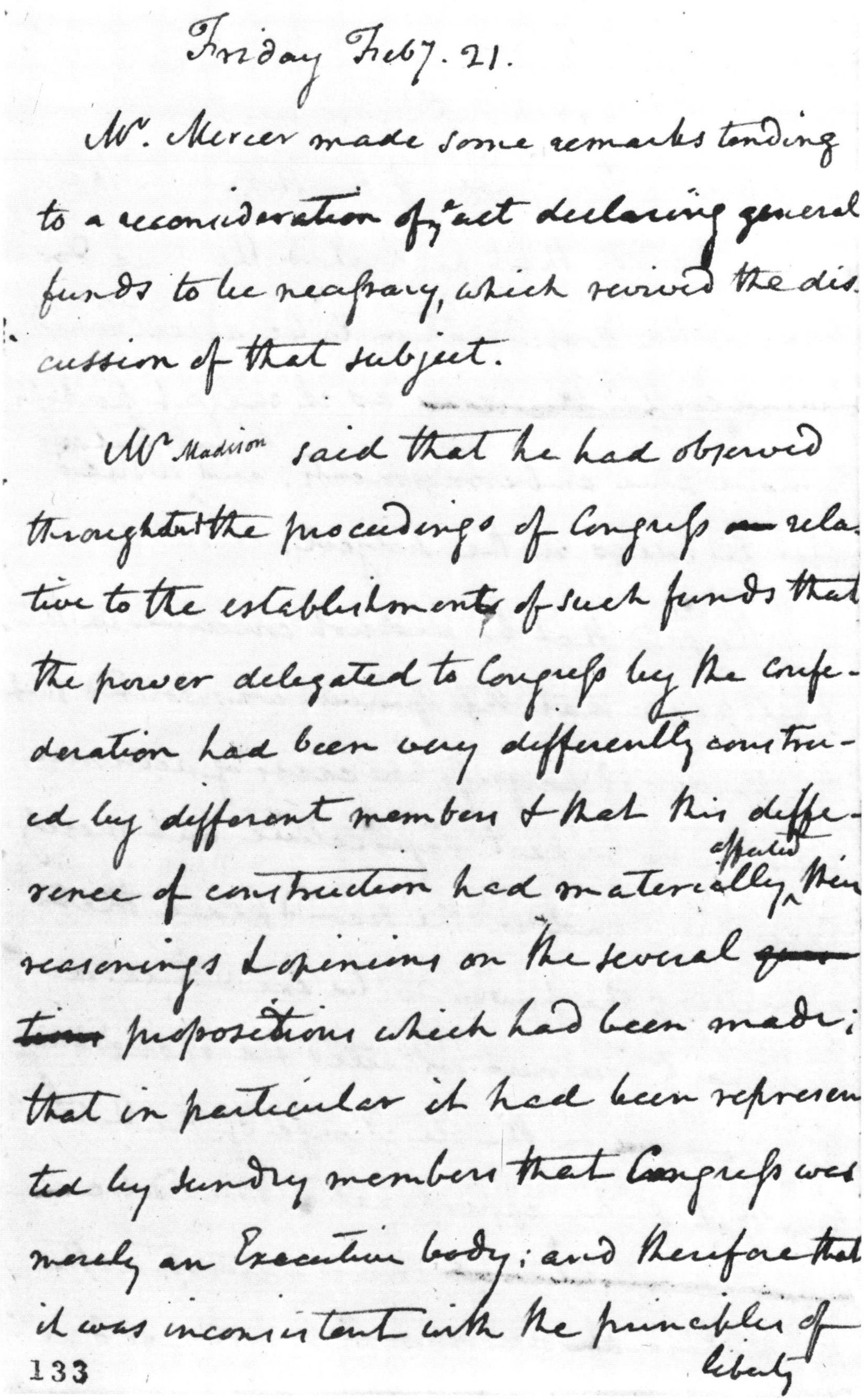

Friday Feby. 21.

Mr. Mercer made some remarks tending to a reconsideration of ye act declaring general funds to be necessary, which revived the discussion of that subject.

Mr Madison said that he had observed throughout the proceedings of Congress ~~on~~ relative to the establishments of such funds that the power delegated to Congress by the Confederation had been very differently construed by different members & that this difference of construction had materially affected their reasonings & opinions on the several ~~ques-tions~~ propositions which had been made; that in particular it had been represented by sundry members that Congress was merely an Executive body; and therefore that it was inconsistent with the principles of liberty

133

James Madison, *Notes of Debates in Continental Congress* (excerpt, Friday, Feb. 21), 1783.
James Madison Papers, Library of Congress.

II

FROM CONFEDERATION TO UNION

The Continental Congress came near to falling apart during the three years of James Madison's first term there.[10] Even the infusion of French gold and military power which led to the final victory at Yorktown was only a brief reprieve for the national legislature, for the Articles of Confederation (our first national constitution) were too flawed to provide for sustained, efficient government. Following the temporary euphoria produced by the celebrated victory at Yorktown, Madison and his colleagues faced a new host of problems. The chief burden on Madison related to the Kentucky district of Virginia, a whole region technically possessed by Virginia but full of emigrants itching for separate statehood. The matter was complicated by navigation rights on the Ohio and thence to the Mississippi, which carried Kentucky produce to New Orleans. Once the war was over, Spanish authorities began to harass Kentucky boatmen and finally closed the vital port altogether. Northern congressmen, seeking a market for New England fisheries, wanted to trade American rights on the Mississippi going into New Orleans for a monopoly on the codfish sales to Spain. Southern and western congressmen made this scheme (along with some mild patter over slavery) the first divisive and sectional issue in our national legislature. Madison's memory of his battles with the northern delegates remained sharp in later life, when he noted: "The right of the U.S. to the navigation of that [Mississippi] River, was maintained by him in every situation & on every

10. Virginia law prohibited delegates to Congress from serving more than three years consecutively and made them strictly accountable for their salary of eight dollars per day while serving. W. W. Hening, ed., *The Statutes . . . of Virginia . . .* 13 vols., (Richmond and Philadelphia, 1819–23), 9:299.

Thomas Colley (attrib.), *The Reconciliation between Britania and her daughter America*, engraving, 10 5/16 in x 14 3/8 in, London, W. Richardson, May 11, 1782. Prints and Photographs Division, Library of Congress.

occasion."[11] His first term in Congress ended in frustration on nearly every score except that one, and ultimately Spain backed down after threatening to deny Americans access to the vital port at New Orleans.

Madison returned to Montpelier and again tried to interest himself in a law career, but the musty pages of Sir Edward Coke's *Commentaries on Littleton* failed to hold his interest. At Jefferson's insistence he began a detailed meteorological record, even noting "strawberries beginning to redden" on May 22, 1785. He was delighted to learn that Jefferson had been persuaded to succeed Dr. Franklin in Paris, for this not only meant his friend was back in

OPPOSITE:

Thomas Hutchins (1730–1789), *A New Map of the Western Parts of Virginia, Pennsylvania, Maryland and North Carolina* (detail), colored engraving, 37 1/8 in x 45 5/16 in, London, T. Cheevers, November 1, 1778. Geography and Map Division, Library of Congress.

11. "James Madison's Autobiography," p. 200.

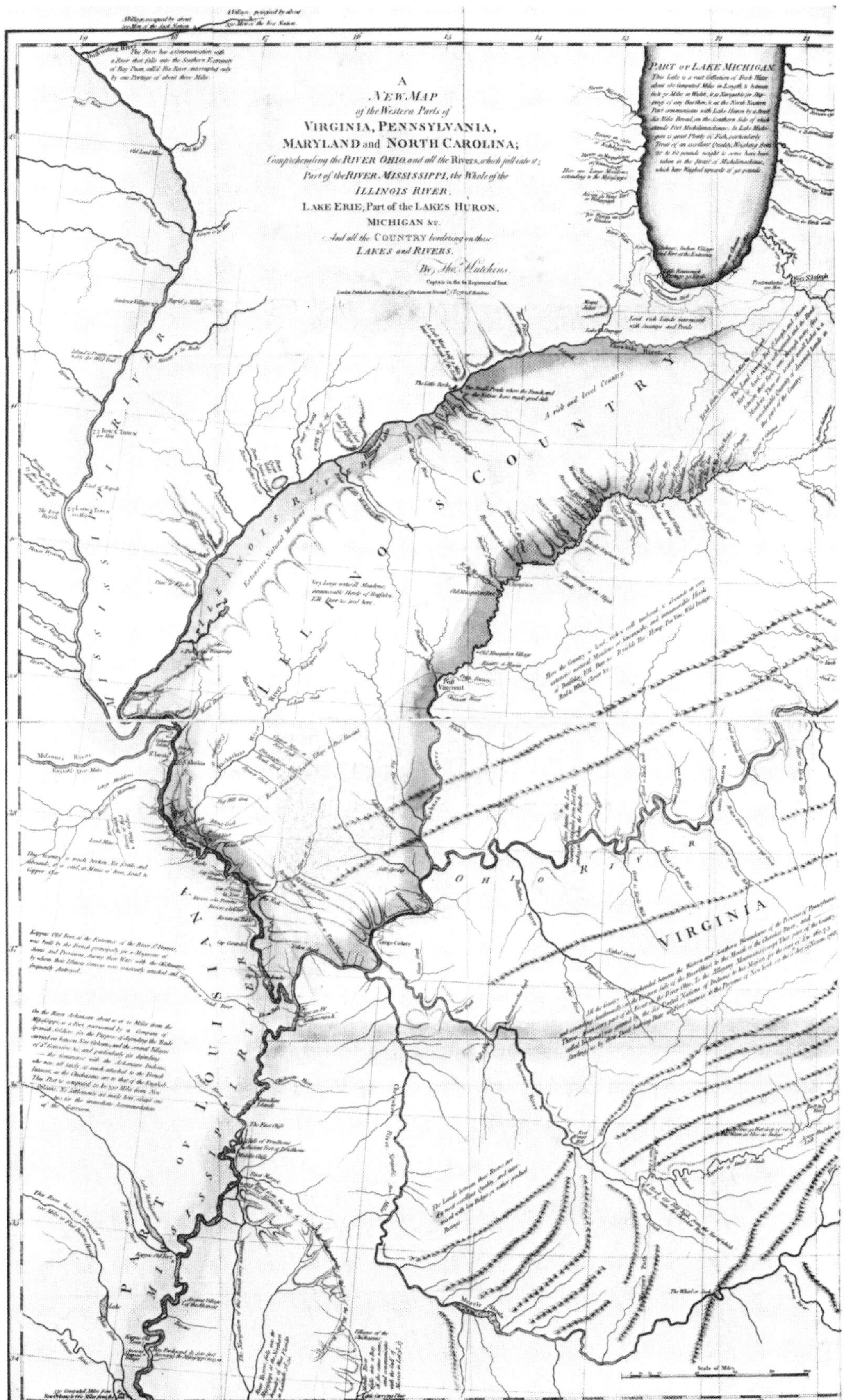
A
NEW MAP
of the Western Parts of
VIRGINIA, PENNSYLVANIA,
MARYLAND and NORTH CAROLINA;
Comprehending the RIVER OHIO, and all the Rivers, which fall into it;
Part of the RIVER MISSISSIPPI, the Whole of the
ILLINOIS RIVER,
LAKE ERIE; Part of the LAKES HURON,
MICHIGAN &c.
And all the COUNTRY bordering on those
LAKES and RIVERS.
By Thos. Hutchins
PART OF LAKE MICHIGAN
VIRGINIA
OHIO RIVER
Scale of Miles

public service but also opened up an opportunity for book purchases in Paris. When first in Williamsburg as a delegate, Madison had begun making modest book purchases, and he now gave Jefferson carte blanche to buy for him any volumes judged proper for his purse and intellectual palate.

Soon their long, informative letters began crossing the Atlantic as Jefferson described France on the eve of its revolution and Madison told of goings-on in Richmond and of Patrick Henry's stranglehold on Virginia politics. Madison was in a position to know, for the Orange County voters had insisted that he represent them in the House of Delegates again. The call of duty provided a good excuse to drop the study of law and sent Madison on the deep-rutted trail back to Richmond. What induced Madison to serve again was an idea forming in his mind that a drastic overhaul of the national government was needed. The country was sliding backwards, with the hard money in circulation disappearing and forcing all transactions to be carried on in warehouse receipts, promissory notes on public securities, and bills of exchange on British commercial houses. Inevitably the planters felt the pinch of a distorted trade, with (in some cases) new debts piling on top of unpaid ones dating back to 1775. Hard-pressed lawmakers in more and more states were falling back on a paper-money solution that jeopardized trade with Europe and horrified the conservative elements in the leading American mercantile houses. Madison looked on paper money and wild inflation as a threat to the country of the first magnitude, for during his term in Congress he had seen the ruin caused by the collapse of the Continental currency.

"We all look up to Virginia for examples," John Adams had told Patrick Henry during the halcyon days of 1776.[12] The remark included both flattery and truth, for Virginia—the largest state in area—had, from the outset of the Revolution, consistently provided the ideas and men that moved the thirteen colonies toward their destiny as an independent republic. In Congress Madison was aware that nothing could succeed if Virginia wanted to block it and that other state delegations watched his moves before they made a decision. Thus Madison viewed his return to the House of Delegates as quite different from

OPPOSITE:
Charles Willson Peale (1741–1827), *George Washington* (1732–1799), mezzotint, 9⅞ in x 11⅞ in, America, 1780. Courtesy National Portrait Gallery, Smithsonian Institution, Washington, D.C., gift of the Barra Foundation.

12. Adams to Henry, June 3, 1776, in Charles Francis Adams, *The Works of John Adams* . . . 10 vols., (Boston, 1850–56), 9:387.

Chas. Willson Peale Pinxt. et fecit.
His Excellency George Washington Esquire, Commander in Chief of the Fœderal Army.
This Plate is humbly Inscribed to the Honorable the Congress of the United States of America,
By their Obedient Servant, Chas. Willson Peale

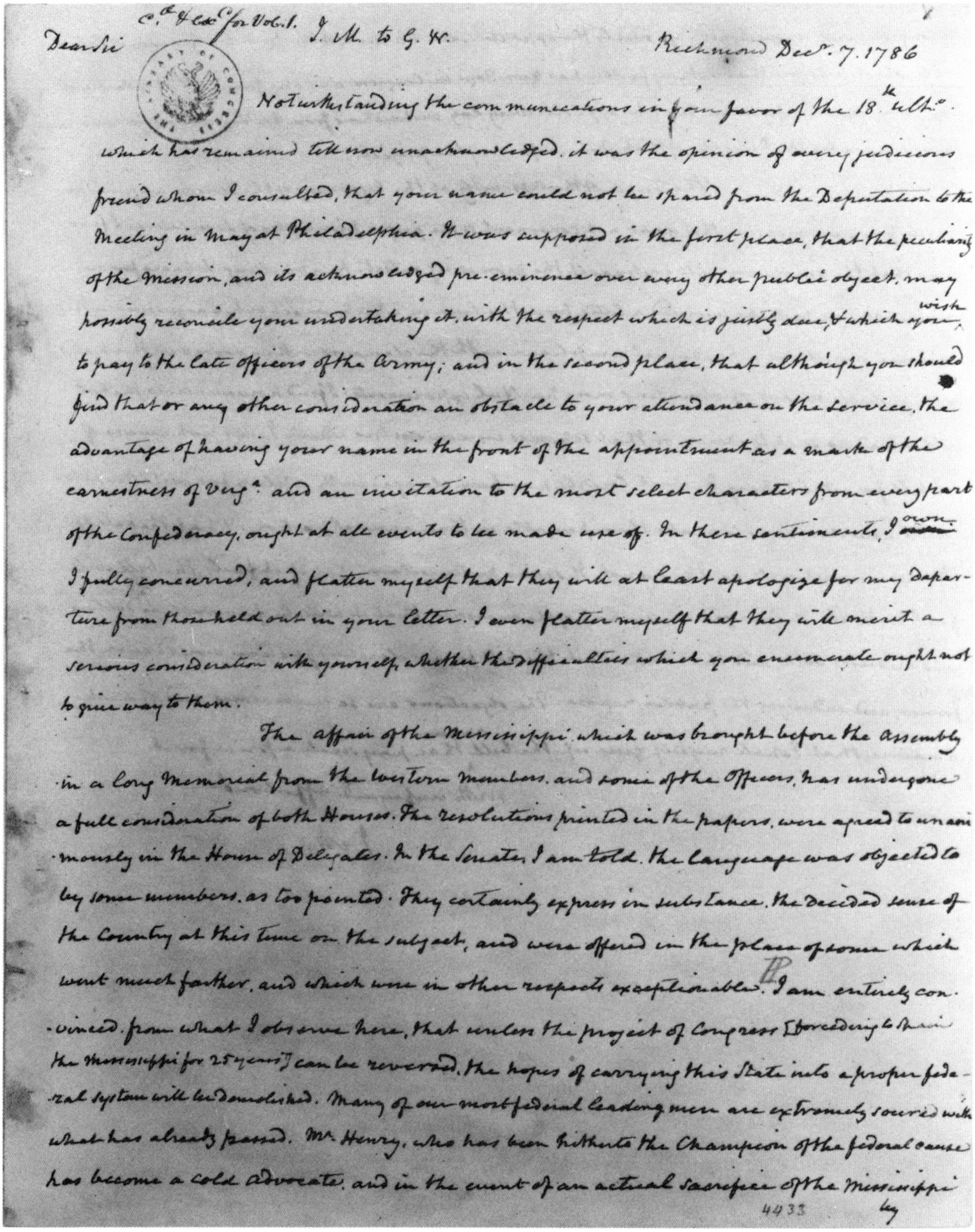

Dear Sir   C.d & ex.d for Vol. 1.   J. M. to G. W.   Richmond Decr. 7. 1786

Notwithstanding the communications in your favor of the 18th ulto. which has remained till now unacknowledged, it was the opinion of every judicious friend whom I consulted, that your name could not be spared from the Deputation to the Meeting in May at Philadelphia. It was supposed in the first place, that the peculiarity of the mission, and its acknowledged pre-eminence over every other public object, may possibly reconcile your undertaking it, with the respect which is justly due, & which you wish to pay to the late officers of the Army; and in the second place, that although you should find that or any other consideration an obstacle to your attendance on the service, the advantage of having your name in the front of the appointment as a mark of the earnestness of Virga. and an invitation to the most select characters from every part of the Confederacy, ought at all events to be made use of. In these sentiments, I own I fully concurred, and flatter myself that they will at least apologize for my departure from those held out in your letter. I even flatter myself that they will merit a serious consideration with yourself, whether the difficulties which you enumerate ought not to give way to them.

The affair of the Mississippi which was brought before the Assembly in a long Memorial from the Western members and some of the Officers, has undergone a full consideration of both Houses. The resolutions printed in the papers, were agreed to unanimously in the House of Delegates. In the Senate I am told, the language was objected to by some members, as too pointed. They certainly express in substance, the decided sense of the Country at this time on the subject, and were offered in the place of some which went much farther, and which were in other respects exceptionable. I am entirely convinced, from what I observe here, that unless the project of Congress [for ceding to Spain the Mississippi for 25 years] can be reversed, the hopes of carrying this State into a proper federal system will be demolished. Many of our most federal leading men are extremely soured with what has already passed. Mr. Henry, who has been hitherto the Champion of the federal cause, has become a cold advocate, and in the event of an actual sacrifice of the Mississippi by

4433

James Madison, *Letter to George Washington* (excerpt), Richmond, December 7, 1786. James Madison Papers, Library of Congress.

his earlier arrival in the chamber as a novice. He may have been bored with the plantation life at Montpelier (he began dissecting small mammals and found plenty of farm varmints around for his experiments), but it was not boredom that prompted the return to public life. To the voters' call "he yielded with the less reluctance, as it would give him an opportunity of pleading in a favorable position, the cause of reform in our federal system, then in the paroxism of its infirmities, and filling every well informed patriot with the most acute anxieties," Madison recalled.[13] In his mind it was a major challenge, for the question was still unanswered: Had the American Revolution succeeded?

For the shaping battle that would carry Madison to Annapolis in 1786 and Philadelphia in 1787, Madison gained one powerful ally—George Washington—and one formidable enemy—Patrick Henry. Washington thought the leaky ship of state needed new constitutional rigging, while Henry liked the jerry-built vessel just fine and said he would not go to Philadelphia because he "smelt a rat." There was no better man in America to have on your side than George Washington. The general had returned to civilian life in 1783 (or as he put it, to rest under his "own vine and figtree"), thinking he was through with politics forever. The unrest known in history as Shays's Rebellion jolted him. Madison had done the general some favors in Congress and in Richmond, and increasingly Washington wrote to him in the frankest terms. Their fears that the Revolution might be jeopardized by internal strife were in unison as Washington wrote:

> *No morn ever dawned more favourable than ours did—and no day was ever more clouded than the present! Wisdom, & good examples are necessary at this time to rescue the political machine from the impending storm. Virginia has now an opportunity to set the latter, and has enough of the former, I hope, to take the lead in promoting this great & arduous work. Without some alteration in our political creed, the superstructure we have been seven years raising at the expence of much blood and treasure, must fall. We are fast verging to anarchy & confusion!*[14]

For his part, Madison was ready to move even before Washington's call to action came. He, too, shared a feeling that "ignorance and the arts of self interested designing disaffected & desperate characters . . . [will] involve this rising empire in wretchedness & contempt" as Washington feared. The long-

13. "James Madison's Autobiography," p. 201.

14. Washington to Madison, November 5, 1786, in Madison *Papers*, 9:161.

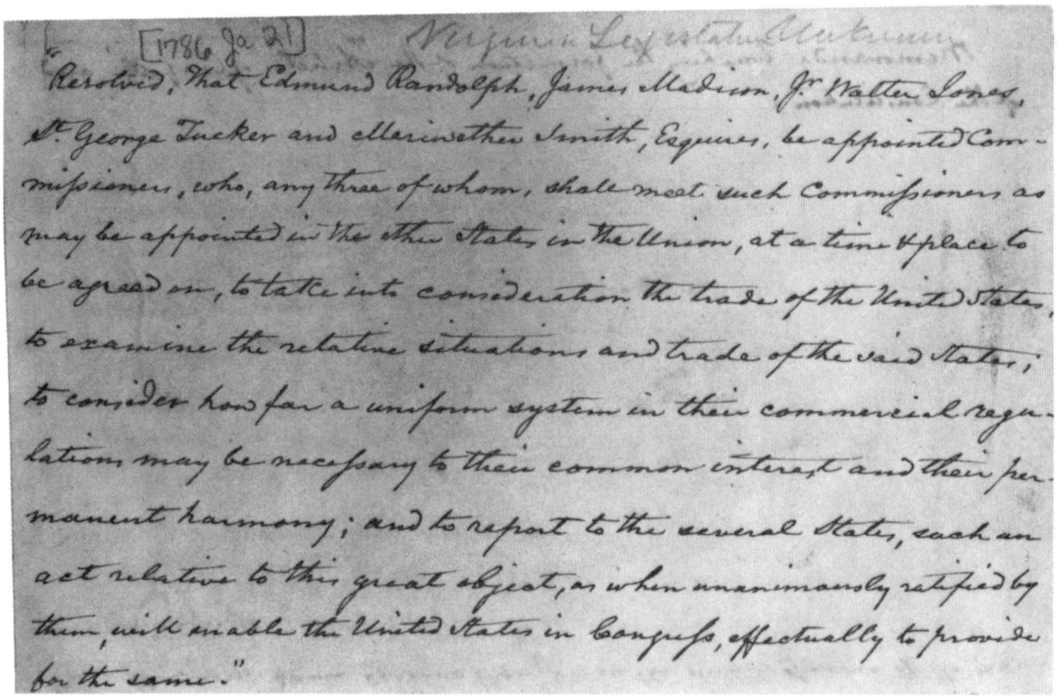

[1786 Ja 21]

"Resolved, That Edmund Randolph, James Madison, Jr. Walter Jones, St. George Tucker and Meriwether Smith, Esquires, be appointed Commissioners, who, any three of whom, shall meet such Commissioners as may be appointed in the other States in the Union, at a time & place to be agreed on, to take into consideration the trade of the United States, to examine the relative situations and trade of the said States; to consider how far a uniform system in their commercial regulations may be necessary to their common interest and their permanent harmony; and to report to the several States, such an act relative to this great object, as when unanimously ratified by them, will enable the United States in Congress, effectually to provide for the same."

Resolution proposing Virginia Delegates to the Annapolis Convention, ca. January 21, 1786. James Madison Papers, Library of Congress.

John Vallance (ca. 1770–1823) after Charles Willson Peale (1741–1827), *A Front View of the State-House &c. at Annapolis the Capital of Maryland,* engraving, 3⅝ in x 6$^{11}/_{16}$ in, in the *Columbian Magazine,* Philadelphia, February 3, 1789. Courtesy Maryland Historical Society, Baltimore.

time political enemy, Patrick Henry, went along with Madison for a while, but bided his time.

What soon followed is the now familiar role Madison played in pushing his Virginia friends into calling for meetings to discuss and act on interstate squabbling and national insolvency. A first meeting at Mount Vernon was held before Madison could reach it, but at the Annapolis Convention in 1786 (called at the urging of the Virginia General Assembly) he helped Alexander Hamilton urge the few states which sent delegates to aim for a larger gathering with every state in attendance. Indeed, the Virginia act which Madison wrote authorizing delegates to attend the Philadelphia convention voiced his latent fears that time was running out for the young republic. "The crisis is arrived at which the good people of America are to decide the solemn question, whether they will by wise and magnanimous efforts reap the just fruits of that Independence which they have so gloriously acquired . . . or whether by giving way to unmanly jealousies and prejudices, or to partial and transitory interests, they will renounce the auspicious blessings prepared for them by the Revolution." Thus was Madison's heart laid on the half shell, for he knew, and Jefferson's letters confirmed, the talk from England that the high Tories there were saying the time would come when the United States would collapse. Then, "were America to petition parliament to be again received on their former footing the petition would be very generally rejected," Jefferson was told by a haughty Scotsman.[15]

Because of current events, such warnings cut Madison to the quick. Some impatient men quietly pushed the notion that an American version of the British constitution, with one of George III's distant cousins on a Yankee throne, was the only workable solution to the young nation's ills. A distressed Madison took to his library, as he often did in stressful times, and pored through his copies of Greek and Roman history for an inkling of how the infant republic might be rescued. His research on "Ancient and Modern Confederacies" convinced Madison that the Articles of Confederation could not be mended, patched, or reconstructed in any way. Only with a fresh start, based on the wisdom of the past and "the lamp of experience" in America, could the Union be preserved and the Revolution affirmed. Like all the leading men of his era, Madison was captivated by the Newtonian idea that if the basic propositions of a plan were sound, the whole concept would fit and

15. Bill Providing for Delegates to the Convention of 1787, November 6, 1786, in Madison *Papers*, 9:163-64; Jefferson to Richard Henry Lee, April 22, 1786, in Jefferson *Papers*, 9:398-99.

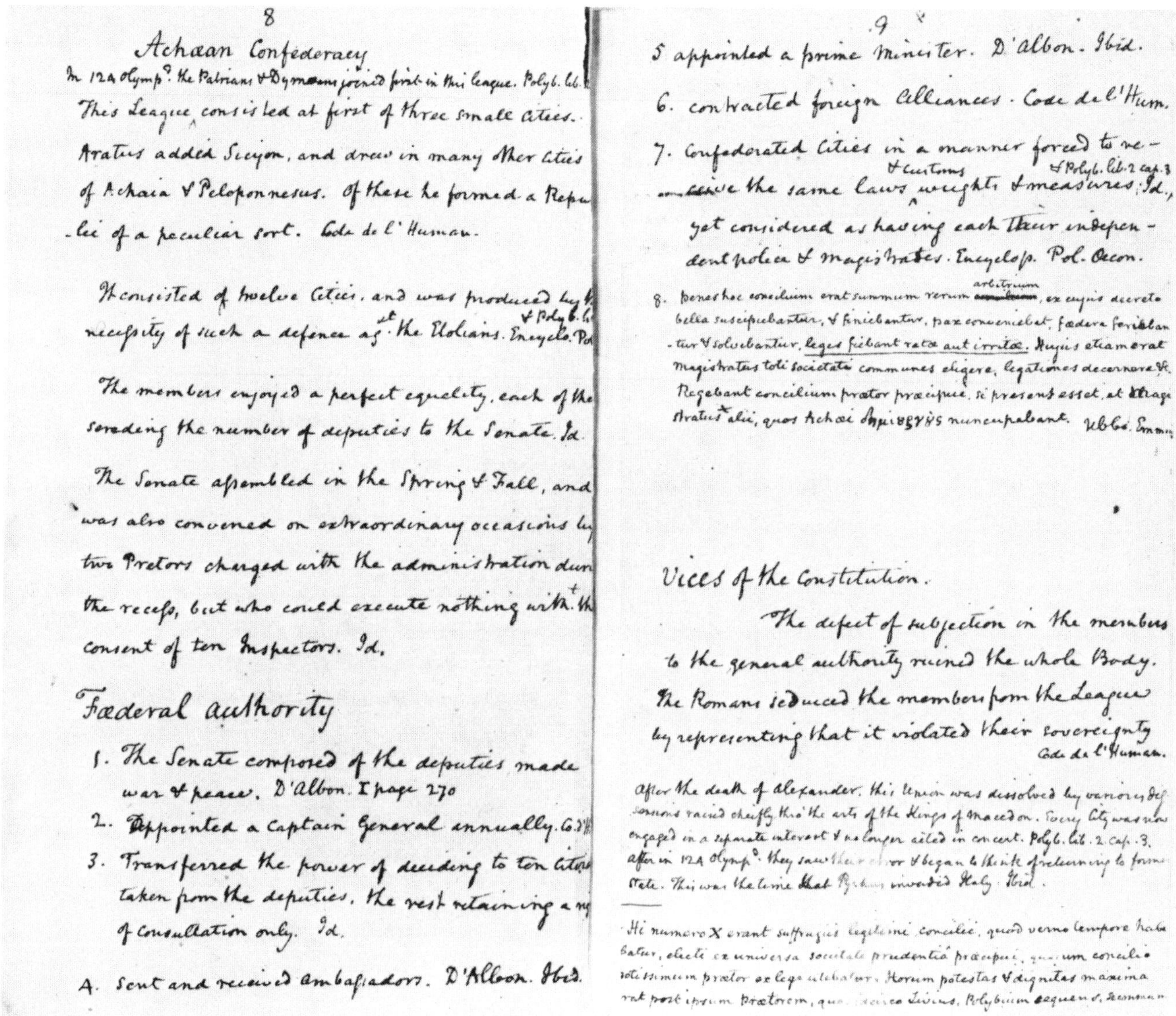
8

Achaan Confederacy

In 124 olymp.d the Patrians & Dymaeans joined first in this league. Polyb. lib.

This League consisted at first of three small cities. Aratus added Sicyon, and drew in many other cities of Achaia & Peloponnesus. Of these he formed a Republic of a peculiar sort. Code de l'Human.

It consisted of twelve Cities, and was produced by the necessity of such a defence agst the Etolians. Encyclo. Pol. & Polyb. lib.

The members enjoyed a perfect equality, each of them sending the number of deputies to the Senate. Id.

The Senate assembled in the Spring & Fall, and was also convened on extraordinary occasions by two Pretors charged with the administration during the recess, but who could execute nothing witht the consent of ten Inspectors. Id.

Fœderal authority

1. The Senate composed of the deputies made war & peace. D'Albon. I page 270
2. Appointed a Captain General annually. Cod. H.
3. Transferred the power of deciding to ten Cities taken from the deputies, the rest retaining a voice of consultation only. Id.
4. Sent and received ambassadors. D'Albon. Ibid.

9

5. appointed a prime Minister. D'Albon. Ibid.
6. contracted foreign Alliances. Code de l'Hum.
7. Confederated Cities in a manner forced to receive the same laws & customs, weights & measures. Id. & Polyb. lib. 2 cap. 3 yet considered as having each their independent police & magistrates. Encyclop. Pol. Oecon.
8. Penes hoc concilium erat summum rerum arbitrium, ex cujus decreto bella suscipiebantur, & finiebantur, pax conveniebat, fœdera feriebantur & solvebantur, leges fiebant ratæ aut irritæ. Hujus etiam erat magistratus toti societati communes eligere, legationes decernere &c. Regebant concilium prætor præcipue, si præsens esset, et [illegible] alii, quos Achæi δημιουργους nuncupabant. Ubbo Emmius

Vices of the Constitution.

The defect of subjection in the members to the general authority ruined the whole Body. The Romans seduced the members from the League by representing that it violated their sovereignty. Code de l'Human.

After the death of Alexander, this Union was dissolved by various dissensions raised chiefly thro' the arts of the Kings of Macedon. Every City was then engaged in a separate interest & no longer acted in concert. Polyb. lib. 2 cap. 3. After in 124 olymp. they saw their error & began to think of returning to former state. This was the time that Pyrrhus invaded Italy. Ibid.

Hi numero X erant suffragiis legitimi concilii, quod verno tempore habebatur, electi ex universa societate prudentia præcipui, [illegible] cum concilio toti [illegible] prætor ex lege utebatur. Horum potestas & dignitas maxima erat post ipsum Prætorem, [illegible] Livius, Polybium sequens, [illegible]

James Madison, *Of Ancient and Modern Confederacies* (excerpt), mss. notebook, ca. May 1787. James Madison Papers, Library of Congress.

work like an exquisite orrery. What applied to the universe at large would work just as well in mapping out a plan of government, and during the winter of 1786-87 Madison turned such a scheme over in his mind many times before he finally wrote an outline for a model republic—Virginia style. When Madison stopped by for a chat with Washington on his way northward, the general's endorsement was already assured. "Influence is no government," Washington had thundered when someone suggested that his name alone could bring Americans to their senses. Not influence, but a sound plan based on republican principles, was Madison's answer to America's crisis.

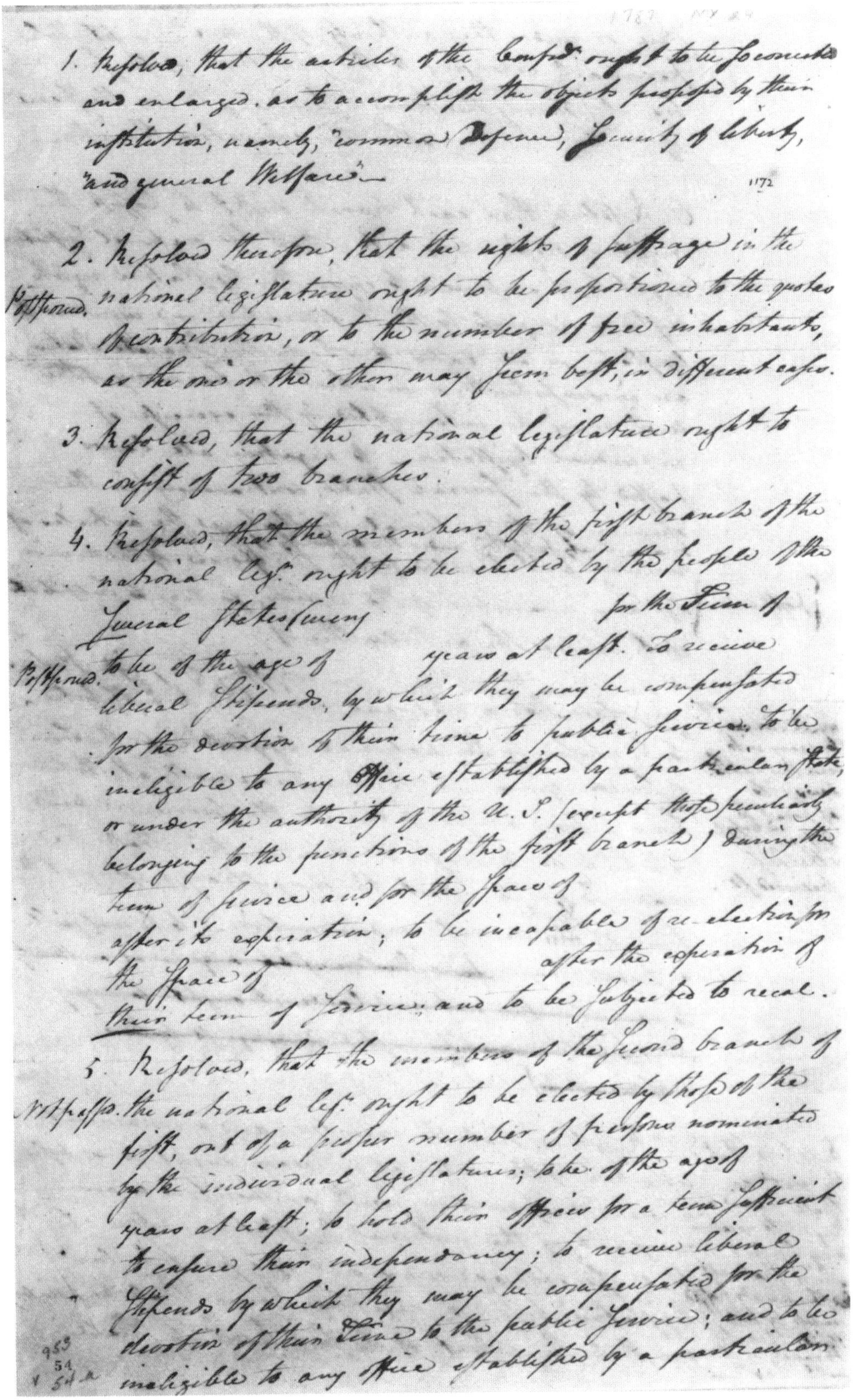

1. Resolved, that the articles of the Confedn. ought to be so corrected and enlarged, as to accomplish the objects proposed by their institution; namely, "common Defence, Security of liberty, and general Welfare."

1172

2. Resolved therefore, that the rights of suffrage in the national legislature ought to be proportioned to the quotas of contribution, or to the number of free inhabitants, as the one or the other may seem best, in different cases.

Postponed.

3. Resolved, that the national legislature ought to consist of two branches.

4. Resolved, that the members of the first branch of the national leg. ought to be elected by the people of the several States every for the term of to be of the age of years at least. to receive liberal Stipends, by which they may be compensated for the devotion of their time to public service; to be ineligible to any office established by a particular State, or under the authority of the U.S. (except those peculiarly belonging to the functions of the first branch) during the term of service and for the space of after its expiration; to be incapable of re-election for the space of after the expiration of their term of service; and to be subjected to recal.

Postponed.

5. Resolved, that the members of the second branch of the national leg. ought to be elected by those of the first, out of a proper number of persons nominated by the individual legislatures; to be of the age of years at least; to hold their offices for a term sufficient to ensure their independency; to receive liberal stipends by which they may be compensated for the devotion of their time to the public service; and to be ineligible to any office established by a particular

Not pass.

953
54
54a

William Paterson (1745–1806), *The Virginia Plan* (excerpt, working copy), ca. May 29, 1787. William Samuel Johnson Papers, Library of Congress.

The Federal Convention that convened in May 1787 to amend the Articles of Confederation never paused a moment with that business. Instead, the work done in the caucus of Virginians before the actual business began led to a framework known to history as the Virginia Plan. Most of the ideas came from Madison, with just enough help from George Mason to make it appear that the younger man was not trying to run things. As a political doctor Madison had scrapped the old notion that each state would have one vote in the national council, and he also promoted the concept of a two-house legislature working with a chief executive and judiciary. Each of the three branches had separate responsibilities and would check the other's power (the good Montesquieu's influence regarding separation of powers was at its height). Madison also conceived of "a Council of revision made up of the Executive and a Convenient number of the National Judiciary," who could veto laws passed by either the Congress or state legislatures. Provision was made for allowing the western states to become part of the original union, and each state was guaranteed its territorial integrity and "a Republican Government."[16] The whole plan filled only a few pages, but it provided the intellectual fodder for the ensuing summer's debates in Philadelphia, and for this alone Madison deserves to be considered "the Father of the Constitution."

Now thirty-six years old, Madison undertook to carry his plan through a convention that was a hodgepodge of prejudice and suspicion. There was no visitors' gallery in Independence Hall, but from other delegates' notes we learn that Madison carried his points by his easy manner, persuasive oratory (he still spoke so low that those at the end of the hall had to strain to hear), and obvious intellectual vigor. He made endless notes, kept an invaluable record of that historic event as a matter of duty, and as a good loser must have impressed those fussy delegates who always liked to have things go their way. Member Pierce Butler from South Carolina wrote down impressions of his colleagues braving the summer solstice in Philadelphia and said of Madison:

> *Mr. Maddison is a character who has long been in public life; and what is very remarkable every Person seems to acknowledge his greatness. He blends together the profound politician, with the Scholar. In the management of every great question he evidently took the lead in the Convention, and tho' he cannot be called an Orator, he is a most agre[e]able, eloquent, and convincing Speaker. . . . The affairs of the United States, he perhaps, has the most correct knowledge of, of any Man in the Union.*[17]

16. The Virginia Plan, May 29, 1787, in Madison *Papers,* 10:12-17.

James Thackara (1767–1848) after Charles Willson Peale (1741–1827), *A N.W. View of the State House in Philadelphia taken 1778*, engraving, $5^{11/16}$ in x 8 in, in the *Columbian Magazine*, Philadelphia, July 1787. Prints and Photographs Division, Library of Congress.

What is so remarkable about this sketch is not that it was drawn by a South Carolina dandy, but that Butler's comments so nearly reflect the consensus of judgment on Madison's abilities.

Although Madison did not work out the compromise which broke a deadlock threatening the whole proceeding, he saw his plan survive much committee wrangling and emerge as a blueprint for what became the Constitution on September 17, 1787. He spoke 161 times and could hardly be still at others. One of his pet schemes, the unlimited veto by a revisionary council of both congressional and state legislation, fell by the wayside. "On no other point did he argue with greater conviction, tenacity, and originality," but as

17. William Pierce: Character Sketches of Delegates to the Federal Convention, in Max Farrand, ed., *The Records of the Federal Convention of 1787*, 4 vols., (New Haven: Yale University Press, 1911–37), 3:94.

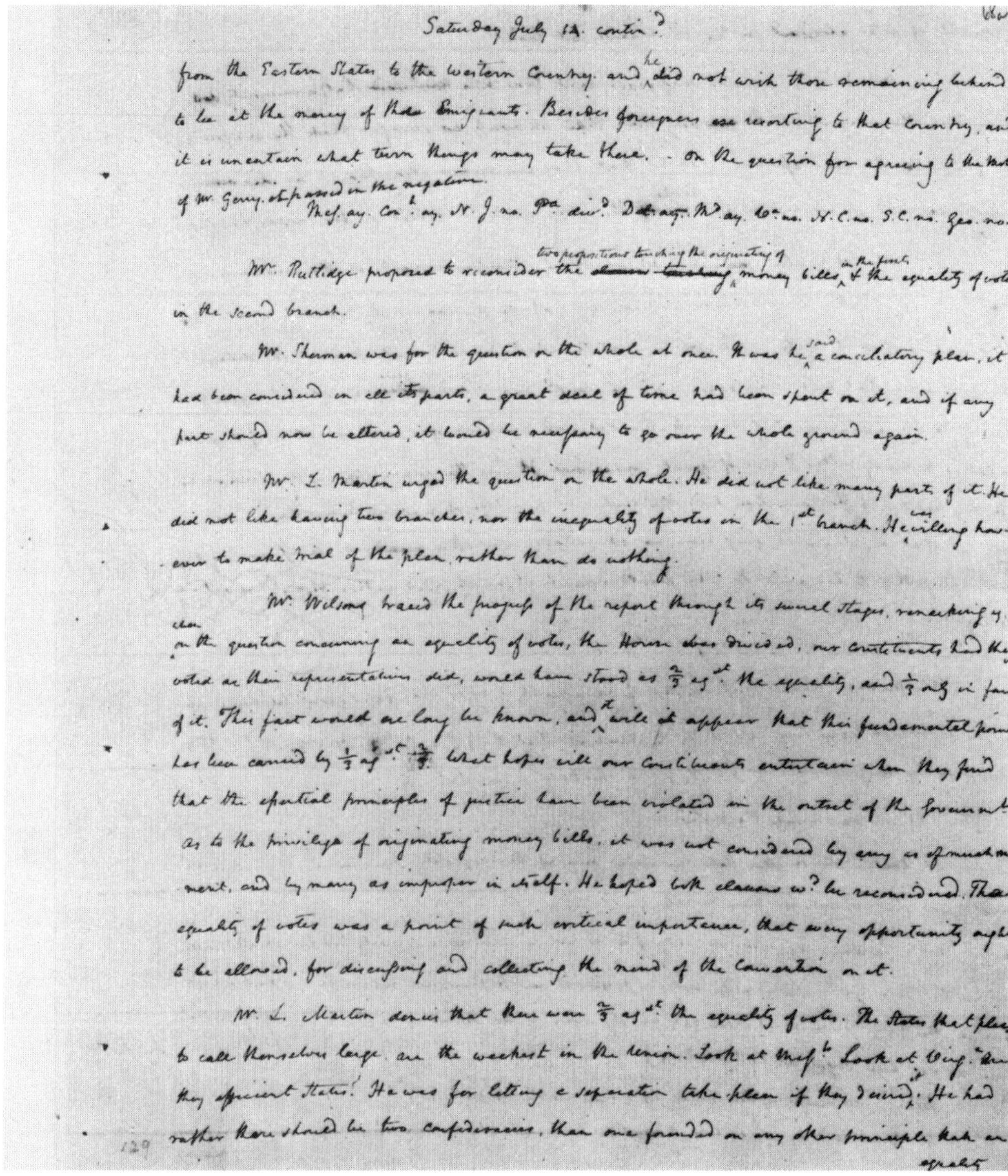

Saturday July 14. contind.

from the Eastern States to the Western Country, and he did not wish those remaining behind to be at the mercy of the Emigrants. Besides foreigners are resorting to that country, and it is uncertain what turn things may take there. – On the question for agreeing to the Motion of Mr. Gerry, it passed in the negative.

Mass. ay. Cont. ay. N. J. no. Pa. divd. Del. ay. Md. ay. Va. no. N. C. no. S. C. no. Geo. no.

Mr. Rutlidge proposed to reconsider the two propositions touching the originating of money bills in the first & the equality of votes in the second branch.

Mr. Sherman was for the question on the whole at once. It was he said a conciliatory plan, it had been considered in all its parts, a great deal of time had been spent on it, and if any part should now be altered, it would be necessary to go over the whole ground again.

Mr. L. Martin urged the question on the whole. He did not like many parts of it. He did not like having two branches, nor the inequality of votes in the 1st branch. He was willing however to make trial of the plan, rather than do nothing.

Mr. Wilson traced the progress of the report through its several stages, remarking yt. when on the question concerning an equality of votes, the House was divided, our Constituents had they voted as their representatives did, would have stood as 2/3 agst. the equality, and 1/3 only in favor of it. This fact would ere long be known, and it will appear that this fundamental point has been carried by 1/3 agst. 2/3. What hopes will our Constituents entertain when they find that the essential principles of justice have been violated in the outset of the Governmt. As to the privilege of originating money bills, it was not considered by any as of much moment, and by many as improper in itself. He hoped both clauses wd. be reconsidered. The equality of votes was a point of such critical importance, that every opportunity ought to be allowed, for discussing and collecting the mind of the Convention on it.

Mr. L. Martin denies that there were 2/3 agst. the equality of votes. The States that please to call themselves large, are the weakest in the Union. Look at Masts. Look at Virga. Are they efficient States? He was for letting a separation take place if they desired it. He had rather there should be two Confederacies, than one founded on any other principle than an equality

James Madison, *Notes on the Debates in the Federal Convention* (excerpt, Saturday, July 14), 1787. James Madison Papers, Library of Congress.

things worked out a solution not unlike what he envisioned came about anyway through the judiciary clauses and their interpretation by John Marshall.[18] At the time, however, Madison wrote Jefferson with something less than optimism. "The plan should it be adopted will neither effectually answer its national object nor prevent the local mischiefs which every where excite disgusts ag[ain]st the state governments," he told his friend Jefferson. The orrery might work, but for how long?

Anonymous, probably after Charles Willson Peale (1741–1827), *Ja^s. Madison*, stipple and line engraving, 3⅜ in x 2¾ in, in Charles Smith, *The Gentleman's Political Pocket Almanack for 1797*, New York, 1796. Courtesy National Portrait Gallery, Smithsonian Institution, Washington, D.C.

A month later Madison realized that he had been too critical. "The great desideratum in Government is, so to modify the sovereignty as that it may be sufficiently neutral between different parts of the Society to controul one part from invading the rights of another, and at the same time sufficiently controuled itself, from setting up an interest adverse to that of the entire Society," he wrote Jefferson in late October 1787.[19] But he was talking now about perfection, and Madison's fine-grained mind discerned the difference between political dreams and practical politics. They were not all the same, he realized. Exercising his common sense, Madison soon dropped all his doubts and entered the propaganda battle raging over ratification of the Constitution. From his convenient vantage point in New York (where he returned to serve in the expiring continental Congress), Madison used his franking privilege to dispatch reams of advice to the pro-Constitution forces in crucial cities.

18. Harold S. Schultz, "James Madison: Father of the Constitution?" *Quarterly Journal of the Library of Congress* 37 (1980): 221.

19. Madison to Jefferson, September 6, October 24, 1787, in Madison *Papers*, 10:163-64, 214.

Joseph Wright (1756–1793), *John Jay* (1745–1829), oil on canvas, 30¼ in x 26 in, New York?, 1786. Courtesy New-York Historical Society, New York City, gift of John Pintard.

Nobody planned it that way, but in the ensuing debate over adoption of the Constitution, Madison teamed with John Jay and Alexander Hamilton to write a masterful work on the purposes of republican government. *The Federalist* articles were originally published in the daily newspapers in New York City as arguments aimed at the anti-Constitution forces in that crucial state. "The Papers were first meant for the important doubtful state of New York and signed a 'Citizen of New York,' " Madison recalled, "afterwards

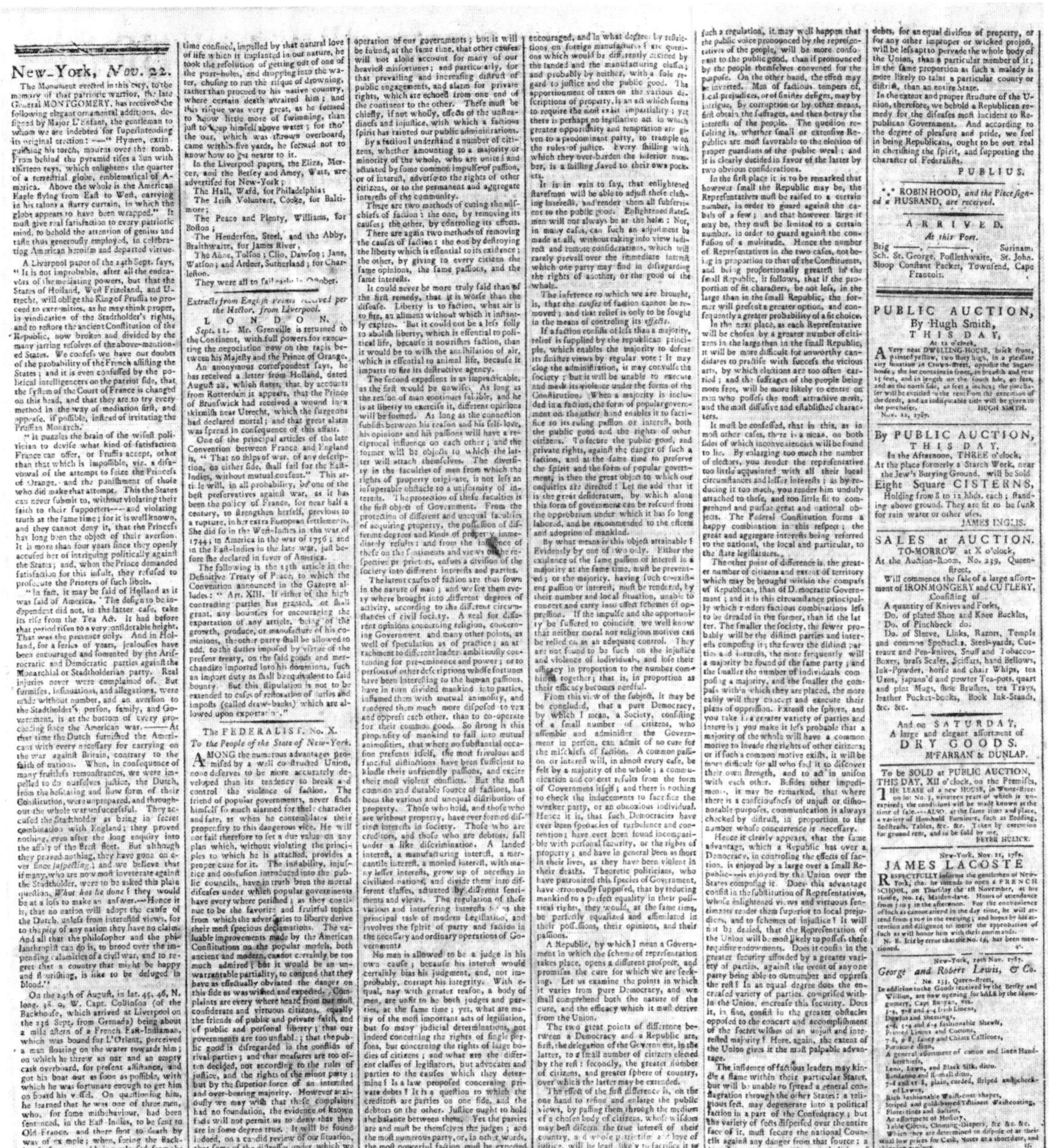
New-York, Nov. 22.

The FEDERALIST. No. X.

To the People of the State of New-York.

PUBLIUS.

PUBLIC AUCTION,

By Hugh Smith,

THIS DAY,

By PUBLIC AUCTION,

THIS DAY,

SALES at AUCTION.

JAMES LACOSTE

Publius (pseudonym for James Madison), *The Federalist. No. X.* in the *Daily Advertiser*, New York, November 22, 1787. Serial and Government Publications Division, Library of Congress.

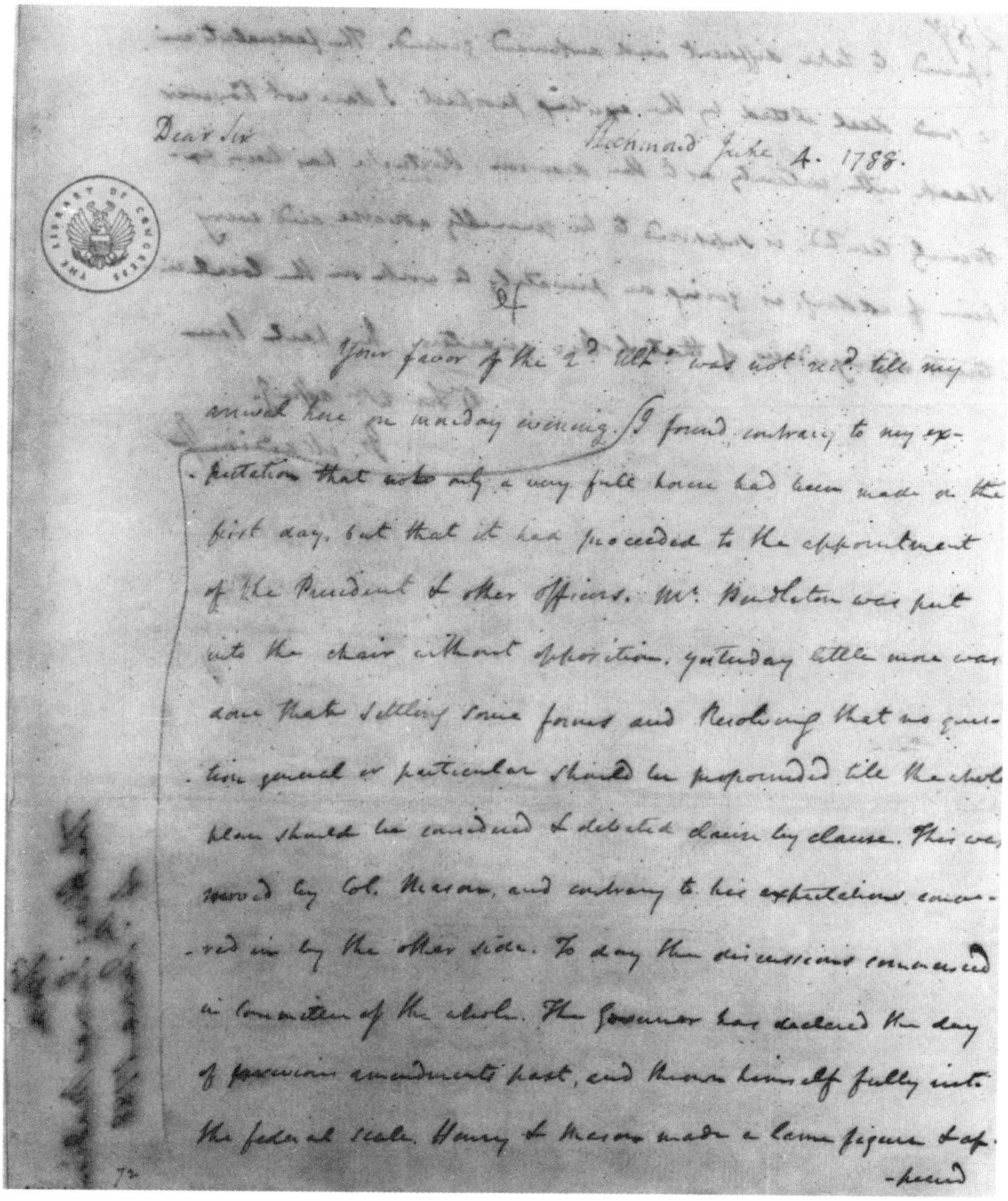
Dear Sir Richmond June 4. 1788.

Your favor of the 2d. ult. was not recd. till my arrival here on monday evening. I found, contrary to my expectation that not only a very full house had been made on the first day, but that it had proceeded to the appointment of the President & other officers. Mr. Pendleton was put into the chair without opposition. yesterday little more was done than settling some forms and Resolving that no question general or particular should be propounded till the whole plan should be considered & debated clause by clause. This was moved by Col. Mason, and contrary to his expectations concurred in by the other side. To day the discussions commenced in Committee of the whole. The Governor has declared the day of previous amendments past, and thrown himself fully into the federal scale. Henry & Mason made a lame figure & appeared

James Madison, *Letter to George Washington* (excerpt), Richmond, June 4, 1788. George Washington Papers, Library of Congress.

meant for all the States under 'Publius.' "[20] No matter that Madison posed as a New Yorker, for such tactics were accepted in those days when it was customary to publish a column anonymously. What was important was that his *Federalist* paper no. 10 became the most reasonable statement ever presented to explain what an expanding nation might do if it accepted the basic premise of majority rule, a balanced government of three separate branches, and a commitment to balance all the diverse interests through a system of checks and

20. "James Madison's Autobiography," p. 202.

John Trumbull (1756–1843), *Alexander Hamilton* (1757–1804), oil on canvas, 30¼ in x 24⅛ in, Philadelphia?, ca. 1792. Courtesy National Gallery of Art, Washington, D.C., gift of the Avalon Foundation, 1952.

balances. The brilliance of his ideas slowly sank in, and although Madison dashed them off (he sent in twenty-nine of the eighty-five essays), his writings remain as one of the most original presentations ever made by an American on the theory of government.

Madison's ability to organize the Federalists who favored the Constitution into a cohesive unit has never been fully recognized. Using his free mailing privilege to full advantage, he wrote day and night to correspondents in every part of the Union, exhorting them to rush along the ratification process as quickly as possible without offending too many powerful men. Called back to Virginia when a rumor mill spread notions that he was against a bill of rights (Mason had sought such a bill in the last moments of the Philadelphia meeting, and Madison had not then seen the point clearly), Madison hurried to Orange County to broadcast a promise that he was second to no one in his commitment to religious freedom and civil rights for all. Once elected to the Virginia ratifying convention, Madison made his own evaluation of the situation. If Virginia as the largest state in the Union should reject the Constitution, then the whole process that began back in 1785 might be torn asunder. The only alternative was to work around the clock to convince a handful of uncommitted delegates from western Virginia that the Constitution was their best bet.

As John Marshall would say later, when it came to persuasive debate there was nobody in Virginia who could match Madison. Patrick Henry had the knack of entertaining his listeners, but later they had trouble remembering what he said. Madison, Marshall recalled, was not known for his volume as a speaker but for his logic and persuasiveness. At the Richmond convention, Madison not only made Gov. Edmund Randolph desert Henry and Mason to endorse the Constitution, he also matched Henry and Mason blow-for-blow in the verbal slugging match that took place in June 1788. The fight ended with an eight-vote victory for Madison and his Federalist friends. Henry skulked and plotted ways to keep Madison out of the Congress, but Madison had done what no Virginian up to that time had done—he had whipped Patrick Henry in a public debate. Thereafter, Madison's credentials in his home state were beyond reproach. His victory in that one battle served him well for the rest of his life.

Patrick Henry still had enough power to keep Madison out of the Senate when the new government began to function. However, when Henry talked James Monroe into running against Madison for a seat in the First Congress, the whole campaign became a kind of Alphonse-Gaston act, with Monroe on the short end of nearly all the ballots. Probably no more gentlemanly campaign was ever conducted, but ultimately the voters from Orange to Spotsylvania decided they liked Madison better than Monroe. The two candidates parted company only briefly and would remain friends until the end of their days.

Madison later said he was glad that he had not been elected to the Senate, and this was a frank rather than a modest statement. He realized that what the nation needed in 1789 was a ramrod in the House, and he was prepared for

We the People of the United States, in Order to form a more perfect Union, establish Justice, insure domestic Tranquility, provide for the common defence, promote the general Welfare, and secure the Blessings of Liberty to ourselves and our Posterity, do ordain and establish this Constitution for the United States of America.

Article. I.

Section. 1. All legislative Powers herein granted shall be vested in a Congress of the United States, which shall consist of a Senate and House of Representatives.

Section. 2. The House of Representatives shall be composed of Members chosen every second Year by the People of the several States, and the Electors in each State shall have the Qualifications requisite for Electors of the most numerous Branch of the State Legislature.

No Person shall be a Representative who shall not have attained to the Age of twenty five Years, and been seven Years a Citizen of the United States, and who shall not, when elected, be an Inhabitant of that State in which he shall be chosen.

Representatives and direct Taxes shall be apportioned among the several States which may be included within this Union, according to their respective Numbers, which shall be determined by adding to the whole Number of free Persons, including those bound to Service for a Term of Years, and excluding Indians not taxed, three fifths of all other Persons. The actual Enumeration shall be made within three Years after the first Meeting of the Congress of the United States, and within every subsequent Term of ten Years, in such Manner as they shall by Law direct. The Number of Representatives shall not exceed one for every thirty Thousand, but each State shall have at Least one Representative; and until such enumeration shall be made, the State of New Hampshire shall be entitled to chuse three, Massachusetts eight, Rhode Island and Providence Plantations one, Connecticut five, New York six, New Jersey four, Pennsylvania eight, Delaware one, Maryland six, Virginia ten, North Carolina five, South Carolina five, and Georgia three.

When vacancies happen in the Representation from any State, the Executive Authority thereof shall issue Writs of Election to fill such Vacancies.

The House of Representatives shall chuse their Speaker and other Officers; and shall have the sole Power of Impeachment.

Section. 3. The Senate of the United States shall be composed of two Senators from each State, chosen by the Legislature thereof for six Years; and each Senator shall have one Vote.

Immediately after they shall be assembled in Consequence of the first Election, they shall be divided as equally as may be into three Classes. The Seats of the Senators of the first Class shall be vacated at the Expiration of the second Year, of the second Class at the Expiration of the fourth Year, and of the third Class at the Expiration of the sixth Year, so that one third may be chosen every second Year; and if Vacancies happen by Resignation, or otherwise, during the Recess of the Legislature of any State, the Executive thereof may make temporary Appointments until the next Meeting of the Legislature, which shall then fill such Vacancies.

No Person shall be a Senator who shall not have attained to the Age of thirty Years, and been nine Years a Citizen of the United States, and who shall not, when elected, be an Inhabitant of that State for which he shall be chosen.

The Vice President of the United States shall be President of the Senate, but shall have no Vote, unless they be equally divided.

The Senate shall chuse their other Officers, and also a President pro tempore, in the Absence of the Vice President, or when he shall exercise the Office of President of the United States.

The Senate shall have the sole Power to try all Impeachments. When sitting for that Purpose, they shall be on Oath or Affirmation. When the President of the United States is tried, the Chief Justice shall preside: And no Person shall be convicted without the Concurrence of two thirds of the Members present.

Judgment in Cases of Impeachment shall not extend further than to removal from Office, and disqualification to hold and enjoy any Office of honor, Trust or Profit under the United States: but the Party convicted shall nevertheless be liable and subject to Indictment, Trial, Judgment and Punishment, according to Law.

Section. 4. The Times, Places and Manner of holding Elections for Senators and Representatives, shall be prescribed in each State by the Legislature thereof; but the Congress may at any time by Law make or alter such Regulations, except as to the Places of chusing Senators.

The Congress shall assemble at least once in every Year, and such Meeting shall be on the first Monday in December, unless they shall by Law appoint a different Day.

Section. 5. Each House shall be the Judge of the Elections, Returns and Qualifications of its own Members, and a Majority of each shall constitute a Quorum to do Business; but a smaller Number may adjourn from day to day, and may be authorized to compel the Attendance of absent Members, in such Manner, and under such Penalties as each House may provide.

Each House may determine the Rules of its Proceedings, punish its Members for disorderly Behaviour, and, with the Concurrence of two thirds, expel a Member.

Each House shall keep a Journal of its Proceedings, and from time to time publish the same, excepting such Parts as may in their Judgment require Secrecy; and the Yeas and Nays of the Members of either House on any question shall, at the Desire of one fifth of those Present, be entered on the Journal.

Neither House, during the Session of Congress, shall, without the Consent of the other, adjourn for more than three days, nor to any other Place than that in which the two Houses shall be sitting.

Section. 6. The Senators and Representatives shall receive a Compensation for their Services, to be ascertained by Law, and paid out of the Treasury of the United States. They shall in all Cases, except Treason, Felony and Breach of the Peace, be privileged from Arrest during their Attendance at the Session of their respective Houses, and in going to and returning from the same; and for any Speech or Debate in either House, they shall not be questioned in any other Place.

No Senator or Representative shall, during the Time for which he was elected, be appointed to any civil Office under the Authority of the United States, which shall have been created, or the Emoluments whereof shall have been encreased during such time; and no Person holding any Office under the United States, shall be a Member of either House during his Continuance in Office.

Section. 7. All Bills for raising Revenue shall originate in the House of Representatives; but the Senate may propose or concur with Amendments as on other Bills.

Every Bill which shall have passed the House of Representatives and the Senate, shall, before it become a Law, be presented to the President of the

The Constitution of the United States (excerpt), 1788. Courtesy National Archives and Records Service, Washington, D.C.

Amos Doolittle (1754–1832) after Peter LaCour (fl. New York, 1785–1799), *Federal Hall The Seat of Congress*, engraving, 16$\frac{15}{16}$ in x 13½ in, New Haven, 1790. Courtesy Fraunces Tavern Museum, New York City. Nancy Rosing photograph.

that role. President Washington deferred to Madison at every turn, seeking advice on ways and means of keeping the office of the chief executive from turning into a pseudo-monarchy. Madison became a ghostwriter for Washington, preparing both the president's speech to the House and the House's reply, keeping in mind the dignity needed to preserve Washington's high standing and the proper decorum elected representatives of the people should show. Gradually, Washington turned to Hamilton for help on his speeches and his actions, but for the first years of his presidency Washington invariably looked to Madison for guidance on precedent-setting presidential conduct and on constitutional questions. In every instance, Madison favored simplicity and a strict construction of the Constitution.

What was happening (and neither man realized it) was that two points of view were wrestling for control of the nation. The bankers and merchants clustered around Hamilton wanted the national government to do whatever was necessary to restore credit, shore up the weak merchant shipping fleet, and build a navy symbolic of the nation's potential strength. Planters and farmers had Washington's sympathy, but Madison was by far their ablest spokesman as he wanted the Constitution strictly observed to keep taxes low, avoid subsidies to commercial enterprises, and spend as few dollars as possible on forts and frigates. Ultimately, Washington chose to lean toward the view that the general welfare of the people excused a slight bending of constitutional guidelines. Madison turned to Jefferson and they worked out a different philosophy that emerged—after a knock-down-drag-out fight over Jay's 1795 treaty with England—as a two-party system. All of them paid lip service to the idea that political parties were ruinous. "If I could not go to Heaven but with a party," Jefferson sighed in 1789, "I would not go there at all." But seven years later he and Madison were in the thick of a party fight to decide on Washington's successor. John Adams won over Jefferson, but the vote had been far from a landslide. Madison, worn out by the daily battles in the House of Representatives, took a kind of sabbatical leave and went back to Montpelier to become better acquainted with his bride (he had married the pretty widow, Dolley Payne Todd, in 1794) and to gain a perspective on his life. He was forty-six, and he had made more enemies in Congress than he liked to contemplate. Jefferson, as second-best in the 1796 presidential polling, was now vice-president. The mails between the temporary capital in Philadelphia and Montpelier were heavy with letters passing between the two dedicated Republicans, as their ideas took shape and evoked a response among like-minded voters.

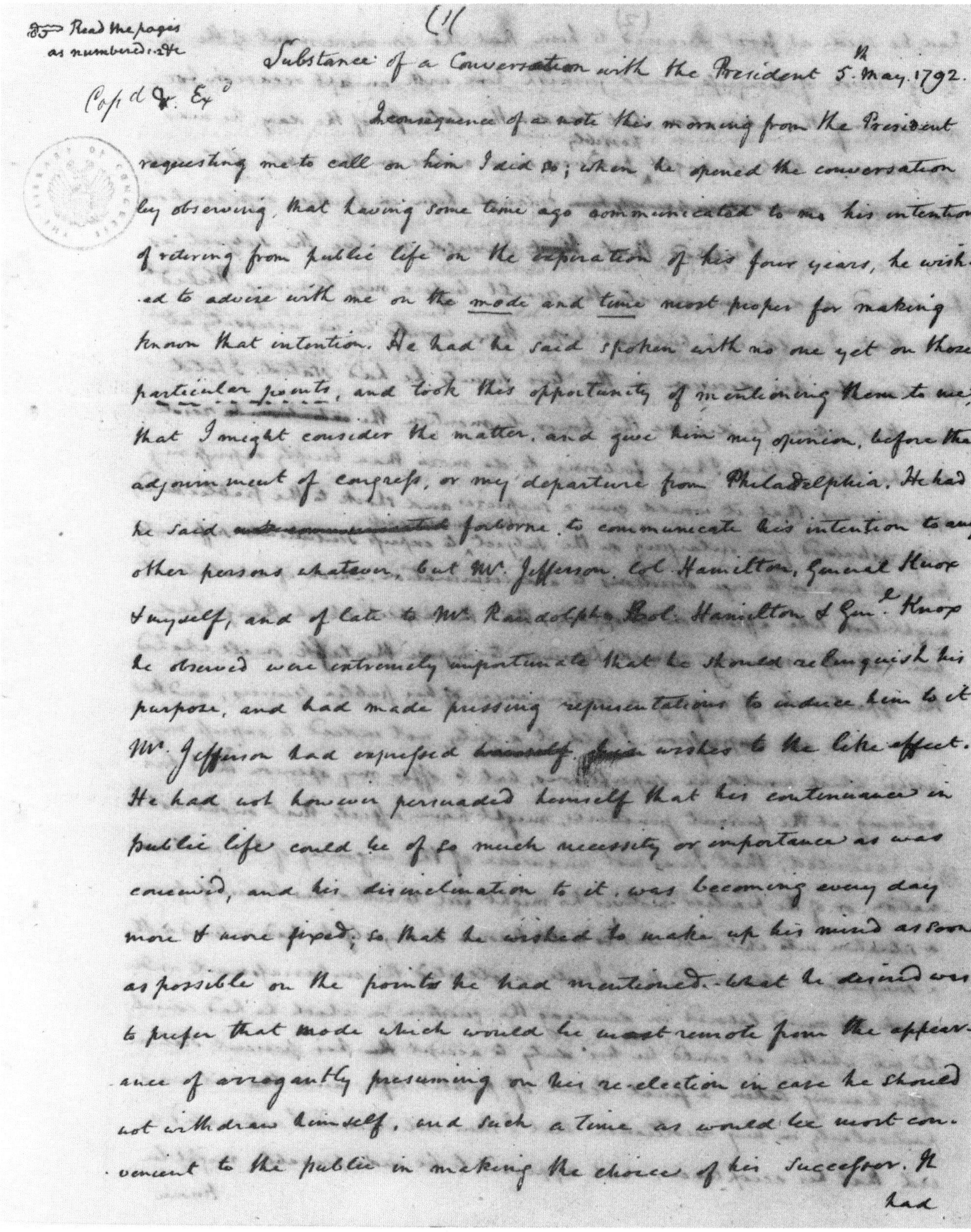

Read the pages as numbered

Cop'd & Ex'd

(1)

Substance of a Conversation with the President 5th May 1792.

In consequence of a note this morning from the President requesting me to call on him I did so; when he opened the conversation by observing, that having some time ago communicated to me his intention of retiring from public life on the expiration of his four years, he wished to advise with me on the mode and time most proper for making known that intention. He had he said spoken with no one yet on those particular points, and took this opportunity of mentioning them to me, that I might consider the matter, and give him my opinion, before the adjournment of Congress, or my departure from Philadelphia. He had he said ~~not communicated~~ forborne to communicate his intention to any other persons whatever, but Mr. Jefferson, Col. Hamilton, General Knox & myself, and of late to Mr. Randolph. Col. Hamilton & Genl. Knox he observed were extremely importunate that he should relinquish his purpose, and had made pressing representations to induce him to it. Mr. Jefferson had expressed ~~himself~~ ~~his~~ wishes to the like effect. He had not however persuaded himself that his continuance in public life could be of so much necessity or importance as was conceived, and his disinclination to it, was becoming every day more & more fixed; so that he wished to make up his mind as soon as possible on the points he had mentioned. What he desired was to prefer that mode which would be most remote from the appearance of arrogantly presuming on his re-election in case he should not withdraw himself, and such a time as would be most convenient to the public in making the choice of his Successor. It had

James Madison, *Substance of a Conversation with the President* (excerpt), May 5–25, 1792. James Madison Papers, Library of Congress.

Charles Willson Peale (1741–1827), *James Madison* (from life), oil on canvas, 23¼ in x 19 in, Philadelphia, ca. 1792. Courtesy Thomas Gilcrease Institute of American History and Art, Tulsa, Oklahoma.

What emerged from the Jefferson-Madison conversations and their voluminous correspondence was the formation of a political party dedicated to the proposition that the United States was the world's best hope for proving that mankind was capable of self-government. It was a startling idea, a seedling that struggled for centuries and finally took root in North America. The American Revolution brought the notion into full bloom, but there had been some pruning and withering on the vine. The whole point boiled down to the idea expressed by Madison in *Federalist* paper no. 51. "It is of great importance in a republic not only to guard the society against the oppression of its rulers, but to guard one part of the society against the injustice of the other part," he wrote. In the United States "all authority . . . will be derived from and dependent on the society, [but] the society itself will be broken into so many parts,

Amos Doolittle (1754-1832), *A New Display of the United States*, engraving, 20⅓₂ in x 16¼ in, New Haven, August 14, 1799. Prints and Photographs Division, Library of Congress.

interests and classes of citizens, that the rights of individuals, or of the minority, will be in little danger from interested combinations of the majority. In a free government the security for civil rights must be the same as that for religious rights."[21]

21. *Federalist* paper no. 51, in Clinton Rossiter, ed., *The Federalist Papers* (New York: New American Library, 1951), pp. 323-24.

Madison had the ideas while Jefferson had the personality and the charm needed to turn those thoughts into an inspired vision of what "liberty" meant to their followers. Soon the two Virginians were challenged by a set of circumstances that forced them into a protest movement based on the principle of states' rights that was as dangerous as the physician's deadliest drug. When the Federalists decided to reverse the trend of civil rights in America by passing a series of bills known as the Alien and Sedition Acts, the Democratic Republican victims of their legislative wrath reacted with anguish and began working on the next election. Narrowly passed by the Federalists and signed by President Adams with glowing approval, the legislation contained noxious provisions that were aimed at stifling all criticism of the Adams administration. Within months a score of Democratic Republican editors, congressmen, and assorted hangers-on had been indicted and some severely punished by vindictive Federalist judges wielding intimidated juries.

Madison and Jefferson believed the Federalists had overreached themselves. Yet it was part of their manner not to meet fire with fire. Instead, Jefferson conceived of a plan to undo the Federalists' harm by exercising majority rule. Into the sixteen states now in the Union they sent torrents of advice on what candidates should be elected in 1800—and their test of competence was simple: Did the candidate subscribe to the tenets of the Virginia and Kentucky Resolutions?

For years Jefferson's tracks were so well covered it was not public knowledge that he goaded Madison into writing the Virginia Resolutions of 1798 and wrote the Kentucky version himself. In these resolutions, the two Republican chieftains convinced followers that an unconstitutional law could be upset by the collective action of the states. The notion that a state legislature could declare an act of Congress unconstitutional was original but loaded with political gunpowder. Somewhat hesitantly Madison went along and in the Virginia Resolutions extolled the rights of states to suspend "unconstitutional" national laws. Democrats read this message at rallies for the next generation, as one of the "true principles of the Democratic party." The treatise became, in other hands, a strong call for states' rights, but Madison also asked for strict construction of the Constitution, expressed concern over civil rights, and pledged to maintain the Union "with the most scrupulous fidelity." His assertion that the states had the right and duty "to interpose" and reject unconstitutional laws was not spelled out—Madison simply said the right had to be exercised to arrest "the progress of evil." Other state legislatures failed to pick up the gauntlet the two Virginia Republicans had tossed down, so the

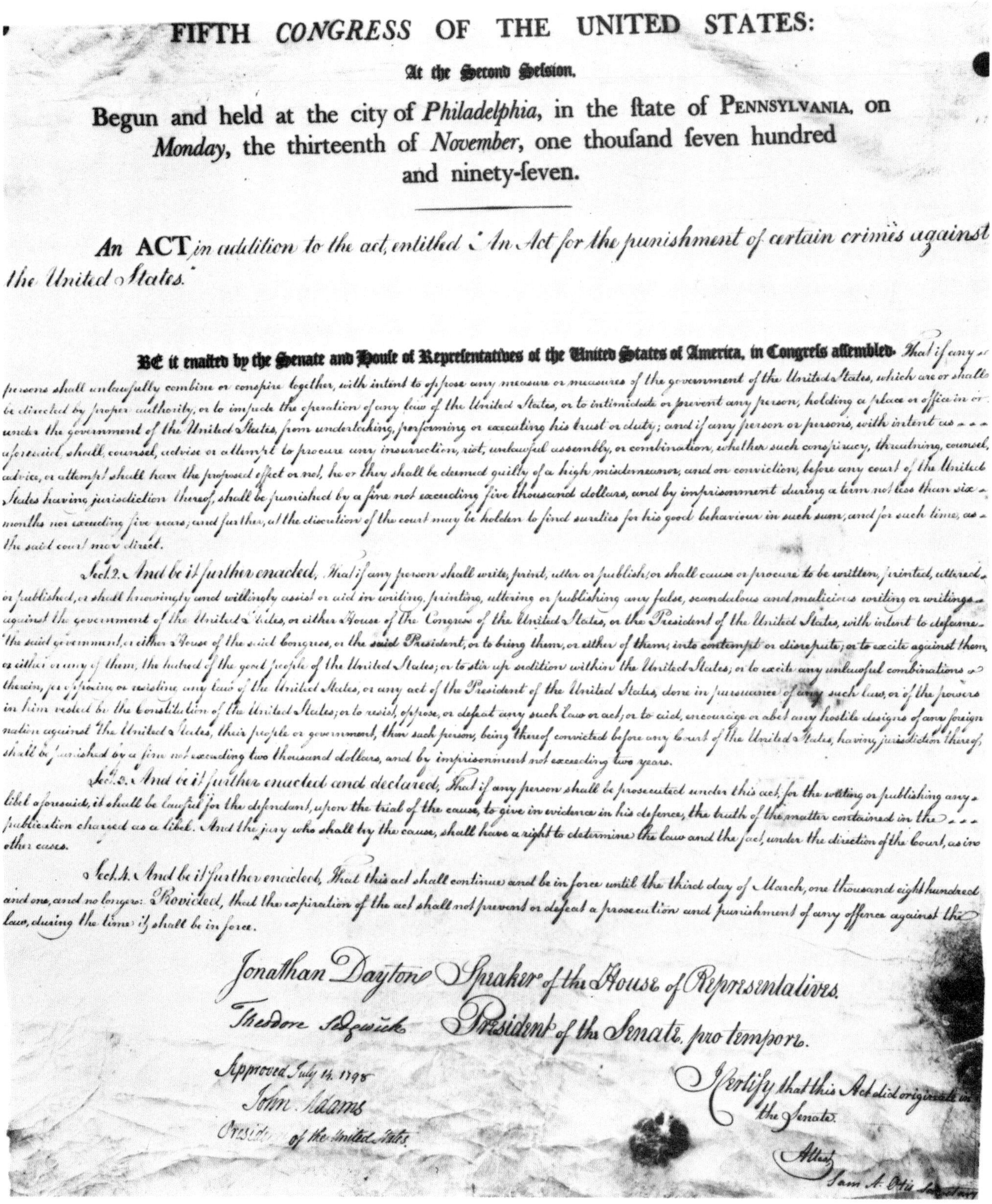

FIFTH *CONGRESS* OF THE UNITED STATES:

At the Second Seſsion,

Begun and held at the city of *Philadelphia*, in the ſtate of PENNSYLVANIA, on *Monday*, the thirteenth of *November*, one thouſand ſeven hundred and ninety-ſeven.

An ACT in addition to the act, entitled "An Act for the punishment of certain crimes against the United States."

Be it enacted by the Senate and House of Representatives of the United States of America, in Congress assembled, That if any persons shall unlawfully combine or conspire together, with intent to oppose any measure or measures of the government of the United States, which are or shall be directed by proper authority, or to impede the operation of any law of the United States, or to intimidate or prevent any person, holding a place or office in or under the government of the United States, from undertaking, performing or executing his trust or duty; and if any person or persons, with intent as aforesaid, shall counsel, advise or attempt to procure any insurrection, riot, unlawful assembly, or combination, whether such conspiracy, threatening, counsel, advice, or attempt shall have the proposed effect or not, he or they shall be deemed guilty of a high misdemeanor, and on conviction, before any court of the United States having jurisdiction thereof, shall be punished by a fine not exceeding five thousand dollars, and by imprisonment during a term not less than six months nor exceeding five years; and further, at the discretion of the court may be holden to find sureties for his good behaviour in such sum, and for such time, as the said court may direct.

Sect. 2. And be it further enacted, That if any person shall write, print, utter or publish, or shall cause or procure to be written, printed, uttered or published, or shall knowingly and willingly assist or aid in writing, printing, uttering or publishing any false, scandalous and malicious writing or writings against the government of the United States, or either House of the Congress of the United States, or the President of the United States, with intent to defame the said government, or either House of the said Congress, or the said President, or to bring them, or either of them, into contempt or disrepute; or to excite against them, or either or any of them, the hatred of the good people of the United States, or to stir up sedition within the United States, or to excite any unlawful combinations therein, for opposing or resisting any law of the United States, or any act of the President of the United States, done in pursuance of any such law, or of the powers in him vested by the Constitution of the United States, or to resist, oppose, or defeat any such law or act, or to aid, encourage or abet any hostile designs of any foreign nation against the United States, their people or government, then such person, being thereof convicted before any Court of the United States, having jurisdiction thereof, shall be punished by a fine not exceeding two thousand dollars, and by imprisonment not exceeding two years.

Sect. 3. And be it further enacted and declared, That if any person shall be prosecuted under this act, for the writing or publishing any libel aforesaid, it shall be lawful for the defendant, upon the trial of the cause, to give in evidence in his defence, the truth of the matter contained in the publication charged as a libel. And the jury who shall try the cause, shall have a right to determine the law and the fact, under the direction of the Court, as in other cases.

Sect. 4. And be it further enacted, That this act shall continue and be in force until the third day of March, one thousand eight hundred and one, and no longer: Provided, that the expiration of the act shall not prevent or defeat a prosecution and punishment of any offence against the law, during the time it shall be in force.

Jonathan Dayton Speaker of the House of Representatives.

Theodore Sedgwick President of the Senate, pro tempore.

Approved July 14. 1798
John Adams
President of the United States

I Certify that this Act did originate in the Senate.
Attest
Sam A. Otis Secretary

The Sedition Act, July 14, 1798. Courtesy National Archives and Records Service, Washington, D.C.

John Vanderlyn (1775–1852), *Aaron Burr* (1756–1836), oil on canvas, 22¼ in x 16½ in, New York, 1802. Courtesy New-York Historical Society, New York City, gift of Dr. John E. Stillwell.

Rembrandt Peale (1778–1860), *Thomas Jefferson*, oil on canvas, 28 in x 23½ in, America, 1805. Courtesy New-York Historical Society, New York City, gift of Thomas J. Bryan.

whole argument soon became academic. But the idea of nullifying unconstitutional laws clung in the southern mind and came back to haunt Madison in his old age.

At the time, however, the Federalists by their intemperate conduct and taxing programs sent voters into the Republican camp in droves. In the 1800 presidential campaign, Madison cheered Jefferson on, was placed on the electoral college ballot in Virginia, and cast a vote that would send Jefferson and Aaron Burr into their 73-73 deadlock. The ensuing events almost disrupted the young nation's political process. Burr's conduct convinced Jefferson (and to some degree Madison) that the new vice-president was a rascal, for there had been plenty of assurances beforehand that Burr's votes would go to Jefferson. But a deadlock developed, Burr reneged on his pledge, and it took a blank ballot in the House to deny the prize to Burr. The outcome remained in doubt until a few weeks before the scheduled March 4, 1800, inauguration. Jefferson's first act was to deliver a conciliatory speech, then he appointed Madison his right-hand man, with the duties and title of secretary of state.

For the next eight years the two Virginians seem never to have strained their friendship for a moment. Instead, they appear to have thought alike on most of the main issues, and the activities of Madison's gregarious wife provided a pleasant contrast to Jefferson's modest social calendar at the White House. In his autobiography, Madison reduced those eight years as the presidential understudy to a single sentence: "In 1801 he was appointed Secretary of State and remained such until 1809."[22] His terseness concealed the heavy drama that unfolded in the recently finished executive mansion as Jefferson and Madison began to dismantle the Federalists' machinery of government and substitute their own. Indeed, Jefferson himself looked back on the events as "the Revolution of 1800," but it was no bloodbath at all. Instead it was a quiet, persistent, and effective effort to cut the cost of government to the bone by employing a minimum number of federal workers, holding taxes down, and letting the army and navy take the scraps from the table. Although Madison's name went down in judicial history when he and the president tried to undo a midnight appointment Adams made for an inconsequential job (resulting in the famous Marbury *v.* Madison case), the Republicans did not fire Federalists right and left. In the first place, there were no droves of officeholders in those days, no "fishes and loaves" for thousands of job-seekers. Instead, the entire federal government in Washington was run by 130 men, and Jefferson figured that he had only 316 jobs in the whole country open to his patronage. By 1803, the president reckoned that 158 of these had been filled by Republicans, 132 by Federalists, and 26 by men he classified as "neutral."[23]

No wonder that the national debt, which was anathema to the Jeffersonian Republicans, started shriveling toward zero. The president and his aide were convinced that the national debt could be eliminated within sixteen years. To prove their point, they took the $83 million debt of 1801 and whittled it down to $57 million by the time Jefferson turned the White House keys over to his trusted friend.

Not all efforts and events led to social and political progress during Jefferson's tenure. The Louisiana Purchase was a coup of enormous dimensions, but when the Peace of Amiens turned sour in 1803 the major European powers began taking potshots at the American ships plying international

22. "James Madison's Autobiography," p. 206.

23. Noble E. Cunningham, Jr., *The Process of Government Under Jefferson* (Princeton: Princeton University Press, 1978), pp. 172-74.

waters. American commerce prospered, as did the farmers who sold their products to the war-torn nations, but hundreds of seamen were yanked off ships and impressed into the British navy on flimsy evidence of British citizenship. The sinking of the frigate *Chesapeake* almost within sight of the American shore sent a shock wave of anger across the country, and Jefferson could have easily obtained a declaration of war from Congress. But he and Madison had another trump to play, or thought they did, in the form of economic sanctions against Great Britain and France. Neither Napoleon nor George III were exactly White House favorites, so that the president and his top cabinet officer seriously pondered the idea of declaring war on both France and England. But Albert Gallatin, the other trusted officer in Jefferson's cabinet, startled the Virginians when he talked about the costs of regiments and war cruisers, so they looked for an honorable way to avoid war and keep the neutral young republic from being swamped by the belligerents.

Eventually, the Jeffersonian Republicans accepted the solution proposed by the party leader-president and his assistant—the Embargo Act. Although it meant throwing a brake on the booming American economy (the peak of 1807 was not reached again until 1835), Jefferson asked for and Congress passed in three days a law which becalmed the shipping industry, sent farm prices tumbling, and roused the fury of Federalists who condemned the measure as "Frenchified," since it was bound to hurt England more than France. The purpose was to dry up English exports to the United States, keep seamen at home and thus stop impressment, and force the warring powers to stop their depredations in order to regain American food, tobacco, and lumber.

Madison was probably the one who planted the idea for the Embargo Act in Jefferson's mind, but it took little urging since both men knew that America was one of England's best customers. They believed England had much more to lose if all Yankee trade ceased. Under a despot, France deserved whatever she got. Moreover, Madison had great faith in economic sanctions. Americans had been using them against England in some form or another since 1765. But the secretary of state had not counted on American disaffection. "The people of this Country *will* bear with chearfulness any sacrifices or inconveniences which these embargo laws will impose upon them," the loyal

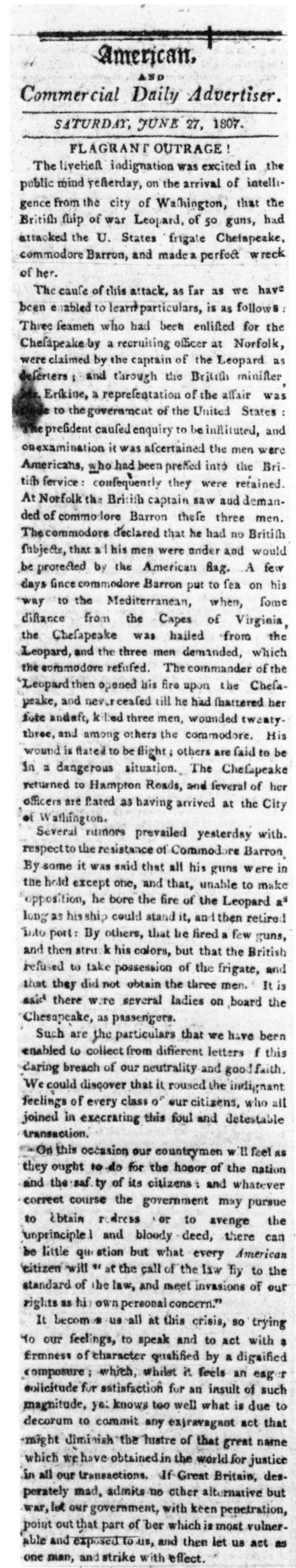

American, AND Commercial Daily Advertiser.

SATURDAY, JUNE 27, 1807.

FLAGRANT OUTRAGE!

The livelieſt indignation was excited in the public mind yeſterday, on the arrival of intelligence from the city of Waſhington, that the Britiſh ſhip of war Leopard, of 50 guns, had attacked the U. States frigate Cheſapeake, commodore Barron, and made a perfect wreck of her.

The cauſe of this attack, as far as we have been enabled to learn particulars, is as follows: Three ſeamen who had been enliſted for the Cheſapeake by a recruiting officer at Norfolk, were claimed by the captain of the Leopard as deſerters; and through the Britiſh miniſter, Mr. Erſkine, a repreſentation of the affair was made to the government of the United States: The preſident cauſed enquiry to be inſtituted, and on examination it was aſcertained the men were Americans, who had been preſſed into the British ſervice: conſequently they were retained. At Norfolk the Britiſh captain saw and demanded of commodore Barron theſe three men. The commodore declared that he had no Britiſh ſubjects, that all his men were under and would be protected by the American flag. A few days ſince commodore Barron put to ſea on his way to the Mediterranean, when, ſome diſtance from the Capes of Virginia, the Cheſapeake was hailed from the Leopard, and the three men demanded, which the commodore refuſed. The commander of the Leopard then opened his fire upon the Cheſapeake, and never ceaſed till he had ſhattered her fore and aft, killed three men, wounded twenty-three, and among others the commodore. His wound is ſtated to be ſlight; others are ſaid to be in a dangerous situation. The Cheſapeake returned to Hampton Roads, and ſeveral of her officers are ſtated as having arrived at the City of Waſhington.

Several rumors prevailed yesterday with respect to the resistance of Commodore Barron. By some it was said that all his guns were in the hold except one, and that, unable to make opposition, he bore the fire of the Leopard as long as his ship could stand it, and then retired into port: By others, that he fired a few guns, and then struck his colors, but that the British refused to take possession of the frigate, and that they did not obtain the three men. It is said there were several ladies on board the Chesapeake, as passengers.

Such are the particulars that we have been enabled to collect from different letters of this daring breach of our neutrality and good faith. We could discover that it roused the indignant feelings of every class of our citizens, who all joined in execrating this foul and detestable transaction.

"On this occasion our countrymen will feel as they ought to do for the honor of the nation and the safety of its citizens; and whatever correct course the government may pursue to obtain redress or to avenge the unprincipled and bloody deed, there can be little question but what every *American* citizen will "at the call of the law fly to the standard of the law, and meet invasions of our rights as his own personal concern."

It becomes us all at this crisis, so trying to our feelings, to speak and to act with a firmness of character qualified by a dignified composure; which, whilst it feels an eager solicitude for satisfaction for an insult of such magnitude, yet knows too well what is due to decorum to commit any extravagant act that might diminish the lustre of that great name which we have obtained in the world for justice in all our transactions. If Great Britain, desperately mad, admits no other alternative but war, let our government, with keen penetration, point out that part of her which is most vulnerable and exposed to us, and then let us act as one man, and strike with effect.

Flagrant Outrage! (the Chesapeake-Leopard incident) in the *American and Commercial Daily Advertiser*, Baltimore, June 27, 1807. Serial and Government Publications Division, Library of Congress.

Richmond *Enquirer* predicted.[24] This turned out to be wishful thinking, for in New England the harbors were filled with idle ships and, even worse, idle seamen. A regular smuggling route from Canada into Boston or down the Hudson to New York jeopardized the embargo, perplexed Madison and Jefferson (how could *Americans* break the law?), and caused discord in the once-harmonious Democratic Republican Congress.

The final months of Jefferson's presidency did him no credit. He more or less served as a caretaker, content to know that Madison's nomination by a congressional caucus virtually assured the continuance of his republican program on the domestic front. As for the international problems, who was better equipped to handle them than Madison?

Luckily, Madison was spared the ordeal of a campaign. His nomination behind closed doors on Capitol Hill had displeased some in the northern wing of the Republican party, for they foresaw a continuance of the "Virginia dynasty" and were dismayed. A few tremors in New York produced only token opposition until James Monroe's friends (or, rather, Jefferson's enemies) in Virginia tried to talk Monroe into being a candidate. However, the Monroe and George Clinton candidacies fizzled, and by early December 1808 Madison realized that he was going to be the nation's fourth president. We can imagine the delight of Dolley Madison, but her husband knew he was headed for some troubled waters and that for the first time since 1790 his tall, red-headed friend would no longer be around to share the joys and trials of public life. Jefferson spoke of "the splendid misery" of the presidency. Madison soon knew what he meant.

24. Quoted in Dumas Malone, *Jefferson the President: Second Term, 1805–1809* (Boston: Little, Brown, 1974), p. 583.

OPPOSITE:

Alexander Anderson (1775–1870) after John Wesley Jarvis (1780–1840), *Death of the Embargo, With All Its 'Restrictive Energies,'* woodcut, 8⅞ in x 5$\frac{3}{16}$ in, in the *New-York Evening Post,* New York, April 25, 1814. Serial and Government Publications Division, Library of Congress.

DEATH OF THE EMBARGO, WITH ALL ITS " RESTRICTIVE ENERGIES."

A wit first celebrated this great event in the FEDERAL REPUBLICAN, in the manner to be seen below; but he has had the politeness to revise and correct the article for the Evening Post, with additions: in this improved state it is now presented to our readers, aided by an appropriate engraving devised by the author and admirably executed by one of our fellow-citizens. Here it comes—

" TO THE GRAVE GO SHAM PROTECTORS OF " FREE TRADE AND SAILORS' RIGHTS"—AND ALL THE PEOPLE SAY AMEN !"

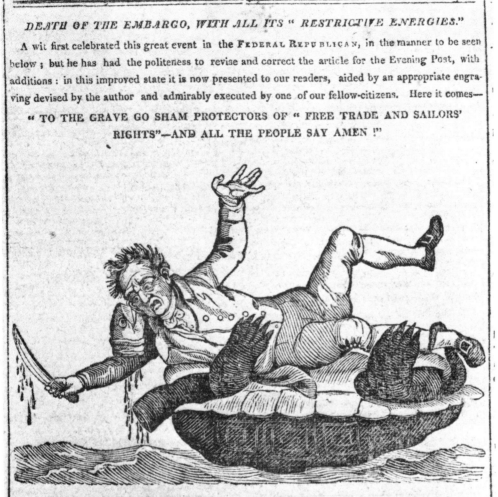

TERRAPIN'S ADDRESS.

Reflect, my friend, as you pass by;
As *you* are, *now*, so, once, was *I*;
As *I* am *now*, so *you* may be:—
Laid on your back to die like me!
I was, indeed, true Sailor born;
To quit my friend, in death, I scorn.
Once Jemmy *seem'd* to be my friend,
But, basely, brought me to my end!
Of head bereft, and light, and breath,
I hold *Fidelity*, in death:—
For "*Sailor's Rights*" I still will tug:
And, Madison to death I'll hug,
For his perfidious zeal display'd,
For "*Sailor's Rights and for Free Trade.*"
This small atonement I will have—
I'll lug down Jemmy to the grave.
Then Trade and Commerce shall be free
And Sailors have their liberty—
Of head bereft, and light, and breath,
The *Terrapin*, still true in death,
Will punish Jemmy's perfidy:
Leave *Trade*, and *brother Sailors Free!*

PASSENGERS REPLY.

Yes Terrapin, bereft of breath,
We see thee faithful still, in death:
Stick to't—"*Free Trade and Sailor's Right*:
Hug Jemmy—press him—hold him—bite—
Ne'er mind thy head—thou'lt live without it,
Spunk will preserve thy life—don't doubt it—
Down to the grave t'atone for sin,
Jemmy must go, with Terrapin.
Bear *him* but off, and we shall see
Commerce restor'd and *Sailors Free!*
Hug, Terrapin, with all thy might,
Now for "*Free Trade* and *Sailor's Right*:"
Stick to him, Terrapin, to thee the nation
Now eager looks:—then die for her salvation.

FLOREAT RESPUBLICA.

Banks of Goose Creek,
City of Washington,
15th April 1814.

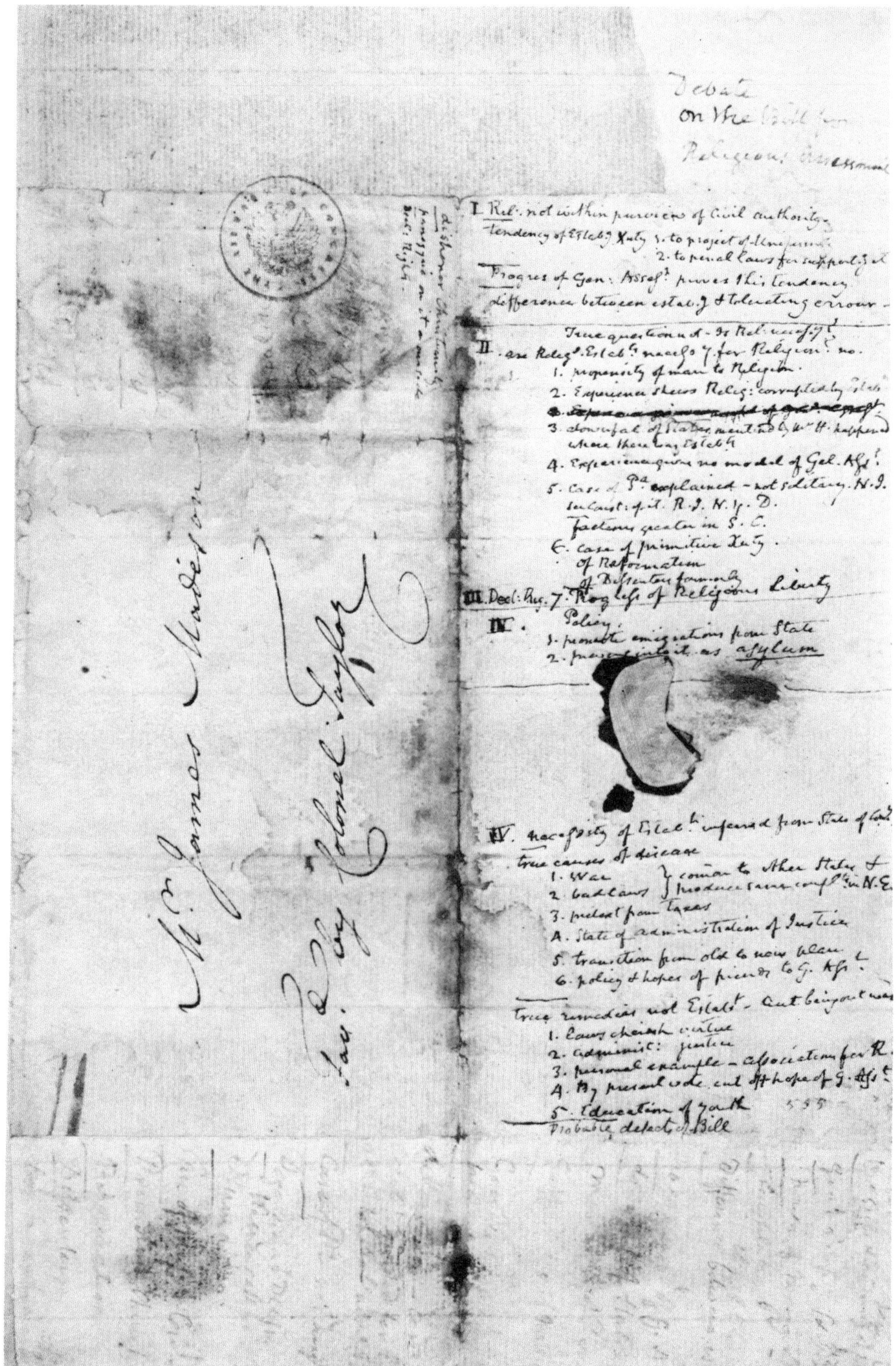
Debate on the Bill for Religious Assessment

I. Rel: not within purview of Civil authority.
tendency of Estabg Xnty 1. to project of Uniformity
2. to penal laws for supportg it
Progress of Gen: Assest proves this tendency
difference between estabg & tolerating errour –
True question not – is Rel: necessy?
II. are Relig. Estabts necessy for Religion? no.
1. propensity of man to Religion.
2. Experience shews Relig: corrupted by Estabt.
3. downfal of States mentd by Mr H. happened where there was Estabt
4. Experience gives no model of Gel. Asst.
5. Case of Pa explained – not solitary. N. J. See Const: of it. R. I. N. Y. D.
Factions greater in S. C.
6. Case of primitive Xnty.
of Reformation
of Dissenters formerly
III. Decl: Rts. Rights of Religious Liberty
IV. Policy.
1. promote emigrations from State
2. prevent [illegible] into it as asylum
IV. necessity of Estabt. inferred from State of Country
true causes of disease
1. War } common to other States &
2. bad laws } produce same compts in N. E.
3. pretext from taxes
4. State of administration of Justice
5. transition from old to new plan
6. policy & hopes of friends to G. Asst.
true remedies not Estabt. – but being out war
1. laws cherish virtue
2. administ: justice
3. personal example – associations for R.
4. By present vote cut off hope of G. Asst.
5. Education of youth
Probable defects of Bill

Mr. James Madison
Fav'd by Colonel Taylor

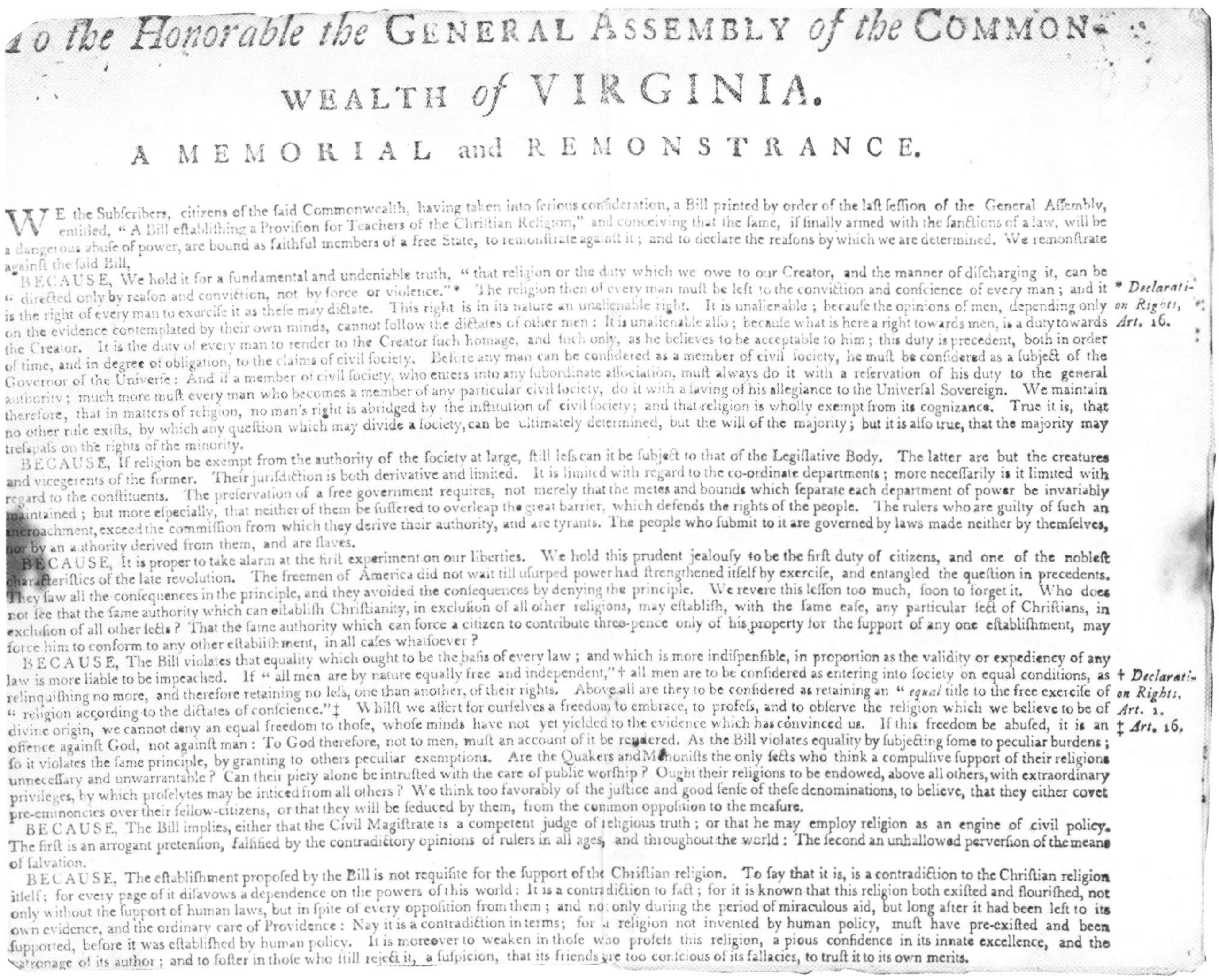

To the Honorable the GENERAL ASSEMBLY *of the* COMMON-WEALTH *of* VIRGINIA.

A MEMORIAL and REMONSTRANCE.

WE the Subſcribers, citizens of the ſaid Commonwealth, having taken into ſerious conſideration, a Bill printed by order of the laſt ſeſſion of the General Aſſembly, entitled, "A Bill eſtabliſhing a Proviſion for Teachers of the Chriſtian Religion," and conceiving that the ſame, if finally armed with the ſanctions of a law, will be a dangerous abuſe of power, are bound as faithful members of a free State, to remonſtrate againſt it; and to declare the reaſons by which we are determined. We remonſtrate againſt the ſaid Bill,

BECAUSE, We hold it for a fundamental and undeniable truth, "that religion or the duty which we owe to our Creator, and the manner of diſcharging it, can be "directed only by reaſon and conviction, not by force or violence."* The religion then of every man muſt be left to the conviction and conſcience of every man; and it is the right of every man to exerciſe it as theſe may dictate. This right is in its nature an unalienable right. It is unalienable; becauſe the opinions of men, depending only on the evidence contemplated by their own minds, cannot follow the dictates of other men: It is unalienable alſo; becauſe what is here a right towards men, is a duty towards the Creator. It is the duty of every man to render to the Creator ſuch homage, and ſuch only, as he believes to be acceptable to him; this duty is precedent, both in order of time, and in degree of obligation, to the claims of civil ſociety. Before any man can be conſidered as a member of civil ſociety, he muſt be conſidered as a ſubject of the Governor of the Univerſe: And if a member of civil ſociety, who enters into any ſubordinate aſſociation, muſt always do it with a reſervation of his duty to the general authority; much more muſt every man who becomes a member of any particular civil ſociety, do it with a ſaving of his allegiance to the Univerſal Sovereign. We maintain therefore, that in matters of religion, no man's right is abridged by the inſtitution of civil ſociety; and that religion is wholly exempt from its cognizance. True it is, that no other rule exiſts, by which any queſtion which may divide a ſociety, can be ultimately determined, but the will of the majority; but it is alſo true, that the majority may treſpaſs on the rights of the minority.

BECAUSE, If religion be exempt from the authority of the ſociety at large, ſtill leſs can it be ſubject to that of the Legiſlative Body. The latter are but the creatures and vicegerents of the former. Their juriſdiction is both derivative and limited. It is limited with regard to the co-ordinate departments; more neceſſarily is it limited with regard to the conſtituents. The preſervation of a free government requires, not merely that the metes and bounds which ſeparate each department of power be invariably maintained; but more eſpecially, that neither of them be ſuffered to overleap the great barrier, which defends the rights of the people. The rulers who are guilty of ſuch an encroachment, exceed the commiſſion from which they derive their authority, and are tyrants. The people who ſubmit to it are governed by laws made neither by themſelves, nor by an authority derived from them, and are ſlaves.

BECAUSE, It is proper to take alarm at the firſt experiment on our liberties. We hold this prudent jealouſy to be the firſt duty of citizens, and one of the nobleſt characteriſtics of the late revolution. The freemen of America did not wait till uſurped power had ſtrengthened itſelf by exerciſe, and entangled the queſtion in precedents. They ſaw all the conſequences in the principle, and they avoided the conſequences by denying the principle. We revere this leſſon too much, ſoon to forget it. Who does not ſee that the ſame authority which can eſtabliſh Chriſtianity, in excluſion of all other religions, may eſtabliſh, with the ſame eaſe, any particular ſect of Chriſtians, in excluſion of all other ſects? That the ſame authority which can force a citizen to contribute three-pence only of his property for the ſupport of any one eſtabliſhment, may force him to conform to any other eſtabliſhment, in all caſes whatſoever?

BECAUSE, The Bill violates that equality which ought to be the baſis of every law; and which is more indiſpenſible, in proportion as the validity or expediency of any law is more liable to be impeached. If "all men are by nature equally free and independent,"† all men are to be conſidered as entering into ſociety on equal conditions, as relinquiſhing no more, and therefore retaining no leſs, one than another, of their rights. Above all are they to be conſidered as retaining an "*equal* title to the free exerciſe of "religion according to the dictates of conſcience."‡ Whilſt we aſſert for ourſelves a freedom to embrace, to profeſs, and to obſerve the religion which we believe to be of divine origin, we cannot deny an equal freedom to thoſe, whoſe minds have not yet yielded to the evidence which has convinced us. If this freedom be abuſed, it is an offence againſt God, not againſt man: To God therefore, not to men, muſt an account of it be rendered. As the Bill violates equality by ſubjecting ſome to peculiar burdens; ſo it violates the ſame principle, by granting to others peculiar exemptions. Are the Quakers and Menoniſts the only ſects who think a compulſive ſupport of their religions unneceſſary and unwarrantable? Can their piety alone be intruſted with the care of public worſhip? Ought their religions to be endowed, above all others, with extraordinary privileges, by which proſelytes may be inticed from all others? We think too favorably of the juſtice and good ſenſe of theſe denominations, to believe, that they either covet pre-eminencies over their fellow-citizens, or that they will be ſeduced by them, from the common oppoſition to the meaſure.

BECAUSE, The Bill implies, either that the Civil Magiſtrate is a competent judge of religious truth; or that he may employ religion as an engine of civil policy. The firſt is an arrogant pretenſion, falſified by the contradictory opinions of rulers in all ages, and throughout the world: The ſecond an unhallowed perverſion of the means of ſalvation.

BECAUSE, The eſtabliſhment propoſed by the Bill is not requiſite for the ſupport of the Chriſtian religion. To ſay that it is, is a contradiction to the Chriſtian religion itſelf; for every page of it diſavows a dependence on the powers of this world: It is a contradiction to fact; for it is known that this religion both exiſted and flouriſhed, not only without the ſupport of human laws, but in ſpite of every oppoſition from them; and not only during the period of miraculous aid, but long after it had been left to its own evidence, and the ordinary care of Providence: Nay it is a contradiction in terms; for a religion not invented by human policy, muſt have pre-exiſted and been ſupported, before it was eſtabliſhed by human policy. It is moreover to weaken in thoſe who profeſs this religion, a pious confidence in its innate excellence, and the patronage of its author; and to foſter in thoſe who ſtill reject it, a ſuſpicion, that its friends are too conſcious of its fallacies, to truſt it to its own merits.

* Declaration on Rights, Art. 16.

† Declaration on Rights, Art. 1.

‡ Art. 16.

James Madison, *A Memorial and Remonstrance* (detail), broadside, 16⅞ in x 21¹⁄₁₆ in, Alexandria, Virginia, Phenix Press, ca. 1785–86. Rare Book and Special Collections Division, Library of Congress.

Madison's reasoned arguments against religious assessments were printed for local circulation. The document remains a key statement advocating man's natural right to liberty of conscience.

OPPOSITE:

James Madison, *Notes for speech against the Religious Assessment Bill,* ca. November 1784. James Madison Papers, Library of Congress.

Madison returned to Orange County from Congress in 1783 and served for the next three years as a delegate to the Virginia Assembly. These notes outline Madison's arguments against a resolution, proposed by Patrick Henry to the Virginia legislature, that the people of the state be taxed annually for the support "of the Christian religion." Religious persecutions in Virginia had been a key factor in persuading Madison to enter politics, and he championed freedom of conscience throughout his life.

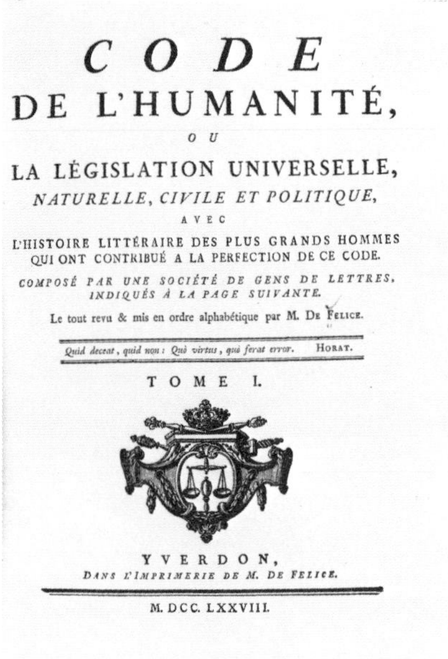

CODE
DE L'HUMANITÉ,
OU
LA LÉGISLATION UNIVERSELLE,
NATURELLE, CIVILE ET POLITIQUE,
AVEC
L'HISTOIRE LITTÉRAIRE DES PLUS GRANDS HOMMES QUI ONT CONTRIBUÉ A LA PERFECTION DE CE CODE.
COMPOSÉ PAR UNE SOCIÉTÉ DE GENS DE LETTRES, INDIQUÉS A LA PAGE SUIVANTE.
Le tout revu & mis en ordre alphabétique par M. De Felice.
Quid deceat, quid non: Quò virtus, quò ferat error. Horat.
TOME I.
YVERDON,
DANS L'IMPRIMERIE DE M. DE FELICE.
M. DCC. LXXVIII.

Fortunato Bartolomeo de Felice (1723–1789), *Code De L'Humanité,* 10 1/16 in x 7 3/8 in, vol. 1, Yverdon, de Felice, 1778. Rare Book and Special Collections Division, Library of Congress.

Before attending the Constitutional Convention, Madison made a detailed study of the history of governments, ancient and modern, using works such as a thirteen-volume set of de Felice. His research into past republics convinced him that a government of "national supremacy" was the key to a successful democracy. Madison's theory of a powerful national government founded on the authority of all the people became the nucleus of the Virginia Plan.

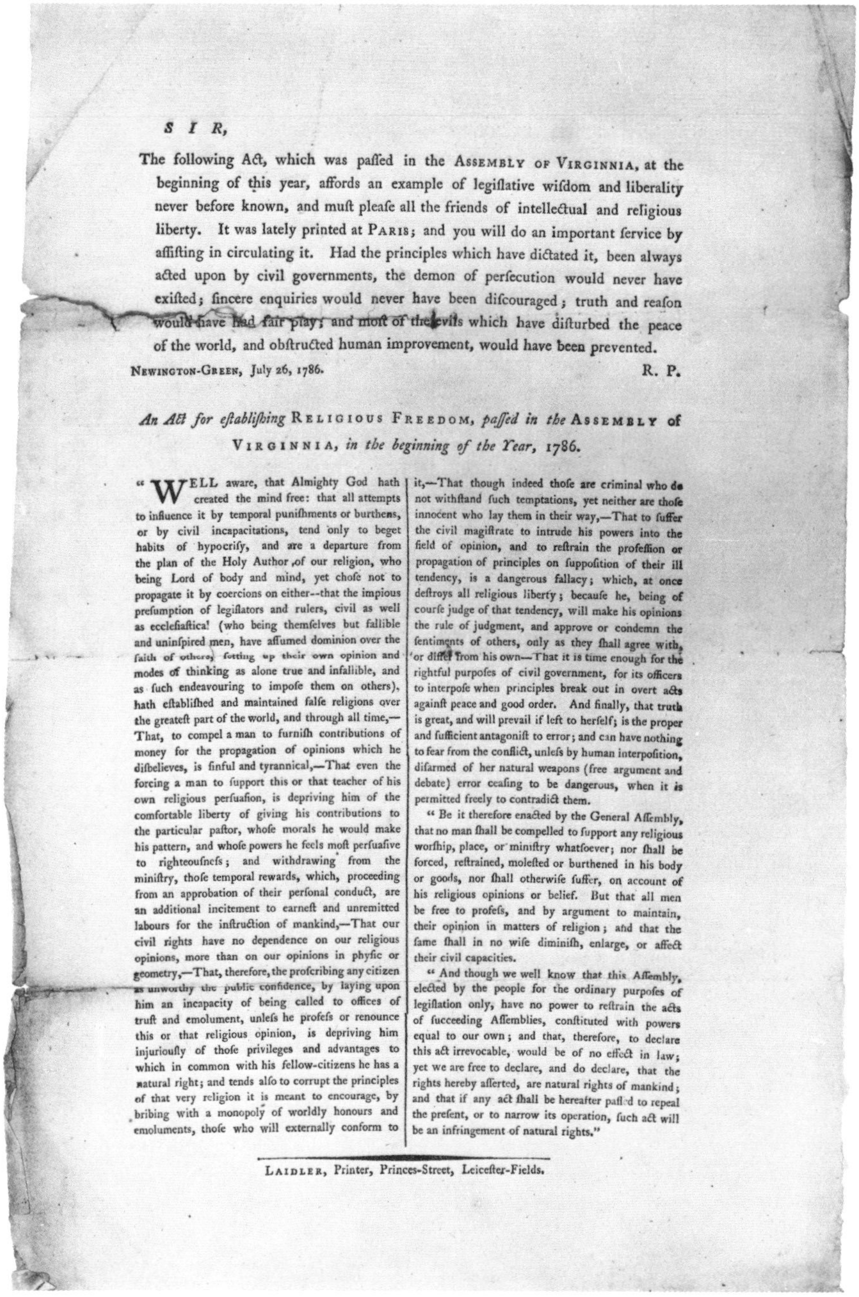

S I R,

The following Aƈt, which was paſſed in the ASSEMBLY OF VIRGINNIA, at the beginning of this year, affords an example of legiſlative wiſdom and liberality never before known, and muſt pleaſe all the friends of intellectual and religious liberty. It was lately printed at PARIS; and you will do an important ſervice by aſſiſting in circulating it. Had the principles which have dictated it, been always acted upon by civil governments, the demon of perſecution would never have exiſted; ſincere enquiries would never have been diſcouraged; truth and reaſon would have had fair play; and moſt of the evils which have diſturbed the peace of the world, and obſtructed human improvement, would have been prevented.

NEWINGTON-GREEN, July 26, 1786. R. P.

An Act for eſtabliſhing RELIGIOUS FREEDOM, *paſſed in the* ASSEMBLY of VIRGINNIA, *in the beginning of the Year,* 1786.

"WELL aware, that Almighty God hath created the mind free: that all attempts to influence it by temporal puniſhments or burthens, or by civil incapacitations, tend only to beget habits of hypocriſy, and are a departure from the plan of the Holy Author of our religion, who being Lord of body and mind, yet choſe not to propagate it by coercions on either--that the impious preſumption of legiſlators and rulers, civil as well as eccleſiaſtical (who being themſelves but fallible and uninſpired men, have aſſumed dominion over the faith of others, ſetting up their own opinion and modes of thinking as alone true and infallible, and as ſuch endeavouring to impoſe them on others), hath eſtabliſhed and maintained falſe religions over the greateſt part of the world, and through all time,—That, to compel a man to furniſh contributions of money for the propagation of opinions which he diſbelieves, is ſinful and tyrannical,—That even the forcing a man to ſupport this or that teacher of his own religious perſuaſion, is depriving him of the comfortable liberty of giving his contributions to the particular paſtor, whoſe morals he would make his pattern, and whoſe powers he feels moſt perſuaſive to righteouſneſs; and withdrawing from the miniſtry, thoſe temporal rewards, which, proceeding from an approbation of their perſonal conduct, are an additional incitement to earneſt and unremitted labours for the inſtruction of mankind,—That our civil rights have no dependence on our religious opinions, more than on our opinions in phyſic or geometry,—That, therefore, the proſcribing any citizen as unworthy the public confidence, by laying upon him an incapacity of being called to offices of truſt and emolument, unleſs he profeſs or renounce this or that religious opinion, is depriving him injuriouſly of thoſe privileges and advantages to which in common with his fellow-citizens he has a natural right; and tends alſo to corrupt the principles of that very religion it is meant to encourage, by bribing with a monopoly of worldly honours and emoluments, thoſe who will externally conform to it,—That though indeed thoſe are criminal who do not withſtand ſuch temptations, yet neither are thoſe innocent who lay them in their way,—That to ſuffer the civil magiſtrate to intrude his powers into the field of opinion, and to reſtrain the profeſſion or propagation of principles on ſuppoſition of their ill tendency, is a dangerous fallacy; which, at once deſtroys all religious liberty; becauſe he, being of courſe judge of that tendency, will make his opinions the rule of judgment, and approve or condemn the ſentiments of others, only as they ſhall agree with, or differ from his own—That it is time enough for the rightful purpoſes of civil government, for its officers to interpoſe when principles break out in overt acts againſt peace and good order. And finally, that truth is great, and will prevail if left to herſelf; is the proper and ſufficient antagoniſt to error; and can have nothing to fear from the conflict, unleſs by human interpoſition, diſarmed of her natural weapons (free argument and debate) error ceaſing to be dangerous, when it is permitted freely to contradict them.

"Be it therefore enacted by the General Aſſembly, that no man ſhall be compelled to ſupport any religious worſhip, place, or miniſtry whatſoever; nor ſhall be forced, reſtrained, moleſted or burthened in his body or goods, nor ſhall otherwiſe ſuffer, on account of his religious opinions or belief. But that all men be free to profeſs, and by argument to maintain, their opinion in matters of religion; and that the ſame ſhall in no wiſe diminiſh, enlarge, or affect their civil capacities.

"And though we well know that this Aſſembly, elected by the people for the ordinary purpoſes of legiſlation only, have no power to reſtrain the acts of ſucceeding Aſſemblies, conſtituted with powers equal to our own; and that, therefore, to declare this act irrevocable, would be of no effect in law; yet we are free to declare, and do declare, that the rights hereby aſſerted, are natural rights of mankind; and that if any act ſhall be hereafter paſſed to repeal the preſent, or to narrow its operation, ſuch act will be an infringement of natural rights."

LAIDLER, Printer, Princes-Street, Leiceſter-Fields.

An Act for Establishing Religious Freedom, broadside, 15 3/16 in x 9 7/8 in, London, Laidler, 1786. Rare Book and Special Collections Division, Library of Congress.

After the death of the assessment legislation, Madison shepherded through the legislature a bill written by Jefferson in 1779 establishing religious liberty in Virginia. He reported to Jefferson, then in Paris, that its passing "extinguished forever the ambitious hope of making laws for the human mind."

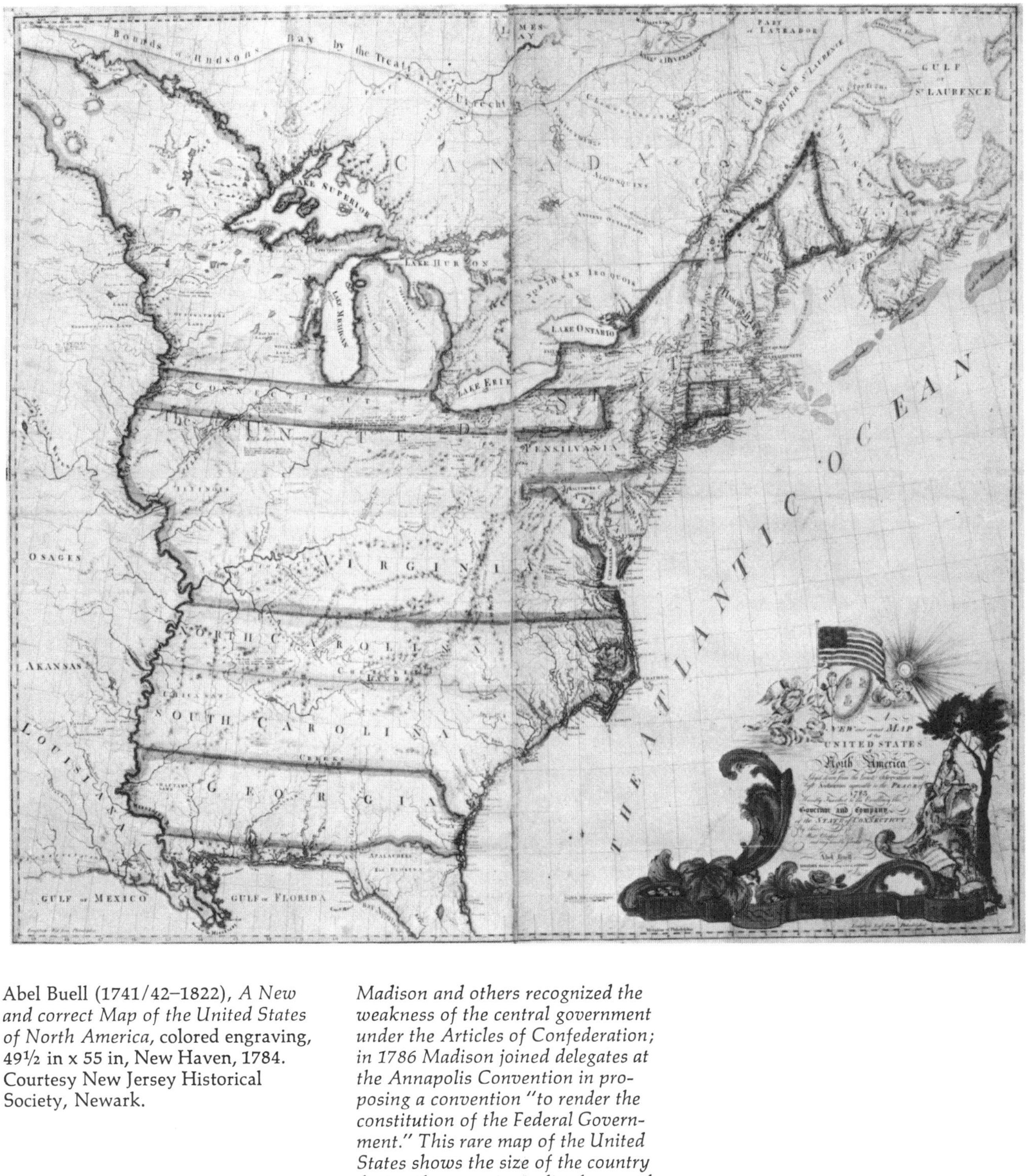

Abel Buell (1741/42–1822), *A New and correct Map of the United States of North America*, colored engraving, 49½ in x 55 in, New Haven, 1784. Courtesy New Jersey Historical Society, Newark.

Madison and others recognized the weakness of the central government under the Articles of Confederation; in 1786 Madison joined delegates at the Annapolis Convention in proposing a convention "to render the constitution of the Federal Government." This rare map of the United States shows the size of the country during the years immediately preceding the Constitutional Convention.

Convention at Philadelphia 1787 (detail), engraving, $2\frac{5}{8}$ in x $3\frac{1}{16}$ in, in Charles A. Goodrich, *A history of the United States of America*, Hartford, Connecticut, Huntington & Hopkins, 1823. Rare Book and Special Collections Division, Library of Congress.

The Constitutional Convention opened in Philadelphia on May 25, 1787. By the end of June, the fifty-five delegates had voted to devise a plan of national government to replace the unworkable Articles of Confederation. Madison worked incessantly, taking detailed notes of the proceedings and studying at night. He addressed the convention 161 times.

OPPOSITE:

The Constitution (excerpt, working draft), broadside with mss. notes (in the hand of James Madison), $14\frac{5}{16}$ in x $10\frac{1}{16}$ in, Philadelphia, Dunlap & Claypoole, September 12, 1787. James Madison Papers, Library of Congress.

The specific provisions of the Constitution were resolved by the beginning of September, after a month-long debate. This printed draft of the final Constitution was commissioned by the Committee on Style, which prepared the language of the amendments agreed upon for presentation to the entire convention. Madison was a member of the five-man committee and his corrections survive on this copy of the document. The final version was signed on September 17 by thirty-nine delegates and sent to the states for ratification.

Bickerstaff's Boston Almanack, Or, The Federal Calendar (detail), pamphlet, $7\frac{1}{4}$ in x $4\frac{15}{32}$ in, third edition, Boston, E. Russell, 1788. Courtesy American Antiquarian Society, Worcester, Massachusetts.

Framing the Constitution was only the first part of the battle; it then had to be ratified by nine of the states. In this print, elder statesmen Washington and Franklin are shown driving the "Federal Chariot," pulled by the thirteen states, toward ratification.

WE, the People of the United States, in order to form a more perfect union, to establish justice, insure domestic tranquility, provide for the common defence, promote the general welfare, and secure the blessings of liberty to ourselves and our posterity, do ordain and establish this Constitution for the United States of America.

A R T I C L E I.

Sect. 1. ALL legislative powers herein granted shall be vested in a Congress of the United States, which shall consist of a Senate and House of Representatives.

Sect. 2. The House of Representatives shall be composed of members chosen every second year by the people of the several states, and the electors in each state shall have the qualifications requisite for electors of the most numerous branch of the state legislature.

No person shall be a representative who shall not have attained to the age of twenty-five years, and been seven years a citizen of the United States, and who shall not, when elected, be an inhabitant of that state in which he shall be chosen.

Representatives and direct taxes shall be apportioned among the several states which may be included within this Union, according to their respective numbers, which shall be determined by adding to the whole number of free persons, including those bound to servitude for a term of years, and excluding Indians not taxed, three-fifths of all other persons. The actual enumeration shall be made within three years after the first meeting of the Congress of the United States, and within every subsequent term of ten years, in such manner as they shall by law direct. The number of representatives shall not exceed one for every forty thousand, but each state shall have at least one representative: and until such enumeration shall be made, the state of New-Hampshire shall be entitled to chuse three, Massachusetts eight, Rhode-Island and Providence Plantations one, Connecticut five, New-York six, New-Jersey four, Pennsylvania eight, Delaware one, Maryland six, Virginia ten, North-Carolina five, South-Carolina five, and Georgia three.

When vacancies happen in the representation from any state, the Executive authority thereof shall issue writs of election to fill such vacancies.

The House of Representatives shall choose their Speaker and other officers; and they shall have the sole power of impeachment.

Sect. 3. The Senate of the United States shall be composed of two senators from each state, chosen by the legislature thereof, for six years: and each senator shall have one vote.

Immediately after they shall be assembled in consequence of the first election, they shall be divided, as equally as may be into three classes. The seats of the senators of the first class shall be vacated at the expiration of the second year, of the second class at the expiration of the fourth year, and of the third class at the expiration of the sixth year, so that one-third may be chosen every second year: and if vacancies happen by resignation, or otherwise, during the recess of the Legislature of any state, the Executive thereof may make temporary appointments until the next meeting of the Legislature.

No person shall be a senator who shall not have attained to the age of thirty years, and been nine years a citizen of the United States, and who shall not, when elected, be an inhabitant of that state for which he shall be chosen.

The Vice-President of the United States shall be, ~~ex officio~~, President of the senate, but shall have no vote, unless they be equally divided.

The Senate shall choose their other officers, and also a President pro tempore, in the absence of the Vice-President, or when he shall exercise the office of President of the United States.

The Senate shall have the sole power to try all impeachments. When sitting for that purpose, they shall be on oath. When the President of the United States is tried, the Chief Justice shall preside: And no person shall be convicted without the concurrence of two-thirds of the members present.

Judgment in cases of impeachment shall not extend further than to removal from office, and disqualification to hold and enjoy any office of honor, trust or profit under the United States: but the party convicted shall nevertheless be liable and subject to indictment, trial, judgment and punishment, according to law.

Sect. 4. The times, places and manner of holding elections for senators and representatives, shall be prescribed in each state by the legislature thereof: but the Congress may at any time by law make or alter such regulations.

The Congress shall assemble at least once in every year, and such meeting shall be on the first Monday in December, unless they shall by law appoint a different day.

Sect. 5. Each house shall be the judge of the elections, returns and qualifications of its own members, and a majority of each shall constitute a quorum to do business: but a smaller number may adjourn from day to day, and may be authorised to compel the attendance of absent members, in such manner, and under such penalties as each house may provide.

Each house may determine the rules of its proceedings; punish its members for disorderly behaviour, and, with the concurrence of two-thirds, expel a member.

Each house shall keep a journal of its proceedings, and from time to time publish the same, excepting such parts as may in their judgment require secrecy; and the yeas and nays of the members of either house on any question shall, at the desire of one-fifth of those present, be entered on the journal.

Neither house, during the session of Congress, shall, without the consent of the other, adjourn for more than three days, nor to any other place than that in which the two houses shall be sitting.

Sect. 6. The senators and representatives shall receive a compensation for their services, to be ascertained by law, and paid out of the treasury of the United States. They shall in all cases, except treason, felony and breach of the peace, be privileged from arrest during their attendance at the session of their respective houses, and in going to and returning from the same; and for any speech or debate in either house, they shall not be questioned in any other place.

No senator or representative shall, during the time for which he was elected, be appointed to any civil office under the authority of the United States, which shall have been created, or the emoluments

* The words by Col. [illegible] not in the Report as printed, but were [illegible] error departing from the text [illegible] the Report referred to the Committee of Stile & arrangement

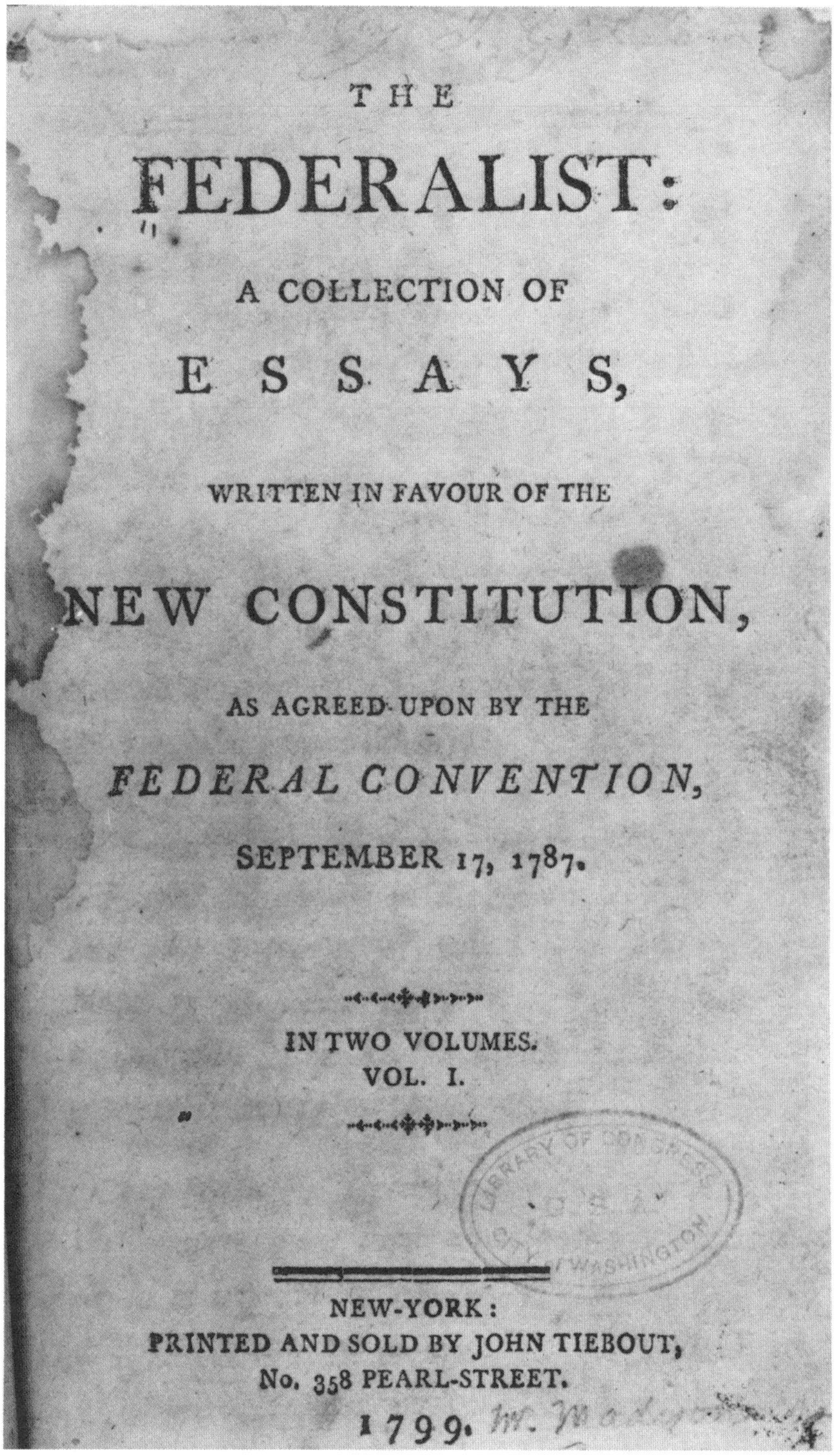

THE

FEDERALIST:

A COLLECTION OF

ESSAYS,

WRITTEN IN FAVOUR OF THE

NEW CONSTITUTION,

AS AGREED UPON BY THE

FEDERAL CONVENTION,

SEPTEMBER 17, 1787.

IN TWO VOLUMES.
VOL. I.

NEW-YORK:
PRINTED AND SOLD BY JOHN TIEBOUT,
No. 358 PEARL-STREET.
1799.

Alexander Hamilton, John Jay, and James Madison, *The Federalist* (Madison's copy), $6\frac{5}{16}$ in x $3\frac{5}{16}$ in, vol. 1, New York, John Tiebout, 1799. Rare Book and Special Collections Division, Library of Congress.

Hoping to sway public opinion, Madison and New Yorkers Hamilton and Jay collaborated in 1787–88 on a series of newspaper essays which they published under the name of "Publius." These seventy-seven essays in support of the Constitution, along with eight more, were later published as The Federalist. *Madison wrote twenty-nine of the original essays.*

Lawrence Sully (1769–1804), *Patrick Henry* (1736–1799), watercolor on ivory, gold, $2\frac{1}{2}$ in x 2 in, America, 1795. Courtesy Mead Art Museum, Amherst College, Massachusetts, bequest of Herbert L. Pratt.

Proponents of the Constitution worked frantically at state conventions to assure ratification. Passage by the Virginia Convention was considered vital to the future of the Constitution. Orator Henry led the fight against the plan, but Madison's reasoned arguments convinced the delegates to ratify. On June 25, 1788, Virginia became the tenth state to approve the document.

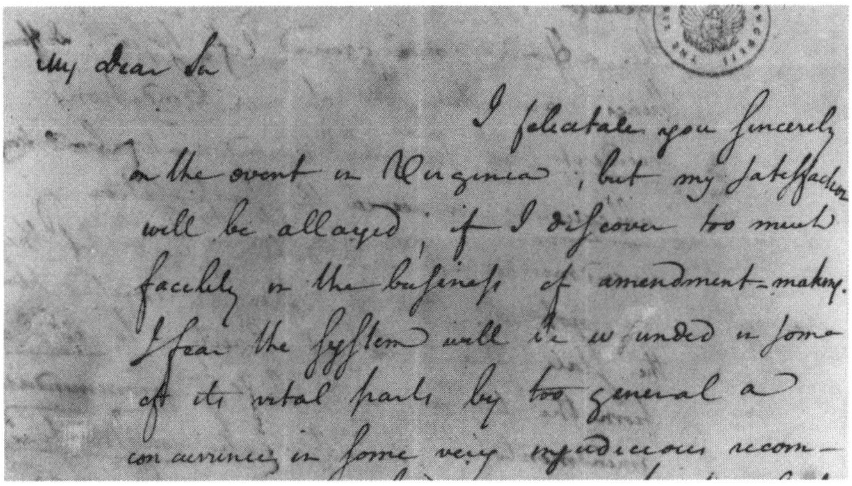

My dear Sir

I felicitate you sincerely on the event in Virginia; but my satisfaction will be allayed, if I discover too much facility in the business of amendment-making. I fear the system will be wounded in some of its vital parts by too general a concurrence in some very injudicious recom-

Alexander Hamilton, *Letter to James Madison* (excerpt), New York, July 8, 1788. James Madison Papers, Library of Congress.

In this note, fellow advocate Hamilton congratulates Madison on the Virginia victory and reports to him on the progress of the New York State Convention.

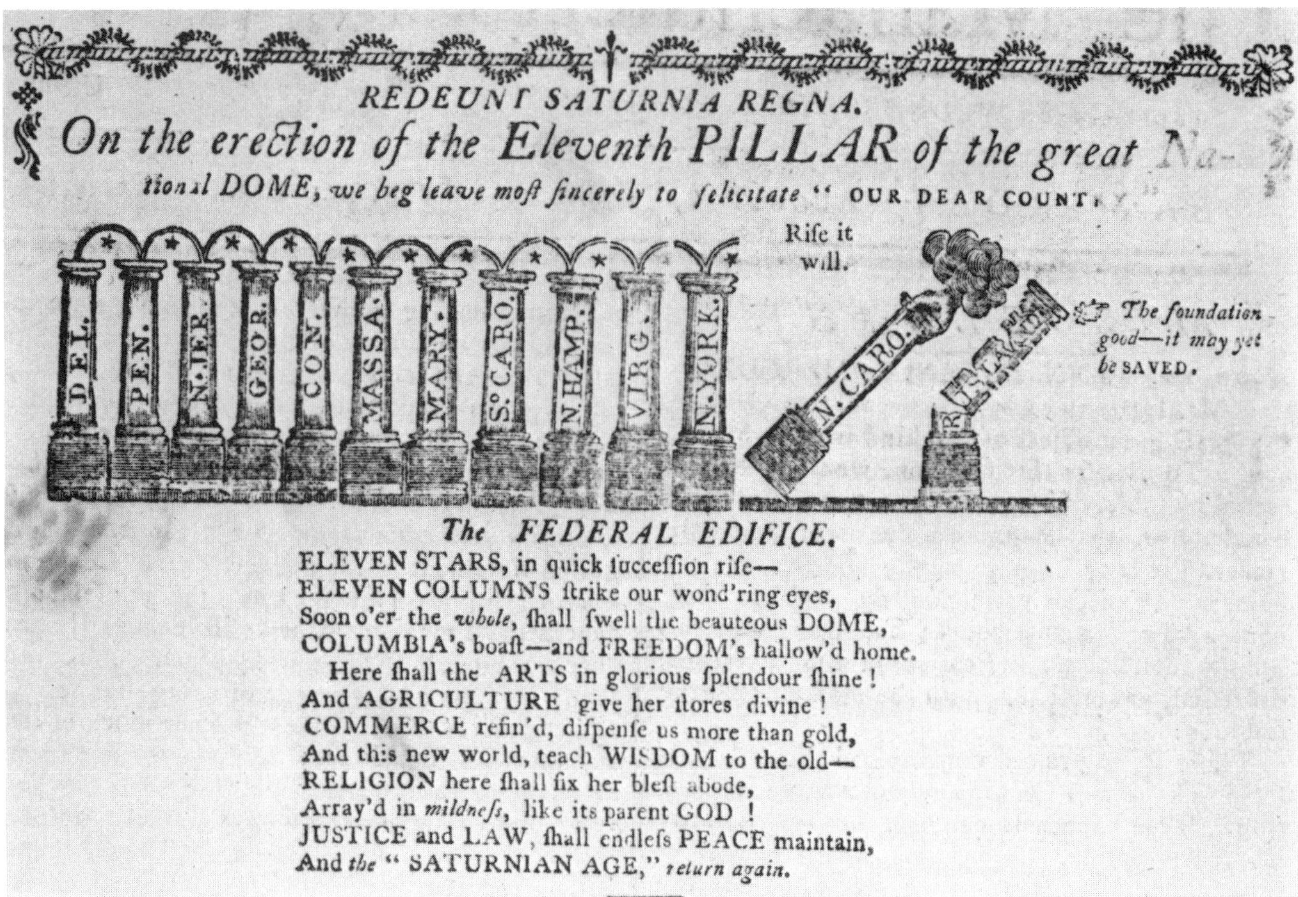

REDEUNT SATURNIA REGNA.

On the erection of the Eleventh PILLAR of the great National DOME, we beg leave most sincerely to felicitate " OUR DEAR COUNTRY."

The FEDERAL EDIFICE.

ELEVEN STARS, in quick succession rise—
ELEVEN COLUMNS strike our wond'ring eyes,
Soon o'er the *whole*, shall swell the beauteous DOME,
COLUMBIA's boast—and FREEDOM's hallow'd home.
Here shall the ARTS in glorious splendour shine!
And AGRICULTURE give her stores divine!
COMMERCE refin'd, dispense us more than gold,
And this new world, teach WISDOM to the old—
RELIGION here shall fix her blest abode,
Array'd in *mildness*, like its parent GOD!
JUSTICE and LAW, shall endless PEACE maintain,
And *the* " SATURNIAN AGE," *return again.*

Anonymous, *The Federal Edifice*, woodcut, 15½ in x 21 in, in *The Massachusetts Centinel*, Boston, August 2, 1788. Serial and Government Publications Division, Library of Congress.

This print, one of a series, was published to celebrate the ratification of the Constitution by the eleventh state, New York.

Joseph Wright (1756–1793), *George Washington* (1732–1799), oil on canvas, 21 in x 17 in, New York?, ca. 1790. Courtesy Cleveland Museum of Art, Ohio, Hinman B. Hurlbut Collection.

The Constitution created the office of president, and Gen. George Washington, former commander of the Continental Forces, was the logical choice to serve as the first chief executive. Inaugurated in 1789, Washington completed two terms before retiring in 1796.

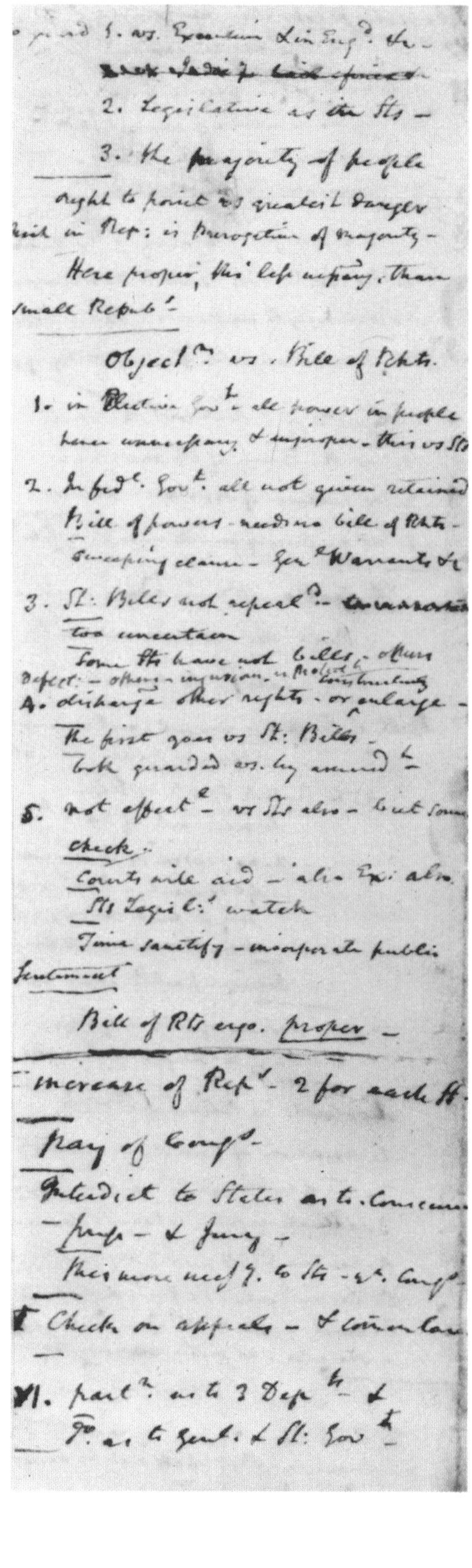

James Madison, *Notes on Debates on the Bill of Rights* (excerpt), 1789. James Madison Papers, Library of Congress.

Five state ratifying conventions had stressed the need for immediate amendments to the Constitution, and particularly for a bill of rights. Accordingly, Madison synthesized the numerous states' demands into twelve amendments and ushered their passage through the new Congress. The first two amendments were never ratified by the states; the other ten survive as the original Bill of Rights.

William Russell Birch (1755–1834), *Back of the State House, Philadelphia,* colored line engraving, 12¼ in x 15½ in, Philadelphia, William Birch & Son, 1798-99. Courtesy Library Company of Philadelphia, Pennsylvania.

After ratification of the Constitution, Madison was elected to serve in the new federal Congress, headquartered first in New York and then in Philadelphia. During his terms in the House of Representatives, Madison was at the center of all political discussions, resolutions, and agreements. Massachusetts representative Fisher Ames remembered Madison as one of the "few shining geniuses" in the House.

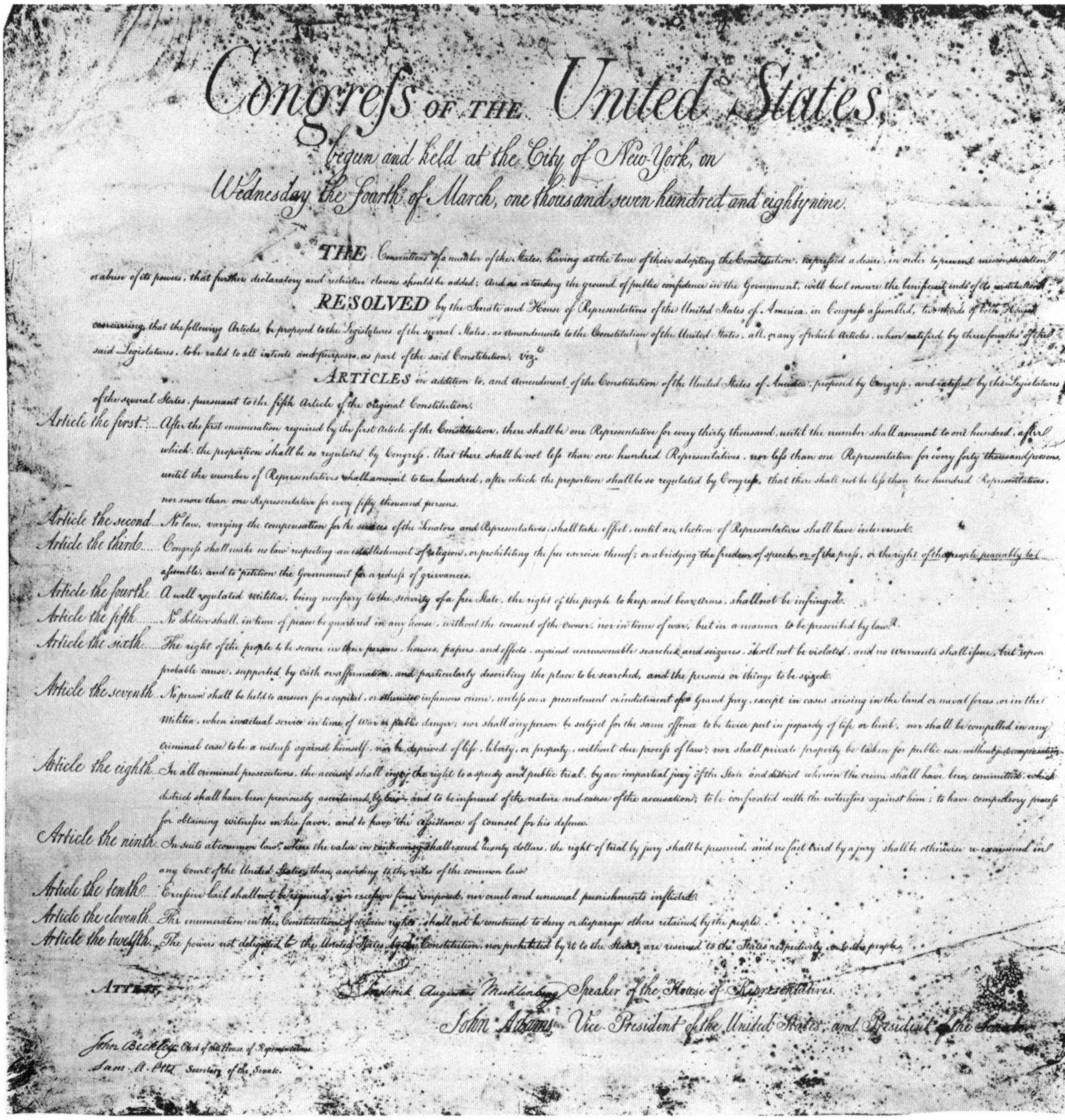
Congress of the United States,
begun and held at the City of New-York, on
Wednesday the Fourth of March, one thousand seven hundred and eighty nine.

THE Conventions of a number of the States, having at the time of their adopting the Constitution, expressed a desire, in order to prevent misconstruction or abuse of its powers, that further declaratory and restrictive clauses should be added: And as extending the ground of public confidence in the Government, will best ensure the beneficent ends of its institution.

RESOLVED by the Senate and House of Representatives of the United States of America, in Congress assembled, two thirds of both Houses concurring, that the following Articles be proposed to the Legislatures of the several States, as amendments to the Constitution of the United States, all, or any of which Articles, when ratified by three fourths of the said Legislatures, to be valid to all intents and purposes, as part of the said Constitution; viz.

ARTICLES in addition to, and Amendment of the Constitution of the United States of America, proposed by Congress, and ratified by the Legislatures of the several States, pursuant to the fifth Article of the original Constitution.

Article the first.... After the first enumeration required by the first Article of the Constitution, there shall be one Representative for every thirty thousand, until the number shall amount to one hundred, after which the proportion shall be so regulated by Congress, that there shall be not less than one hundred Representatives, nor less than one Representative for every forty thousand persons, until the number of Representatives shall amount to two hundred, after which the proportion shall be so regulated by Congress, that there shall not be less than two hundred Representatives, nor more than one Representative for every fifty thousand persons.

Article the second.... No law, varying the compensation for the services of the Senators and Representatives, shall take effect, until an election of Representatives shall have intervened.

Article the third.... Congress shall make no law respecting an establishment of religion, or prohibiting the free exercise thereof; or abridging the freedom of speech, or of the press, or the right of the people peaceably to assemble, and to petition the Government for a redress of grievances.

Article the fourth.... A well regulated militia, being necessary to the security of a free State, the right of the people to keep and bear arms, shall not be infringed.

Article the fifth.... No Soldier shall, in time of peace be quartered in any house, without the consent of the owner, nor in time of war, but in a manner to be prescribed by law.

Article the sixth.... The right of the people to be secure in their persons, houses, papers, and effects, against unreasonable searches and seizures, shall not be violated, and no warrants shall issue, but upon probable cause, supported by oath or affirmation, and particularly describing the place to be searched, and the persons or things to be seized.

Article the seventh.... No person shall be held to answer for a capital, or otherwise infamous crime, unless on a presentment or indictment of a Grand Jury, except in cases arising in the land or naval forces, or in the Militia, when in actual service in time of War or public danger; nor shall any person be subject for the same offence to be twice put in jeopardy of life or limb; nor shall be compelled in any criminal case to be a witness against himself, nor be deprived of life, liberty, or property, without due process of law; nor shall private property be taken for public use without just compensation.

Article the eighth.... In all criminal prosecutions, the accused shall enjoy the right to a speedy and public trial, by an impartial jury of the State and district wherein the crime shall have been committed, which district shall have been previously ascertained by law, and to be informed of the nature and cause of the accusation; to be confronted with the witnesses against him; to have compulsory process for obtaining witnesses in his favor, and to have the assistance of counsel for his defence.

Article the ninth.... In suits at common law, where the value in controversy shall exceed twenty dollars, the right of trial by jury shall be preserved, and no fact tried by a jury shall be otherwise re-examined in any Court of the United States, than according to the rules of the common law.

Article the tenth.... Excessive bail shall not be required, nor excessive fines imposed, nor cruel and unusual punishments inflicted.

Article the eleventh.... The enumeration in the Constitution, of certain rights, shall not be construed to deny or disparage others retained by the people.

Article the twelfth.... The powers not delegated to the United States by the Constitution, nor prohibited by it to the States, are reserved to the States respectively, or to the people.

ATTEST,

Frederick Augustus Muhlenberg Speaker of the House of Representatives.
John Adams, Vice-President of the United States, and President of the Senate.

John Beckley, Clerk of the House of Representatives.
Sam. A. Otis Secretary of the Senate.

The Bill of Rights (as proposed), New York, March 4, 1789. Courtesy National Archives and Records Service, Washington, D.C.

With the addition of the Bill of Rights, the two remaining holdouts, North Carolina and Rhode Island, ratified the Constitution in 1789 and 1790.

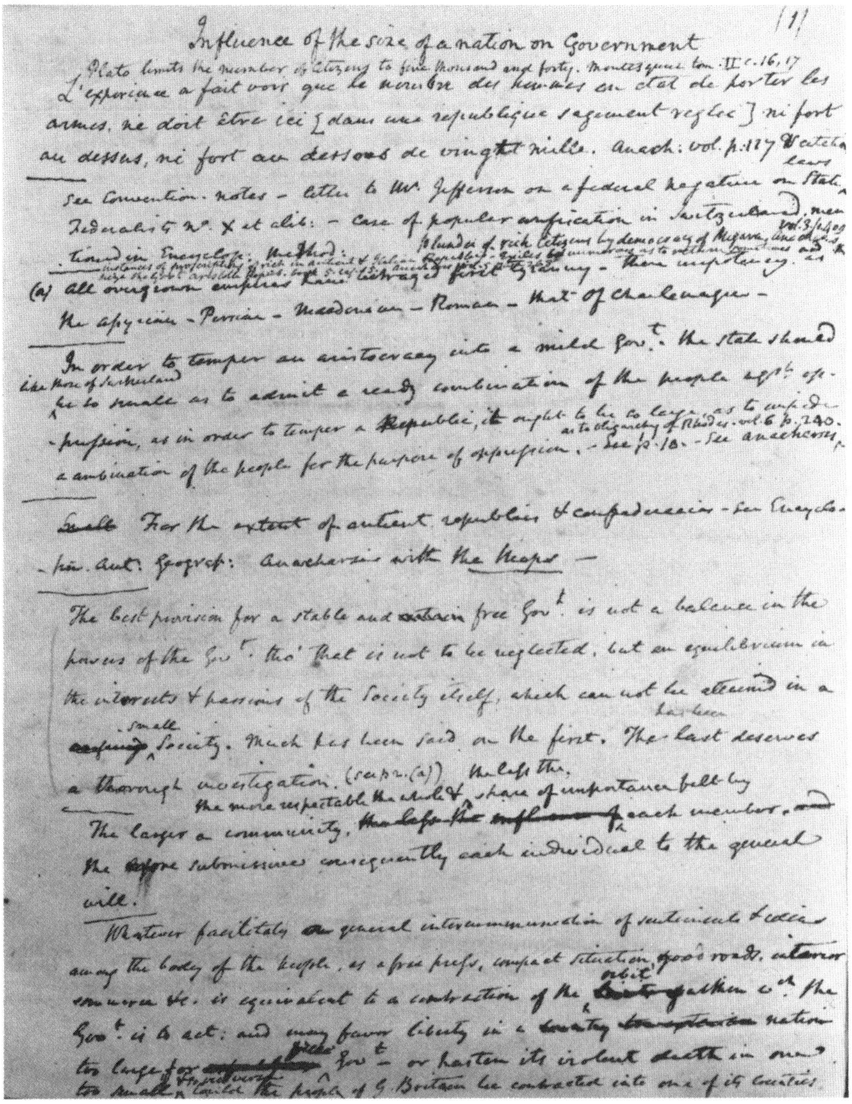

Influence of the size of a nation on Government

Plato limits the number of Citizens to five thousand and forty. Montesquieu tom. II c. 16, 17

L'experience a fait voir que le nombre des hommes en état de porter les armes, ne doit être ici [dans une republique sagement reglée] ni fort au dessus, ni fort au dessous de vingt mille.

The best provision for a stable and free Gov.t is not a balance in the powers of the Gov.t tho' that is not to be neglected, but an equilibrium in the interests & passions of the Society itself, which can not be attained in a small Society. Much has been said on the first. The last deserves a thorough investigation.

James Madison, *Notes on government*, mss. notebook, ca. 1790–91. James Madison Papers, Library of Congress.

Madison wrote a series of unsigned essays which were published in the National Gazette *during 1791 and 1792. Madison's fragmentary notes and early drafts for these articles exemplify the emerging doctrine of the Republican party.*

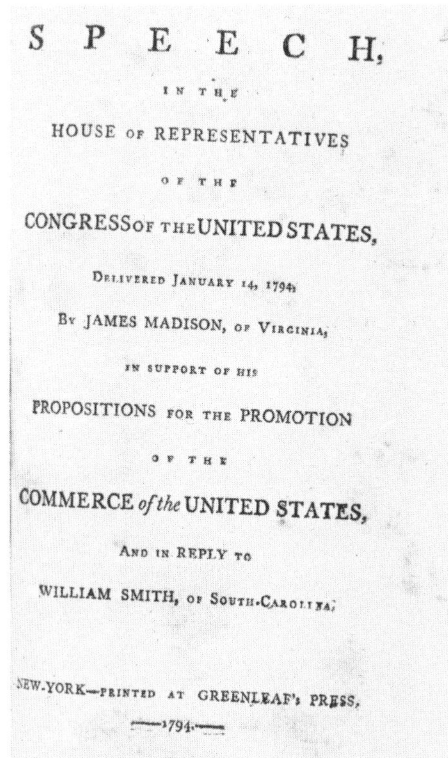

SPEECH,

IN THE

HOUSE OF REPRESENTATIVES

OF THE

CONGRESS OF THE UNITED STATES,

DELIVERED JANUARY 14, 1794;

BY JAMES MADISON, OF VIRGINIA;

IN SUPPORT OF HIS

PROPOSITIONS FOR THE PROMOTION

OF THE

COMMERCE *of the* UNITED STATES,

AND IN REPLY TO

WILLIAM SMITH, OF SOUTH-CAROLINA;

NEW-YORK—PRINTED AT GREENLEAF'S PRESS,

—1794.—

James Madison, *Speech . . . in support of his Propositions for the Promotion of the Commerce of the United States . . .*, pamphlet, 7$\frac{15}{16}$ in x 4$\frac{5}{8}$ in, New York, Greenleaf's Press, 1794. Rare Book and Special Collections Division, Library of Congress.

Throughout the 1790s, American sympathies were sharply divided between France and Great Britain. Jefferson's last act as secretary of state in 1793 was to deliver a report to Congress, assessing the state of American commerce. Madison supported its pro-French stance and subsequently introduced seven resolutions to Congress proposing severe restrictions against trade with Great Britain.

Anonymous, *The Times; a Political Portrait*, engraving, 12¼ in x 17¾ in, America, ca. 1795. Courtesy New-York Historical Society, New York City.

This unique Federalist cartoon illustrates the growing factionalism in American politics. Jefferson, as one of the leaders of the opposition party, is shown trying to stop the wheels of Washington's government.

Anonymous, *Cong. . . ss Embark'd on board the Ship Constitution of America*, engraving, 8$\frac{3}{16}$ in x 13 in, America, 1790. Prints and Photographs Division, Library of Congress.

As a member of Congress, Madison played an active role in the selection of a permanent home for the new government. Like George Washington and other Southerners, he favored a seat on the Potomac River; northern lawmakers divided their preferences between New York and Philadelphia. This pro-Potomac cartoon shows a clear route to Virginia.

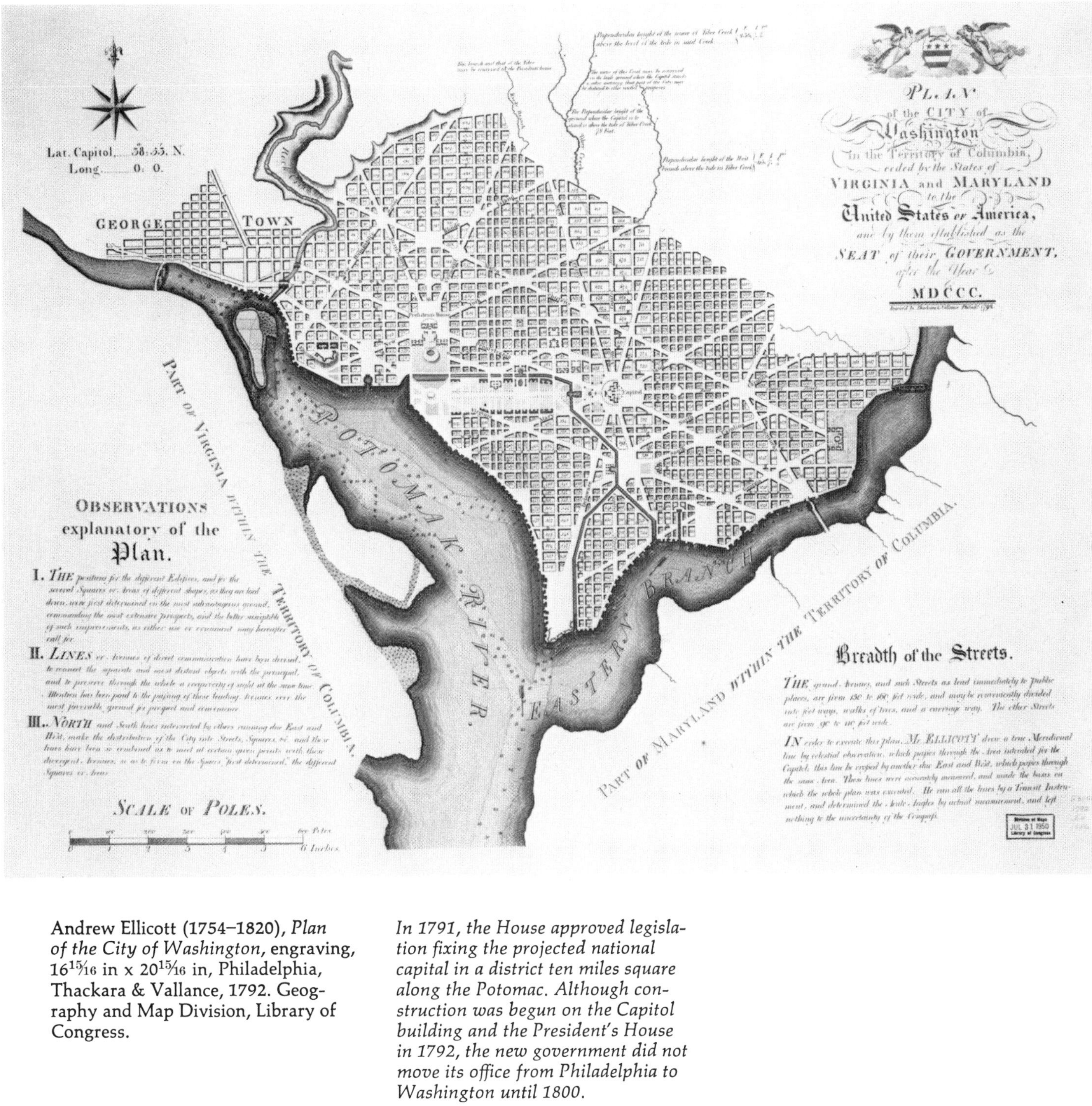

Andrew Ellicott (1754–1820), *Plan of the City of Washington*, engraving, 16 15/16 in x 20 15/16 in, Philadelphia, Thackara & Vallance, 1792. Geography and Map Division, Library of Congress.

In 1791, the House approved legislation fixing the projected national capital in a district ten miles square along the Potomac. Although construction was begun on the Capitol building and the President's House in 1792, the new government did not move its office from Philadelphia to Washington until 1800.

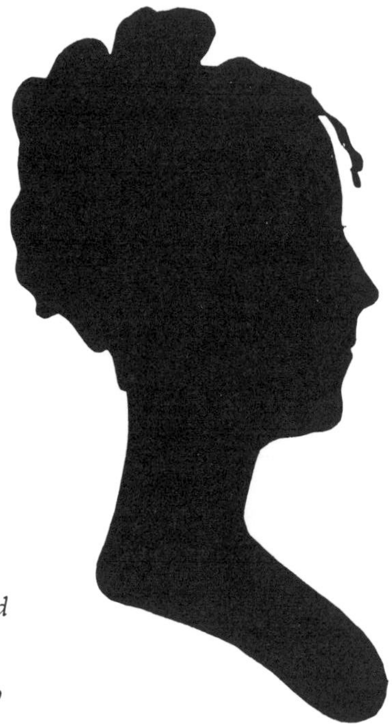

Anonymous, *Dolley Payne* (later Dolley Madison, 1768–1849), paper on black silk, 4 in x 3½ in, America, ca, 1785–90. Courtesy Virginia Historical Society, Richmond.

The daughter of Quaker parents, Dolley Payne grew up in Virginia and Philadelphia. The 1793 yellow fever epidemic in Philadelphia claimed the life of her husband, lawyer John Todd and one of their two infant sons. The young and vivacious widow met James Madison in the spring of 1794. "Thou must come to me," she urged a friend, "Aaron Burr says that the great little Madison has asked to be brought to see me this evening."

James Madison, *Letter to Dolley Payne Todd* (excerpt), Orange, August 18, 1794. James Madison Papers, Library of Congress.

Congressman Madison's courtship of Dolley Payne Todd must have surprised his friends; they were married in September 1794, only a few months after the formal introductions were made. Madison proposed before the end of the summer, and anxiously awaited a reply from his intended, who was visiting in Virginia. This fragment acknowledges receipt of her "precious favor."

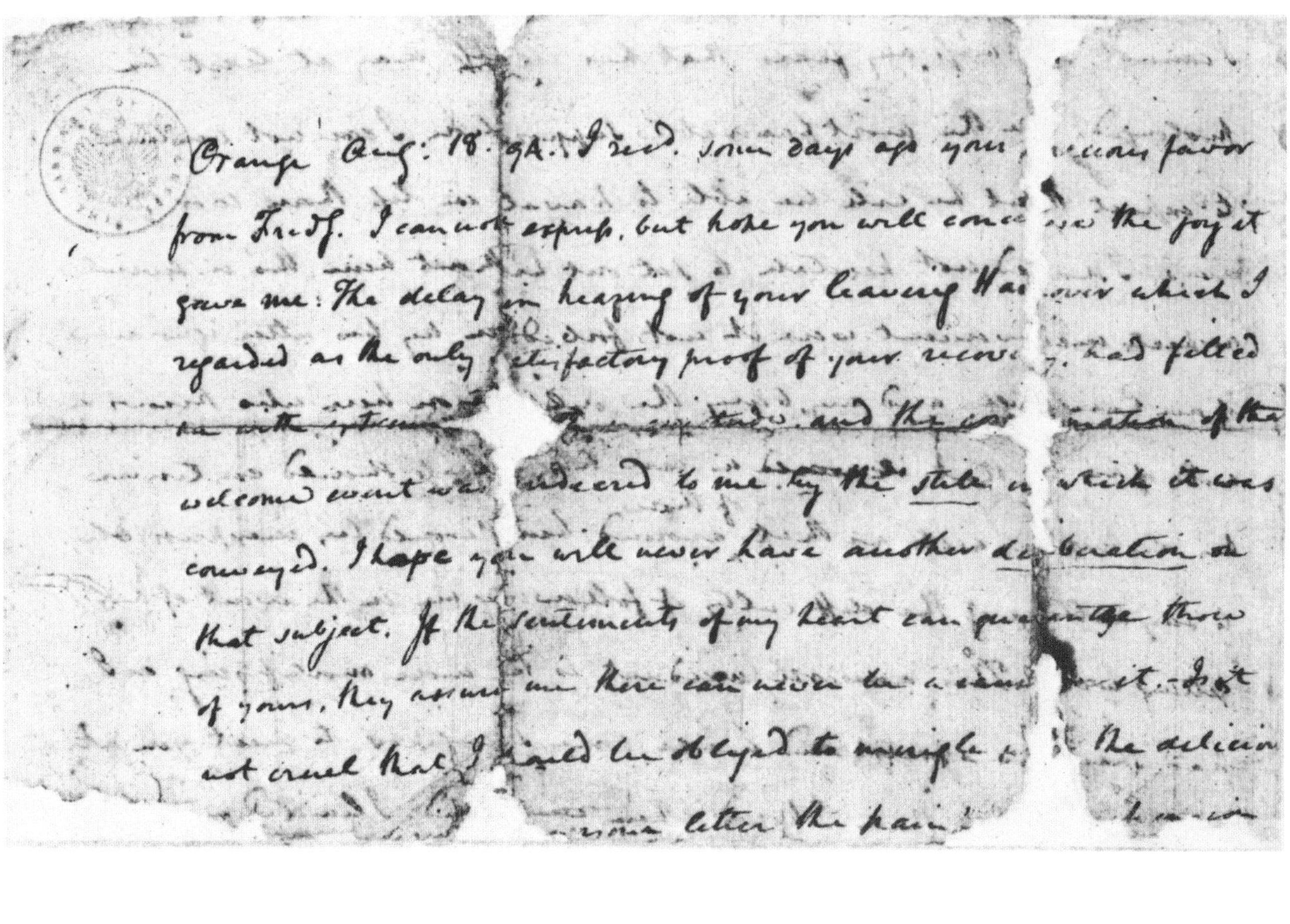

Orange Aug: 18. 94. I recd. some days ago your precious favor from Fredg. I can not express, but hope you will conceive the joy it gave me. The delay in hearing of your leaving Hanover which I regarded as the only satisfactory proof of your recovery, had filled me with extreme inquietude, and the confirmation of that welcome event was endeared to me by the stile in which it was conveyed. I hope you will never have another deliberation on that subject. If the sentiments of my heart can guarantee those of yours, they assure me there can never be a cause for it. Is it not cruel that I should be obliged to mingle with the delicious

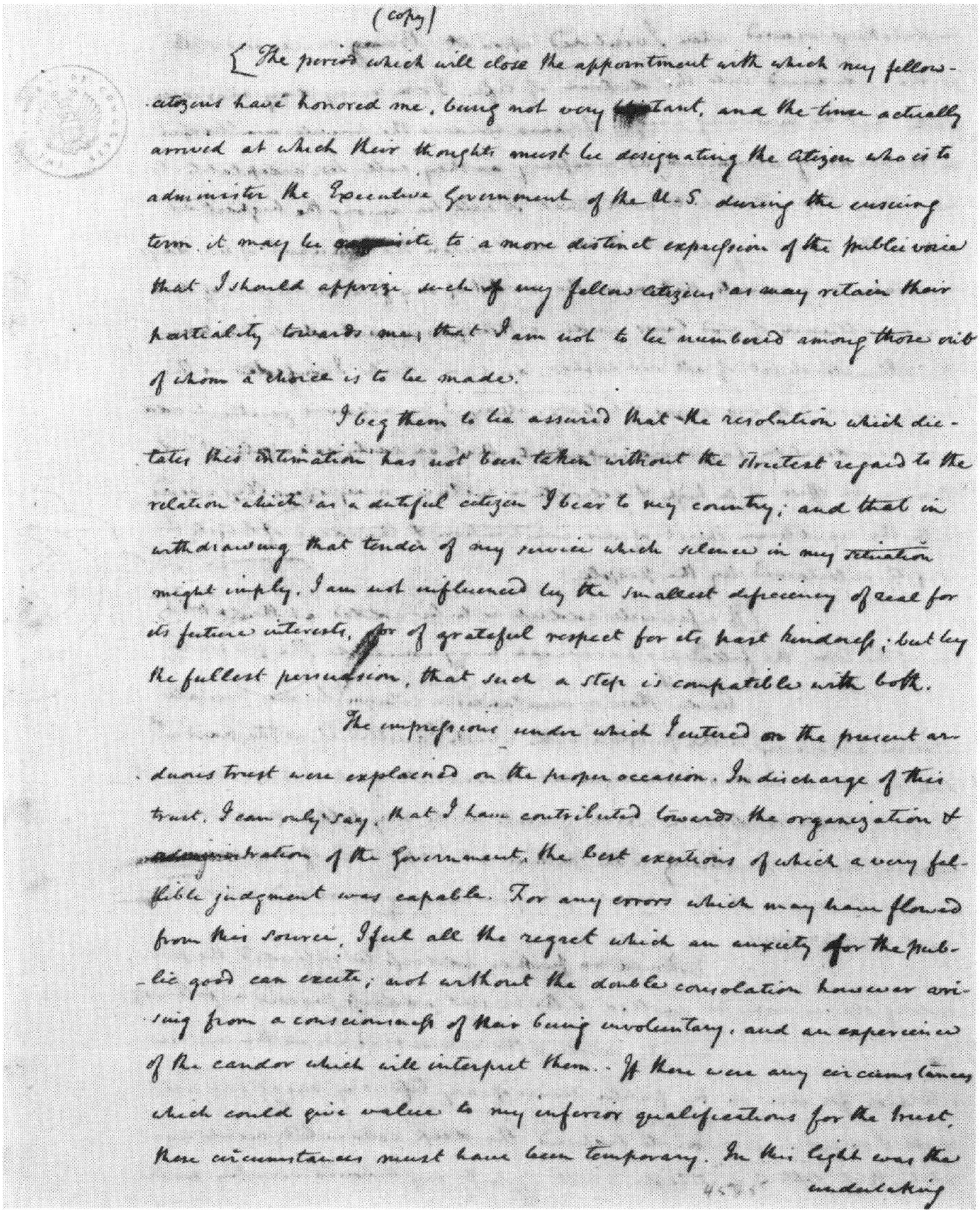
(copy)

[The period which will close the appointment with which my fellow-citizens have honored me, being not very distant, and the time actually arrived at which their thoughts must be designating the citizen who is to administer the Executive Government of the U.S. during the ensuing term, it may be requisite to a more distinct expression of the public voice that I should apprize such of my fellow citizens as may retain their partiality towards me, that I am not to be numbered among those out of whom a choice is to be made.

I beg them to be assured that the resolution which dictates this intimation has not been taken without the strictest regard to the relation which as a dutiful citizen I bear to my country; and that in withdrawing that tender of my service which silence in my situation might imply, I am not influenced by the smallest deficiency of zeal for its future interests, or of grateful respect for its past kindness; but by the fullest persuasion, that such a step is compatible with both.

The impressions under which I entered on the present arduous trust were explained on the proper occasion. In discharge of this trust, I can only say, that I have contributed towards the organization & administration of the Government, the best exertions of which a very fallible judgment was capable. For any errors which may have flowed from this source, I feel all the regret which an anxiety for the public good can excite; not without the double consolation however arising from a consciousness of their being involuntary, and an experience of the candor which will interpret them. If there were any circumstances which could give value to my inferior qualifications for the trust, these circumstances must have been temporary. In this light was the undertaking

James Madison, *Draft for President Washington's Farewell Address* (excerpt), June 21, 1792. James Madison Papers, Library of Congress.

During the first term of his presidency, Washington frequently relied on Madison for advice. When the president considered retiring in 1792, he asked Madison to write an appropriate announcement. Parts of this draft were later incorporated into Washington's Farewell Address in 1796.

Anonymous, *The Providential Detection,* line engraving, 16¼ in x 14 in, America?, ca. 1797. Courtesy Library Company of Philadelphia, Pennsylvania.

This Federalist cartoon portrays Jefferson as the head of a party friendly to France. The bitter presidential campaign of 1796 firmly established a national two-party system in American politics. Madison sided with the Republicans but Federalist John Adams won the race.

James Sharples (ca. 1751–1811), *James Madison* (from life), pastel on paper, 9 in x 7 in, Philadelphia, 1796–97. Courtesy Independence National Historical Park Collection, Philadelphia, Pennsylvania.

After spending a decade as a congressman, Madison retired to Montpelier with his new bride in 1797. They remained in Virginia until Madison's appointment as Jefferson's secretary of state in 1801.

James Sharples (ca. 1751–1811), *Dolley Madison*, pastel on paper, 9 in x 7 in, Philadelphia, 1796–97. Courtesy Independence National Historical Park Collection, Philadelphia, Pennsylvania.

William Russell Birch (1755–1834), *Preparation for War to defend Commerce*, colored line engraving, 11½ in x 13⅝ in, Philadelphia, William Birch & Son, 1798–99. Rare Book and Special Collections Division, Library of Congress.

Interference by the French Directory with American shipping provoked an undeclared war with France from 1798–1800. Frigates such as the Philadelphia *were constructed to strengthen the American naval fleet.*

Ansell, pseudonym for Charles Williams (?–d. after 1830) (attrib.), *Property Protected. a la Françoise*, colored engraving, 10 7/16 in x 16 13/16 in, London, S. W. Fores, June 1, 1798. Prints and Photographs Division, Library of Congress.

In an effort to negotiate a commercial treaty with France, President Adams sent a group of American commissioners to Paris in 1798. An attempt by agents of Talleyrand's government to obtain a large bribe from the Americans in exchange for the treaty precipitated the notorious "XYZ" affair.

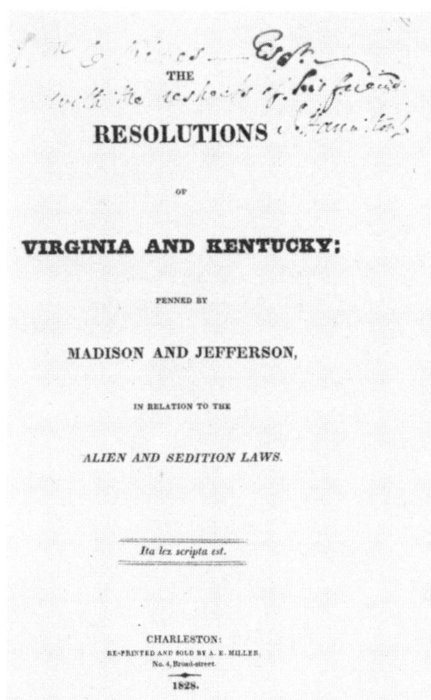

THE

RESOLUTIONS

OF

VIRGINIA AND KENTUCKY;

PENNED BY

MADISON AND JEFFERSON,

IN RELATION TO THE

ALIEN AND SEDITION LAWS.

Ita lex scripta est.

CHARLESTON:
RE-PRINTED AND SOLD BY A. E. MILLER,
No. 4, Broad-street.
1828.

The Resolutions of Virginia and Kentucky; penned by Madison and Jefferson, 8 5/16 in x 5 3/8 in, Charleston, South Carolina, A. E. Miller, 1828 (1798 reprint). Rare Book and Special Collections Division, Library of Congress.

In 1798, the Federalist government enacted the repressive Alien and Sedition Acts, which were viewed by the Republicans as censorious measures against their party and the French. Jefferson drafted the Kentucky Resolutions, whereby a state could declare null and void any federal law that it considered a violation of its constitutional rights. Madison wrote similar measures for Virginia.

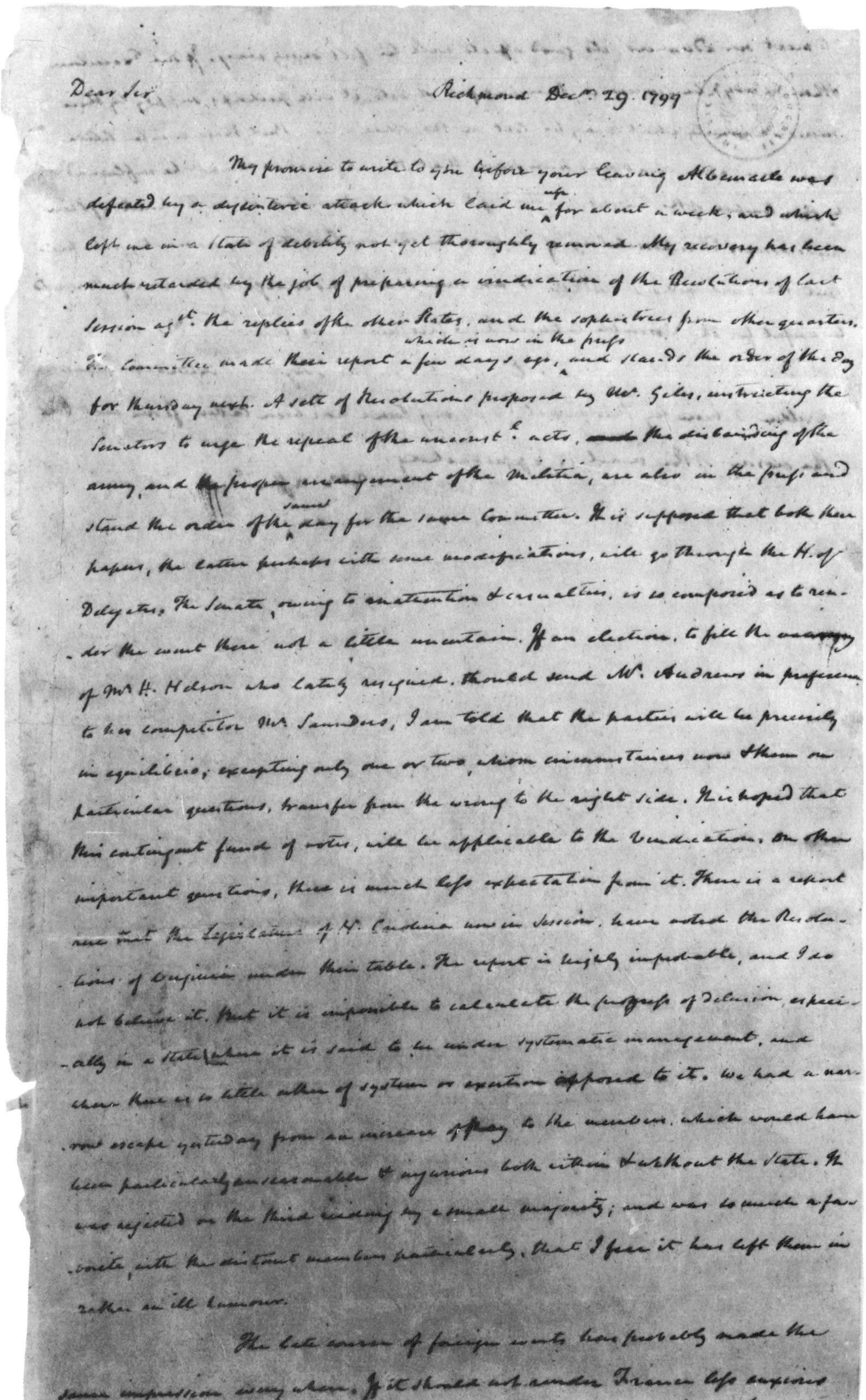

Dear Sir   Richmond Decr. 29. 1799

My promise to write to you before your leaving Albemarle was defeated by a dysentery attack which laid me up for about a week, and which left me in a state of debility not yet thoroughly removed. My recovery has been much retarded by the job of preparing a vindication of the Resolutions of last Session agst. the replies of the other States, and the sophistries from other quarters. The Committee made their report a few days ago, which is now in the press and stands the order of the day for Thursday next. A sett of Resolutions proposed by Mr. Giles, instructing the Senators to urge the repeal of the unconstl. acts, the disbanding of the army, and the proper arrangement of the Militia, are also in the press and stand the order of the same day for the same Committee. It is supposed that both these papers, the latter perhaps with some modifications, will go through the H. of Delegates. The Senate, owing to inattention & casualties, is so composed as to render the event there not a little uncertain. If an election to fill the vacancy of Mr H. Nelson who lately resigned, should send Mr. Andrews in preference to his competitor Mr. Saunders, I am told that the parties will be precisely in equilibrio; excepting only one or two, whom circumstances now & then on particular questions, transfer from the wrong to the right side. It is hoped that this contingent fund of votes, will be applicable to the Vindication. On other important questions, there is much less expectation from it. There is a report here that the Legislature of N. Carolina now in Session, have voted the Resolutions of Virginia under their table. The report is highly improbable, and I do not believe it. But it is impossible to calculate the progress of delusion, especially in a State where it is said to be under systematic management, and where there is so little either of system or exertion opposed to it. We had a narrow escape yesterday from an increase of pay to the members, which would have been particularly unseasonable & injurious both within & without the State. It was rejected on the third reading by a small majority; and was so much a favorite with the distant members particularly, that I fear it has left them in rather an ill humour.

The late course of foreign events have probably made the same impression every where. If it should not render France less anxious to

OPPOSITE:

James Madison, *Letter to Thomas Jefferson* (excerpt), Richmond, December 29, 1799. James Madison Papers, Library of Congress.

Reacting to criticism of the Virginia Resolutions, Madison wrote a brilliant exposition of the constitutional and moral principles of Republican freedom, known as the "Report of 1800."

Charles Balthazar Julien Févret de St.-Mémin (1770–1852), *Thomas Jefferson*, black and white crayon and tinted washes on paper, 23 13/16 in x 17 in, Washington, November 27, 1804. Courtesy Worcester Art Museum, Massachusetts.

Jefferson was elected president in 1800 after a bitter and emotional campaign. His victory placed the Republican party in power.

Gilbert Stuart (1755–1828), *James Madison* (from life), oil on canvas, 29 in x 24 in, Washington, 1804. Courtesy Colonial Williamsburg Foundation, Virginia.

Jefferson chose his good friend James Madison as secretary of state. Delayed by the death of his father early in 1801, Madison did not arrive in Washington until the spring. Madison was the new president's most trusted counselor and Jefferson was to write in 1809 of their collaboration, "our principles were the same, and we never differed sensibly in the application of them."

Gilbert Stuart (1755–1828), *Dolley Madison*, oil on canvas, 29 in x 24 in, Washington, 1804. Courtesy Pennsylvania Academy of the Fine Arts, Philadelphia.

Madison and his wife sat for portrait painter Gilbert Stuart in 1804. During Madison's terms as secretary of state, the sociable Dolley frequently served as hostess for the widowed Jefferson at the White House.

T. Cartwright after George Beck (ca. 1748–1812), *GeorgeTown and Federal City, or City of Washington*, colored aquatint, 18 in x 23 in, London, 1801. Prints and Photographs Division, Library of Congress.

When the Madisons moved to Washington, the new Federal City was still a series of small villages joined by muddy pathways.

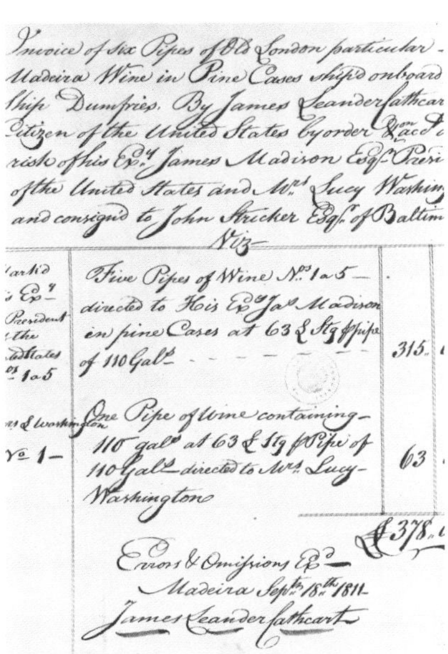

Invoice of Six Pipes of Old London particular Madeira Wine in Pine Cases shipp'd on board Ship Dumfries. By James Leander Cathcart Citizen of the United States by order & acc't & risk of his Ex'y James Madison Esq'r Presi of the United States and Mrs Lucy Washin and consign'd to John Stricker Esq'r of Baltim

Five Pipes of Wine No 1 a 5 — directed to His Ex'y Jas Madison in pine Cases at 63 £ Stg p Pipe of 110 Gal's — 315.

One Pipe of Wine containing 110 gal's at 63 £ Stg p Pipe of 110 Gal's directed to Mrs Lucy Washington — 63

£378.

Errors & Omissions Ex'd
Madeira Sept 18th 1811
James Leander Cathcart

James L. Cathcart, *Invoice for a Shipment of Wines*, September 18, 1811. James Madison Papers, Library of Congress.

The Madisons set standards for entertaining that dominated Washington social life until the Civil War. Madison enjoyed fine wines and kept a variety of foreign agents in pursuit of good vintages.

Anonymous, *Side Chair* (one of a set), painted wood, 34¾ in x 18½ in x 16½ in, France, ca. 1770–80. Courtesy Moses Myers House, Chrysler Museum, Norfolk, Virginia.

Although James and Dolley Madison never visited France, they enthusiastically imported fashionable Gallic articles for their home. This Louis XVI side chair was part of a shipment from Paris, acquired through the efforts of James Monroe.

Roch-Louis Dany, *Candlestick* (one of a set), silver, 11¼ in x 4 in, Paris, ca. 1789. Courtesy White House Collection, Washington, D.C.

When Monroe returned to France as minister in 1803, he offered the Madisons over two hundred pieces of French silver and a large assortment of china and glassware. These candlesticks were part of the transaction.

Nast manufactory, *Ice Cream Vase* (part of a set), porcelain, 9½ in, Paris, ca. 1805–6. Courtesy White House Collection, Washington, D.C.

Frozen ice cream was among the French dishes that graced Dolley Madison's table. The piece shown here was part of a large dinner and dessert service ordered from Paris in 1805.

Sevrès manufactory, *Cup and saucer*, porcelain, 2½ in x 2½ in (cup); 1⅛ in x 4⅞ in (saucer), Paris, late eighteenth century. Courtesy White House Collection, Washington, D.C.

This example of French china survives from a set the Madisons purchased from Monroe in 1803.

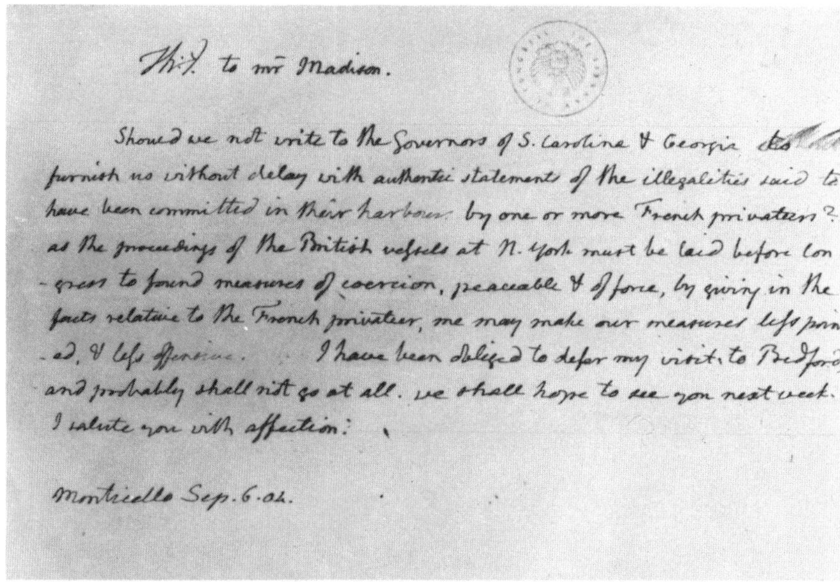

Th: J. to mr Madison.

Should we not write to the Governors of S. Carolina & Georgia to furnish us without delay with authentic statements of the illegalities said to have been committed in their harbours by one or more French privateers? as the proceedings of the British vessels at N. York must be laid before Congress to found measures of coercion, peaceable & of force, by giving in the facts relative to the French privateer, we may make our measures less pointed, & less offensive. I have been obliged to defer my visit to Bedford, and probably shall not go at all. we shall hope to see you next week. I salute you with affection.

Monticello Sep. 6. 04.

Thomas Jefferson, *Memo to James Madison*, Monticello, September 6, 1804. James Madison Papers, Library of Congress.

Jefferson and Madison conducted the affairs of state from Virginia during the warm-weather months; it was the president's habit to communicate to his secretary of state through short notes, such as the example shown here.

John L. Boqueta de Woiseri (fl. America, 1797–1815), *A View of New Orleans taken from the Plantation of Marigny—November 1803*, oil on canvas, 58½ in x 7 feet, 6½ in, New Orleans, 1803. Courtesy Chicago Historical Society, Illinois, gift of Charles B. Pike.

Among the government's triumphs during Madison's first term as secretary of state was the acquisition of France's Louisiana Territory for fifteen million dollars. The Louisiana Purchase, which extended the United States to the Rocky Mountains, doubled the size of the country.

Gilbert Stuart (1755–1828), *James Madison,* oil on canvas, 46½ in x 38¾ in, Boston, 1805. Courtesy Bowdoin College Museum of Art, Brunswick, Maine.

A gull for the People
WEST FLORIDA
EAST FLORIDA
Two Millions!
J. Akin fec.t
The PRAIRIE DOG sickened at the sting of the HORNET
or a Diplomatic Puppet exhibiting his Deceptions!

James Akin (ca. 1773–1846), *The Prairie Dog sickened at the sting of the Hornet*, engraving, 11¼ in x 16 in, Philadelphia?, ca. 1806–8. Prints and Photographs Division, Library of Congress.

The territorial boundaries set by the Louisiana Purchase were not exact and the ownership of eastern and western Florida became an issue in 1806. During Madison's administration, the United States took possession of West Florida in 1810 and East Florida in 1811.

John James Barralet (ca. 1747–1815), *John Pierce who was murderd* [sic] *by a Shot from the Leander,* etching and engraving, $16\frac{7}{16}$ in x $21\frac{5}{16}$ in, Philadelphia?, ca. 1806. Prints and Photographs Division, Library of Congress.

The arbitrary impressment of American seamen by the British was a leading cause of the War of 1812. Public uproar followed the death of sailor John Pierce, killed by a cannon shot from an English squadron off the coast of Long Island, New York, in 1806.

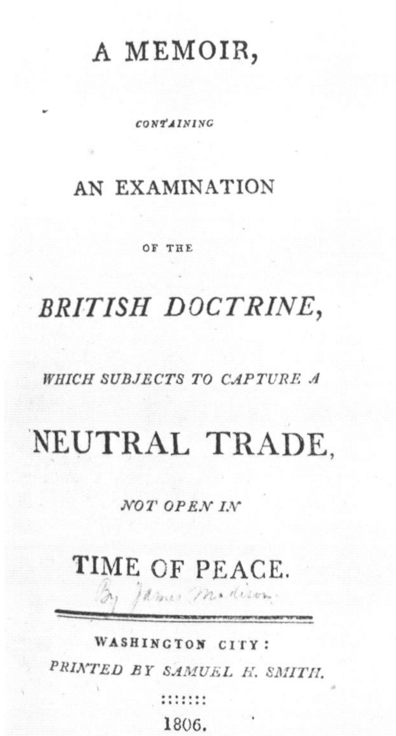

A MEMOIR,

CONTAINING

AN EXAMINATION

OF THE

BRITISH DOCTRINE,

WHICH SUBJECTS TO CAPTURE A

NEUTRAL TRADE,

NOT OPEN IN

TIME OF PEACE.

By James Madison

WASHINGTON CITY:

PRINTED BY SAMUEL H. SMITH.

1806.

James Madison, *A Memoir, Containing An Examination of the British Doctrine,* pamphlet, $8\frac{7}{16}$ in x $4\frac{1}{2}$ in, Washington City, Samuel Smith, 1806. Rare Book and Special Collections Division, Library of Congress.

Madison upheld America's claims to neutral commerce in this 1806 report to Congress. England's aggressive actions against American vessels trading in the West Indies had resumed after the resumption of the Napoleonic wars.

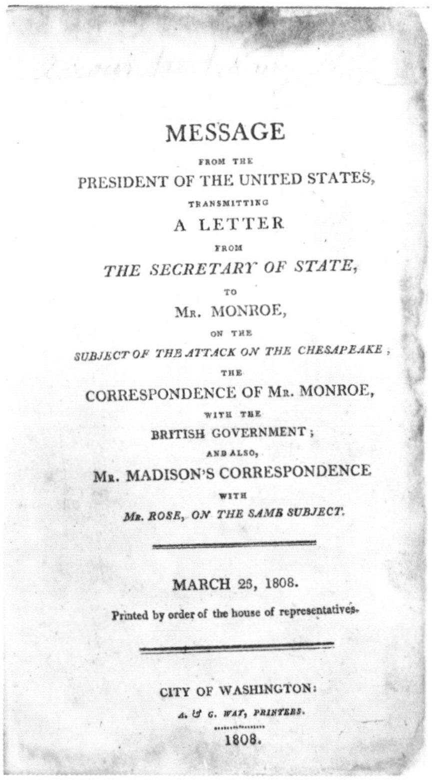

MESSAGE
FROM THE
PRESIDENT OF THE UNITED STATES,
TRANSMITTING
A LETTER
FROM
THE SECRETARY OF STATE,
TO
MR. MONROE,
ON THE
SUBJECT OF THE ATTACK ON THE CHESAPEAKE,
THE
CORRESPONDENCE OF MR. MONROE,
WITH THE
BRITISH GOVERNMENT;
AND ALSO,
MR. MADISON'S CORRESPONDENCE
WITH
MR. ROSE, ON THE SAME SUBJECT.

MARCH 26, 1808.
Printed by order of the house of representatives.

CITY OF WASHINGTON:
A. & G. WAY, PRINTERS.
1808.

Message from the President of the United States . . . On the Subject of the Attack on the Chesapeake, pamphlet, 8 3/16 in x 4 3/4 in, Washington, A & G Way, 1808. Rare Book and Special Collections Division, Library of Congress.

A flagrant violation of the neutral rights of the United States almost precipitated war with Britain in 1807. An attempt by the H.M.S. Leopard *to board the U.S.S.* Chesapeake, *cruising off the coast of Virginia, and search for deserters resulted in the death of three American sailors. Jefferson and Madison hastened to cool the country's ardor for war. They hoped the crisis could be resolved diplomatically. Despite an official apology from the government of Great Britain, the impressment of American seamen continued.*

Charles B. J. F. de St.-Mémin (1770–1852), *George Clinton* (1739–1812), black and white crayon and tinted washes on paper, 21 3/8 in x 14 3/8 in, New York, ca. 1797–98. Courtesy Metropolitan Museum of Art, New York City.

Vice-President during Jefferson's second term, New Yorker George Clinton was elected to the same office on Madison's ticket during the 1808 presidential campaign. He died in office in 1812.

Anonymous, *An old philosopher teaching his mad son economical Projects*, colored etching, 12⅞ in x 17 in, America?, ca. 1809. Courtesy Free Library of Philadelphia, Pennsylvania.

Using a tactic which had succeeded during the American Revolution, an absolute prohibition on foreign commerce, Jefferson and Madison hoped to insure the neutral rights of the United States. This rare cartoon illustrates the views of opponents of the Embargo Bill, who accused Madison of French sympathies. Here his caricature proclaims, "France wants an embargo & must have it!"

Gilbert Stuart (1755–1828), *James Madison* (from life), oil on canvas, 29 in x 24 in, Washington, 1804. Courtesy Colonial Williamsburg Foundation, Virginia.

III

THE EMERGENCE OF NATIONHOOD

As Madison took office, the United States was a country with freely circulating gold and silver, a bountiful food supply produced by a nation of farmers who had no conception whatever of unemployment, and an efficient post office functioning as the one governmental agency that touched most people. The young nation also supported an archaic banking system where any interest rate above eight percent was regarded as usurious. The pace of life was fitted to the farming routine and the seasons of growth and harvest. In a day when all taxes were considered burdensome, the touch of the tax gatherer was light, since land was assessed at a low rate and most of the expenses of government came from the indirect revenue generated by the tariff on imported goods. A twelve-hour workday did not seem oppressive to the farmer tilling his own fields, the smithy at his own forge, or the merchant behind his own counter. Foreign travelers remarked on the widespread literacy of the common man, gawked at his pretty daughters, and marveled at his bounteous table. In short, the country was prospering under a political system which admirably reflected the people's desires, and the politicians who were disconsolate were not unhappy with the times so much as they were grieved at their own loss of power. Madison understood all this and was never able to share Jefferson's strong disdain for the arch-Federalists. Beholding the blessings of nature and the results of the Revolution, Madison was more inclined toward magnanimity than was his neighbor from Monticello.

The fact that Madison was not a good hater probably hurt him as a politician. Then Jefferson's last days in office turned into a shambles, when congressmen allowed their frustrations to surface after years of executive leadership. They showed their defiance by rejecting Jefferson's appointments, intrigued to weaken enforcement of the embargo, and applauded when reports of widespread smuggling from Canada made continuance of the unpopular measure untenable. The crowning insult was repeal of the embargo, to take effect on Jefferson's last day in office (until an amendment set March 15 as the expiration date).

Madison must have realized that he was going to have to pick up the pieces deftly. Jefferson dutifully attended Madison's inauguration and then took off for Monticello, leaving his successor to face a snarling pack of jackals in the Senate who thirsted for power. Although Madison had known most of them for decades and served in Congress with more than a few, he did not comprehend their capacity for pettiness. Committed as he was to republican ideals and to constitutional government, Madison saw himself not as "a man on horseback" ready to lead Congress (as for example Franklin D. Roosevelt did in 1933), but rather as a chief executive bound to a passive policy. If one understands Madison's approach to the presidency as an office for guidance rather than assertive leadership, then the events from 1809 onward make more sense.

All of the signs that the harmony in Congress was over were evident within days after Madison's election as president was unofficially confirmed. The trick for the president-elect was to keep the dissenters in Congress from insulting Jefferson and still to frame a policy that would replace the discredited embargo. A powerful Senate faction intimidated Madison by refusing to allow his nomination of Albert Gallatin as secretary of state (Swiss-born Gallatin was condemned as a smart-aleck "furriner"), forcing the president to begin his administration with a crippled cabinet made up of has-beens, would-bes, and never-wases. His spine stiffened sufficiently to insist that Gallatin remain as secretary of the treasury, but the Senate intriguers had a field day by denying the new president help where he needed it most. Thus forced to compromise, Madison in effect became his own secretary of state and conducted the delicate negotiations with England by keeping his appointee for the job, Robert Smith, at arm's length.

For a time, the makeshift plan worked. David Erskine, the British minister in Washington, had married an American girl and was anxious to provide grounds for an Anglo-American *detente.* A diplomatic whirlwind early in April 1809 produced an agreement that seemed to offer the Americans all they

Gilbert Stuart (1755–1828), *Dolley Madison* (1768–1846), oil on canvas, 29 in x 24 in, Washington, 1804. Courtesy Pennsylvania Academy of the Fine Arts, Philadelphia.

sought: end of the Orders in Council, reparations for the *Chesapeake* incident, and a resumption of normal trade relations. Eager to believe that the embargo policy had been vindicated, Madison carried on the negotiations with Erskine, then hastily signed a proclamation ending the clamp on British-American commerce. For a few months the country was jubilant, as it appeared that a slight twisting of the British lion's tail had brought all America sought in the way of

Gilbert Stuart (1755–1828), *Albert Gallatin* (1761–1848), oil on canvas, 29⅜ in x 23⅞ in, Washington, ca. 1803. Courtesy Metropolitan Museum of Art, New York City, gift of Frederic W. Stevens, 1908.

concessions. But when the British foreign office read the agreement, Canning was less than pleased, and Madison's indelicate wording of the *Chesapeake* matter had offended George III (at least that was the story passed around Whitehall). Madison's note no longer insisted that the offending British commander be punished but said that the president "is not the less sensible of the justice and utility of such an example, nor the less persuaded that it would best comport with what is due from His Britannic majesty to his own honor."[25]

25. *American State Papers*, 38 vols., (Washington: Gales & Seaton, 1832-61), *Foreign Relations*, 3:295-96.

The joy of April turned to ashes in June when the whole agreement was repudiated by Canning in a sharply worded statement that included Erskine's recall. From that moment on, Madison apparently realized war with England was inevitable.

The pace of life being slower when there were no Atlantic cables or fast mail ships, the cauldron of Anglo-American problems boiled for another three years. First, Madison threw the whole initiative back into the hands of Congress. The troubled lawmakers, not certain of what they wanted but sure they did not want another embargo, finally patched together a makeshift program known as Macon's Bill Number 2—simply a weak-kneed answer to continued British and French depredations. The point was that a carrot would be dangled, and if either power chose to relax its decrees or edicts the United States would level its aim at the other. Napoleon, clever if not honest, told the American minister he was repealing his Milan decree so that American ships would have the rights of neutrals in European waters. In fact, Napoleon's move was a sham intended only to force America's hand.

Beleaguered by young congressmen who were sick and tired of England's haughtiness, Madison took Napoleon's revocation at face value. He also paid $50,000 in hard cash for a set of documents which was said to prove that England had been hoping to interfere in United States affairs by spying activities and treasonous overtures with New England Federalists. While outraged Federalists ranted and raved, Madison and his newly appointed secretary of state, James Monroe, insisted they had proof of British duplicity and chalked up another black mark against the English.

They did not need to spend the $50,000 on such dubious evidence, for the mood of the country was swinging toward war anyway. As Rep. Richard M. Johnson said in December 1811, the list of England's mistakes was long:

> *I wish to see Great Britain renounce the piratical system of paper blockades; to liberate our captured seaman on board her ships of war; relinquish the practice of impressment on board our merchant vessels; to repeal her Orders in Council; and cease, in every other respect, to violate our neutral rights; to treat us as an independent people. . . . I should not wish to extend the boundary of the United States by war if Great Britain would leave us to the quiet enjoyment of independence. . . . Her disposition is unfriendly; her enmity is implacable; she sickens at our prosperity and happiness.*[26]

26. Speech in House, December 11, 1811.

John Vanderlyn (1775–1852), *James Monroe* (1751–1831), oil on canvas, 35¼ in x 31½ in, America, 1816. Courtesy Colonial Williamsburg Foundation, Virginia.

Madison was heartened by such talk, but the New England Federalists were insistent upon a policy that would reopen trade with England as well as France. A kinsman wrote him that Federalist newspapers around Boston teemed with outspoken attacks on the administration, and their intemperate remarks proved "that Great Britain with much justice counts upon a [friendly] party among us. War alone can furnish a remedy for this deplorable malady in the body politic." [27]

27. John G. Jackson to Madison, March 30, 1812, Manuscript Division, Library of Congress.

Almost in despair, Madison pinned his hopes on one last appeal to the English to stop their interference with American shipping in international waters. Anxiously he awaited the arrival of the *Hornet*, which might bring diplomatic dispatches from London with news of British concessions. Alas, the *Hornet* arrived with no good news at all. Everything was left just as it was, and the prospects for a break in the British wall of intransigence seemed more remote than ever.

The leading Republican newspaper in Washington hinted at what was in store when it observed: "If the reports we now hear are true, that with England all hope of honorable accomodation is at an end, and that with France our negotiations are in a forwardness encouraging expectations of a favorable result, where is the motive for longer delay? The final step ought to be taken, and that step is WAR." [28] With many regrets, Madison sat down and wrote a war message for Congress.

The idea of war was so repugnant to Madison that he turned the possible alternatives over in his mind, wrote Jefferson of his misgivings about a declaration of war, and probably even prayed that England would provide an excuse not to fight (his religious tendencies were notably covert). But when the *Hornet* returned almost empty-handed, Madison realized that as president he could no longer remain a republican dove in the White House.

One thing Madison could count on was public support. Patriotism would rise over petty politics, he believed, and with much reason. Despite the Federalists' carping, Madison's files were jammed with proof that even in New England the people were united in their defiance of British aggression. From Litchfield, Connecticut, a citizens' meeting had sent a message that called upon the president to resist "the outrages of Great Britain & France." It took particular aim at England. Insisting they were ready for war if that step was needed, the Connecticut citizens upbraided England for a long train of abuses and concluded she was "*daring again* to claim a right to tax us, an independent people, as though we were yet her colonies. . . . England by these unexampled wrongs, has violated our right to *property*, to *liberty* and to *life*; has directly attacked our national sovereignty & independence." [29] Month after month these testimonials of readiness for any action gave Madison a sense of national unity that opposition editorials and long-winded speeches in Congress could

28. Washington *National Intelligencer*, April 12, 1812.

29. Republican Committee of Litchfield, Conn., to the President, March 13, 1809, Madison Papers, Manuscript Division, Library of Congress.

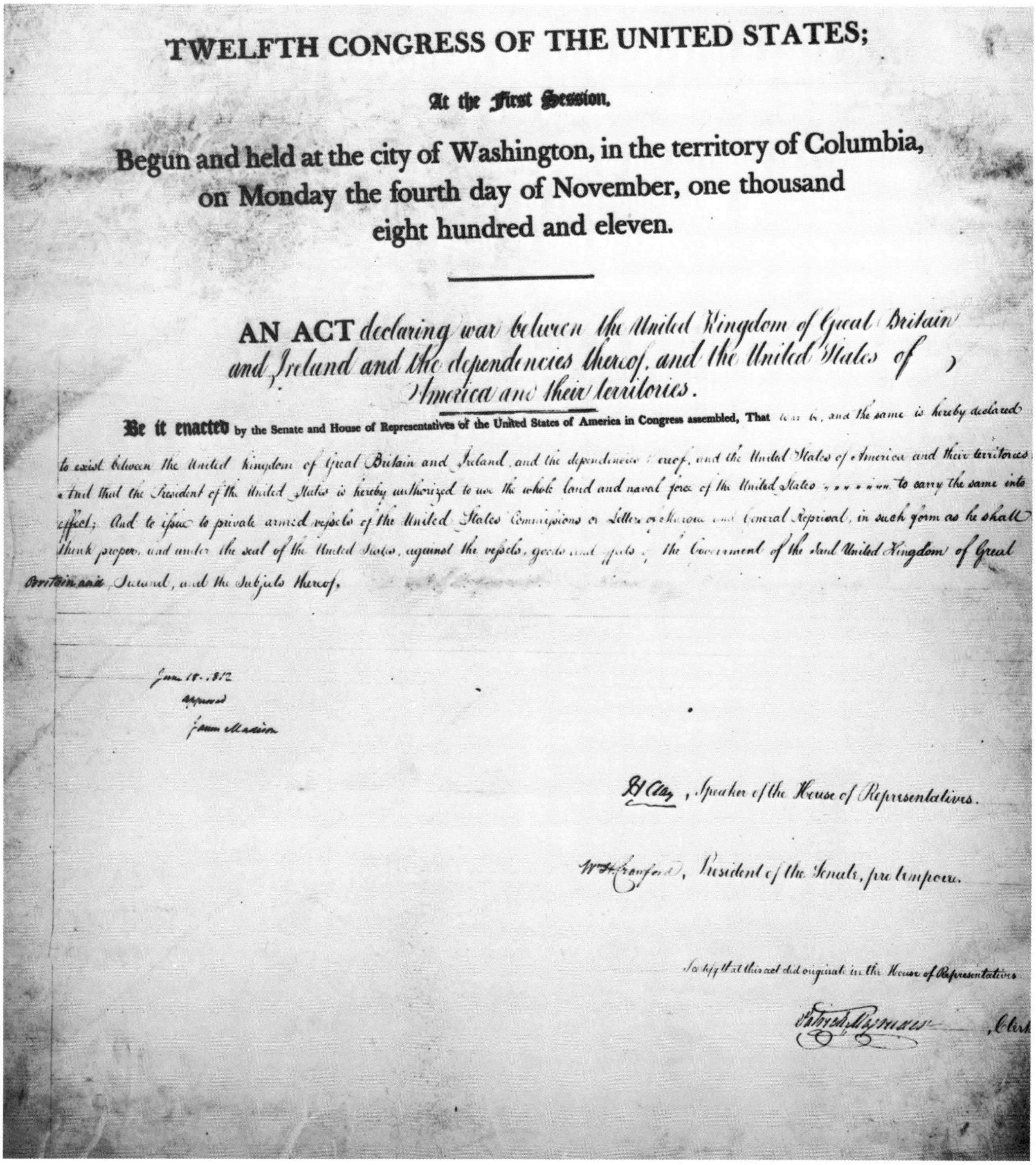

TWELFTH CONGRESS OF THE UNITED STATES;

At the First Session,

Begun and held at the city of Washington, in the territory of Columbia, on Monday the fourth day of November, one thousand eight hundred and eleven.

AN ACT declaring war between the United Kingdom of Great Britain and Ireland and the dependencies thereof, and the United States of America and their territories.

Be it enacted by the Senate and House of Representatives of the United States of America in Congress assembled, That war be, and the same is hereby declared to exist between the United Kingdom of Great Britain and Ireland, and the dependencies thereof, and the United States of America and their territories; and that the President of the United States is hereby authorized to use the whole land and naval force of the United States to carry the same into effect; And to issue to private armed vessels of the United States Commissions or Letters of Marque and General Reprisal, in such form as he shall think proper, and under the seal of the United States, against the vessels, goods and effects of the Government of the said United Kingdom of Great Britain and Ireland, and the Subjects thereof.

June 18. 1812
Approved
James Madison

H Clay, Speaker of the House of Representatives.

Wm H. Crawford, President of the Senate, pro tempore.

I certify that this act did originate in the House of Representatives.

Patrick Magruder, Clerk

Declaration of war, June 18, 1812. Courtesy National Archives and Records Service, Washington, D.C.

not jar. England's only slight bending of her tough position on American commerce, the one crumb aboard the *Hornet*, was an offer to license Yankee ships for a share of European trade. But England also insisted that Napoleon's revocation of the Milan decree be recognized as a French trick.

Madison was in no mood for a British lesson in diplomacy. For at the moment when Americans had proved themselves as good as or better than any sailors in the world, and when the average man still believed that England was gloating over America's distress, it was time for the president to say to Congress that war was a better course than further delay. With this last British note, Madison said later, "no choice remained but between war and degradation, a degradation inviting fresh provocation & rendering war sooner or later inevitable." Indeed, England's policy toward the United States repeatedly confirmed Madison's suspicion that America was still regarded as a third or fourth-rate power with no more of a place in the community of nations than Jamaica or Grenada.

In his war message, Madison said at the outset that England, "by the conduct of her government, presents a series of acts, hostile to the United States, as an Independent and neutral nation." He said a great deal more, but that sentence summed up the main point of Madison's war cry. Congress, after much warlike talk, took two weeks to pass a declaration of war. Ultimately the younger members from the South and West were too much for the conservative New England representatives who did not want a war with England on any terms (and would have preferred a declaration against France, if they had been granted their rathers). But the fat was now in the fire, and after some melodramatic debating the House passed the declaration by a 79 to 49 count. The Senate eased into the picture by a 19 to 13 vote. On June 18, 1812, the United States was finally at war with England.

Ironically, the British cabinet revoked the Orders in Council on June 23, but the news was too late in coming. By the time that word had reached America the hotheads were clamoring for an invasion of Canada, the New England Federalists were whispering in private about dragging their feet, and Madison was hoping that he had some generals and admirals who knew what they were doing.

As it turned out, nobody in charge of the American military apparatus knew much about anything. The much-touted invasion of Canada fizzled, General Hull surrendered Detroit to the British with hardly a shot being fired,

Michel Félice Corné (ca. 1752–1845) (attrib.), *The Battle of the Constitution and the Guerrière*, oil on canvas, 32¾ in x 47¾ in, Boston, ca. 1812. Courtesy New Haven Colony Historical Society, Connecticut.

Capture of the City of Washington, colored engraving, 10⅛ in x 14⅝ in, in Paul Rapin-Thoyras, *History of England*, vol. II, London, J & J Cundee, 1815. Courtesy Anne S. K. Brown Military Collection, Brown University Library, Providence, Rhode Island.

and by the end of 1812 it looked as though "Mr. Madison's War" was the beginning of the end of the United States. Except for the heroic victories on the Great Lakes and some side action by intrepid seamen on the *Constellation* and *Constitution*, the war was not going well at all. Then, to confirm the predictions of Anglophiles who flocked to town meetings to condemn Madison, the British landed in Chesapeake Bay and in August 1814 were marching down the streets of Washington. The story of Madison's abandonment of the White House and Dolley's courageous efforts to save some of the nation's meager cultural heritage from the British torch is now part of our folklore. Madison never lost control, however, although he was cursed with some extremely incompetent military leadership. From a safe haven up the Potomac, he waited until his wife reached him, then they watched the smoke billow from the fires set at public buildings by the king's marines. After burning the Capitol, including the Library of Congress, the White House, the War and Treasury buildings, the office of the *National Intelligencer*, and a federal arsenal, the British returned to their ships. They hauled anchor and departed on August 30, 1814.

One of the low points of American history had been reached, but Madi-

Charles Williams (?–d. after 1830) (attrib.), *The Fall of Washington—or Maddy in full flight*, colored engraving, 10⅝ in x 14⅞ in, London, S. W. Fores, October 4, 1814. Prints and Photographs Division, Library of Congress.

son never for a moment contemplated surrender. The resistance at Fort McHenry soon produced more than a wave of feeling for the enormous "star spangl'd banner" that was never hauled down. The British came to perceive that America was not to be humiliated into signing a peace treaty that would deny the experience of 1776-83. Peace negotiations had been under way for months in Ghent, Belgium, as the British headed out to sea again. Meanwhile, news of an American victory on Lake Champlain was salve for the nation's wounded pride and also nipped a planned British invasion of the Hudson Valley. Clearly, the war was bringing little distinction to either side.

While Madison wearily shifted commanders and fretted over the problems of wartime finance that were piled on his desk at the Octagon House (near the blackened shell of the executive mansion), a dramatic meeting of angry Federalists in Hartford was under way. Convinced the war was going badly, they determined to make more trouble by calling for nullification of a pending conscription bill and sought other steps that would hamstring the federal government. A gigantic British fleet was reportedly plowing through the Caribbean, headed for New Orleans, and only token American resistance was available there. So the rumors went, and one of the leading lights at the Hartford Convention (called by the Massachusetts legislature, attended only by New England Federalists) crowed with delight. "From the moment the British possess New Orleans, the Union is severed," smug Timothy Pickering predicted.[30] Before the Hartford meeting broke up, the delegates urged adoption of a set of proposed constitutional amendments, including one that limited presidents to a single term. Federalists insisted Madison had engineered the war in 1812 to make his reelection certain—and they were desperate to end the stream of Virginians going into the White House. Indeed, one of the Hartford delegates hinted in the *Connecticut Mirror* that the best thing Madison could do to restore national harmony would be to resign.

The miracle that was needed hit Washington just as the Federalist newspapers were about to demand an explanation for the presumed loss of New Orleans. First came the genuine news from New Orleans on February 4. The British had been defeated by Gen. Andrew Jackson and his men, with over 2,600 British troops killed, wounded, or captured. The cost to Jackson's army was seven killed, six wounded. Bonfires and ringing church bells that night brought a smile of relief to Madison's lined face, and there was more good news in store. Three tardy delegates from the Hartford convention arrived to deliver their ultimatum to Madison, behind the glad tidings from Ghent. On February 14, 1815, the peace treaty reached Washington, giving the populace

William Charles (1776–1820), *The Hartford Convention or Leap No Leap*, etching and colored aquatint, 11⅛ in x 16¾ in, Philadelphia?, ca. 1816. Prints and Photographs Division, Library of Congress.

more cause for celebrating. Although the British had conceded nothing, neither had the Americans. In fact the war had ended in a stalemate—or would have if the Battle of New Orleans had not been fought after the treaty was signed. With Jackson's victory behind him and the peace treaty in hand, Madison saw two of the Hartford delegates at a social gathering where all the talk was of victory and peace. The whole point of their mission had collapsed in America's joyous reception of the New Orleans and European messages, so they tossed aside their demands and awkwardly excused themselves. Republican catcalls followed their trail and one of Madison's supporters gleefully wrote a mock-verse for the dismayed Hartford coterie:

30. Quoted in Irving Brant, *James Madison: Commander in Chief* (Indianapolis: Bobbs-Merrill, 1961), p. 359.

WASHINGTON:

TUESDAY, FEBRUARY 21.

The following most interesting Message was yesterday transmitted, by the President of the United States, to both Houses of Congress:

To the Senate and
House of Representatives of the U. S.

I lay before Congress copies of the treaty of peace and amity between the United States and his Britannic Majesty, which was signed by the commissioners of both parties at Ghent, on the 24th of December, 1814, and the ratifications of which have been duly exchanged.

While performing this act, I congratulate you, and our constituents, upon an event which is highly honorable to the nation, and terminates with peculiar felicity a campaign signalised by the most brilliant successes.

The late war, although reluctantly declared by Congress, had become a necessary resort, to assert the rights and independence of the nation. It has been waged with a success which is the natural result of the legislative counsels, of the patriotism of the people, of the public spirit of the militia, and of the valor of the military and naval forces of the country. Peace, at all times a blessing, is peculiarly welcome, therefore, at a period when the causes for the war have ceased to operate; when the government has demonstrated the efficiency of its powers of defence; and when the nation can review its conduct without regret, and without reproach.

I recommend to your care and beneficence, the gallant men whose achievements, in every department of military service, on the land and on the water, have so essentially contributed to the honor of the American name, and to the restoration of peace. The feelings of conscious patriotism and worth will animate such men, under every change of fortune and pursuit; but their country performs a duty to itself, when it bestows those testimonials of approbation and applause, which are, at once, the reward, and the incentive, to great actions.

The reduction of the public expenditures to the demands of a peace establishment will, doubtless, engage the immediate attention of Congress. There are, however, important considerations which forbid a sudden and general revocation of the measures that have been produced by the war. Experience has taught us, that neither the pacific dispositions of the American people, nor the pacific character of their political institutions, can altogether exempt them from that strife which appears, beyond the ordinary lot of nations, to be incident to the actual period of the world; and the same faithful monitor demonstrates that a certain degree of preparation for war, is not only indispensable to avert disaster in the onset, but affords also the best security for the continuance of peace. The wisdom of Congress will, therefore, I am confident, provide for the maintenance of an adequate regular force; for the gradual advance of the naval establishment; for improving all the means of harbor defence; for adding discipline to the distinguished bravery of the militia, and for cultivating the military art, in its essential branches, under the liberal patronage of government.

The resources of our country were, at all times, competent to the attainment of every national object; but they will now be enriched and invigorated by the activity which peace will introduce into all the scenes of domestic enterprize and labour. The provision that has been made for the public creditors, during the present session of Congress, must have a decisive effect in the establishment of the public credit, both at home and abroad. The reviving interests of commerce will claim the legislative attention at the earliest opportunity; and such regulations will, I trust, be seasonably devised as shall secure to the U. States their just proportion of the navigation of the world. The most liberal policy towards other nations, if met by corresponding dispositions, will, in this respect, be found the most beneficial policy towards ourselves. But there is no subject that can enter with greater force and merit into the deliberation of Congress, than a consideration of the means to preserve and promote the manufactures which have sprung into existence, and attained an unparalleled maturity throughout the United States during the period of the European wars. This source of national independence and wealth, I anxiously recommend to the prompt and constant guardianship of Congress.

The termination of the legislative session will soon separate you, fellow-citizens, from each other, and restore you to your constituents. I pray you to bear with you the expressions of my sanguine hope, that the peace which has been just declared will not only be the foundation of the most friendly intercourse between the United States and Great Britain, but that it will also be productive of happiness and harmony in every section of our beloved country. The influence of your precepts and example must be every where powerful: and while we accord in grateful acknowledgements for the protection which Providence has bestowed upon us, let us never cease to inculcate obedience to the laws, and fidelity to the union, as constituting the palladium of the national independence and prosperity.

JAMES MADISON.

Washington, Feb. 18, 1815.

Announcement of the end of the war in the *Daily National Intelligencer,* Washington, February 21, 1815. Serial and Government Publications Division, Library of Congress.

You've disconcerted all our plots,
And this the world will know,
Since Peace *has come we are undone,*
James Madison, my jo.[31]

The month that began thick with gloom ended with Madison's name emblazoned on victory banners at rallies everywhere but in New England. Madison had the satisfaction of knowing his policies had worked. The Republic had been preserved.

In the congratulatory days that followed, Republican newspaper editors praised Madison and attempted to find a deep meaning in the triumph over England. "Peace finds us covered with glory, elevated in the scale of nations, enlightened by experience," the Richmond *Enquirer* noted. "The native stamina of a young and free people will now shoot forth with greater luxuriance. We shall take a fresh start in the race of internal improvement, of literature, and of the arts. The sun never shone upon a people whose destinies promised to be grander." [32]

31. Quoted in Marshall Smelser, *The Democratic Republic, 1801–1815* (New York: Harper & Row, 1968), p. 311.

32. Richmond *Enquirer,* February 18, 1815.

Madison remained in Washington two more years, his burdens as president lightened by the sudden revival of American prospects. Imprisoned seamen returned home, American shipyards echoed to the noises of prosperity, and a ready world market for farmers' products was revived. Thereafter, Madison worked with Monroe to ensure the continuity of Republican doctrines in the presidential office and longingly looked toward retirement near Jefferson so that they might both be practicing farmers as former presidents. John Adams, the only other living former president, had resumed his correspondence with Jefferson, and from his Quincy study he offered an assessment of Madison's eight years in the White House. "Notwithstanding a thousand Faults and blunders," Adams told Jefferson, Madison's "administration has acquired more glory, and established more union; than all his three predecessors . . . put together."[33] The gracious and fair judgment, rendered by one leader of the American Revolution to another, must have caused his old friend on Monticello mountaintop to nod in agreement.

Trunks were packed and teams were hitched in March 1817, and by the month's end the Madisons were back at Montpelier, this time to stay. For decades scores of travelers found excuses to stop at Madison's Orange County retreat. There they found tables groaning with food, a full cellar of wine, and a retired president whose eyes twinkled when he reminisced about the men and events since that first time when he had walked unnoticed into the Virginia Convention of 1776. He spent long afternoons arranging thousands of letters and notes, chatted with nieces and nephews, and took an occasional turn around the plantation on horseback to check on the crops. Like all farmers, Madison was hit hard by the severe depression of 1819. When corn fell to 39 cents a bushel in 1820, Madison cut back on some of the luxuries at Montpelier and advised fellow planters to seek ways of improving their yields. As president of the Albemarle Agricultural Society, he urged American farmers to cease wasteful practices that were exhausting the soil. More time should be spent seeking methods to improve fertility "rather than in further impoverishing" the soil, he counseled, and he warned against shallow plowing that could only increase soil erosion. These efforts caused Jefferson to speak of Madison as the nation's best farmer—an overstatement, of course, but an affectionate tribute from his famous neighbor.

33. Adams to Jefferson, February 2, 1817, in Lester Cappon, ed., *The Adams-Jefferson Letters*, 2 vols., (Chapel Hill: University of North Carolina Press, 1959), 2:508.

Joseph Wood (1780–1845), *James Madison*, oil on wood, 9½ in x 7¾ in, America, ca. 1816–1819. Courtesy Virginia Historical Society, Richmond.

Joseph Wood (1780–1845), *Dolley Madison*, oil on wood, 9 in x 7 in, America, ca. 1816–1819.
Courtesy Virginia Historical Society, Richmond.

J. F. E. Prud'homme (1800–1892) after John G. Chapman (1808–1889), *Montpelier, Va., the Seat of the late James Madison*, engraving, 4¼ in x 4½ in, in James B. Longacre and James Herring, *The National Portrait Gallery of Distinguished Americans*, vol. III, Philadelphia, Henry Perkins, 1836. Prints and Photographs Division, Library of Congress.

The remainder of Madison's life was spent in a leisurely pace of social calls, letter-writing, and less frequent visits to Monticello or other neighboring plantations. When Jefferson died in 1826, Madison succeeded him as rector of the University of Virginia, and in 1829 he made his last public appearance at the Richmond convention called to replace the commonwealth's 1776 constitution. Increasingly he was asked for calming statements concerning the growing sectional tension, and he took office as president of the American Colonization Society in the belief that its plan to return slaves to Africa represented the most sensible way out of that long-festering crisis.

Crippled by old age, Madison celebrated his eighty-fourth birthday content in the belief that his fellow Americans had fulfilled many of those dreams

W. L. B. (?), *Chas Cramer's Trip through the Mountains of Virginia to visit Mr. Madison, the Ex President of the U.S.*, engraving, 3⅝ in x 6¼ in, May 26, 1827, in Charles Cramer, *General Tour thru the United States and British Provinces of North America*, vol. V, St. Petersburg, 1830. James S. Copley Library, La Jolla, California. Photograph courtesy of the American Institute of Architects Foundation/the Octagon, Washington, D.C.

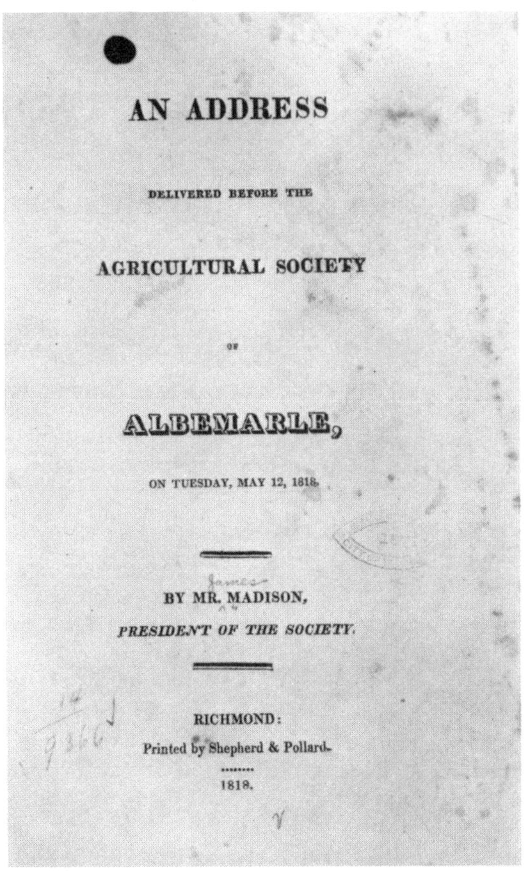

AN ADDRESS

DELIVERED BEFORE THE

AGRICULTURAL SOCIETY

OF

ALBEMARLE,

ON TUESDAY, MAY 12, 1818.

BY MR. MADISON,

PRESIDENT OF THE SOCIETY.

RICHMOND:

Printed by Shepherd & Pollard.

1818.

James Madison, *An Address Delivered before the Agricultural Society of Albemarle*, 9⅜ in x 5¾ in, Richmond, Virginia, Shepherd & Pollard, 1818. Rare Book and Special Collections Division, Library of Congress.

George Catlin (1796–1872), *The Virginia Constitutional Convention* (life portrait of James Madison, standing), watercolor on paper, 21⅝ in x 32⅞ in, Richmond, 1830. Courtesy New-York Historical Society, New York City.

he had discussed with great men at Monticello, Mount Vernon, and Gunston Hall. He must have smiled as he thought of the scars of past party battles, and of "Mr. Madison's War" that had seemed lost and yet ended as a diplomatic and military triumph.

The War of 1812, as Madison knew, had settled for all time the question of American independence. A generation of Americans since then had been reared amidst a rising nationalism that unleashed the talents of Cooper, Hawthorne, Audubon, and a whole new school of American artists and writers. Under presidents who proclaimed themselves to be Democratic Republicans in the tradition of Jefferson and Madison, the national debt had been all but erased, and American farms fed the nation bountifully and had enough left over to send to ports on every ocean.

America's two wars with England earned her respect in every European court. The Congress of Vienna in 1815 had a different tone after news spread that Castlereagh had settled the American war, and the peace which followed had far-reaching effects. A century would pass before the United States would

James Madison's *Certificate of Membership, American Colonization Society*, engraving, $6\frac{9}{16}$ in x $9\frac{11}{16}$ in, Washington, Henry Stone, ca. 1816. James Madison Papers, Library of Congress.

become enmeshed in a major war with a European power—simply one of the blessings made possible by events in America between 1812 and 1815. And the Monroe Doctrine, which was a symbolic manifestation of this whole nationalistic movement, would not have been possible had "Mr. Madison's War" not been fought. Only the blight of slavery remained, but Madison kept his faith that even that problem would disappear provided the Republic would adhere to the good old principles of '76—life, liberty, property, and the pursuing and obtaining of happiness and safety. His last public message, Madison's "Advice to My Country," was dictated to and lovingly copied by Dolley. In the brief statement, he beseeched Americans to stay loyal to the Union he had helped create:

> *The advice nearest to my heart and deepest in my convictions is that the Union of the States be cherished and perpetuated. Let the open enemy to it be regarded as a Pandora with her box opened; and the disguised one, as the serpent creeping with his deadly wiles into Paradise.*

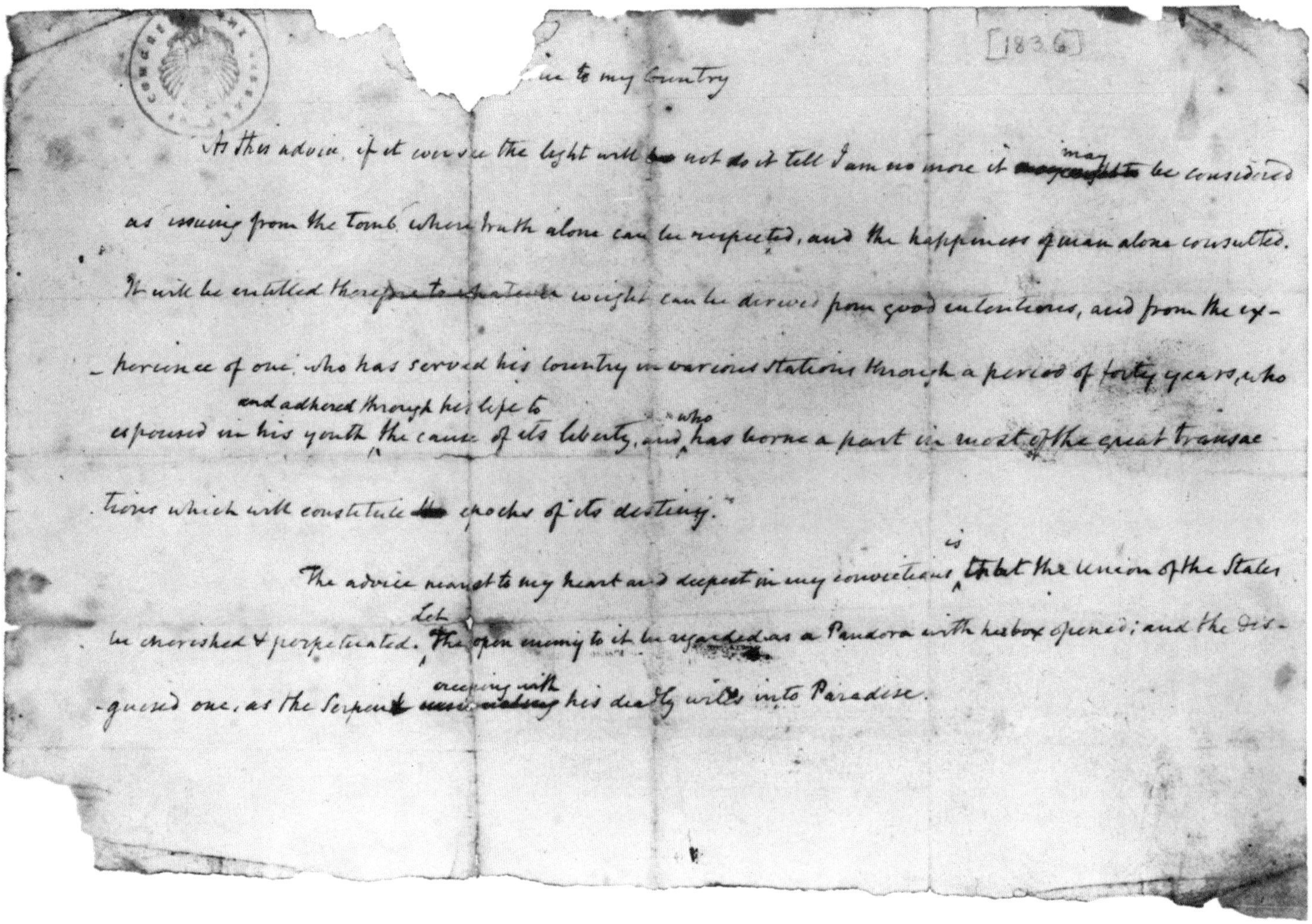

[1836]

...ice to my Country

As this advice, if it ever see the light will not do it till I am no more it may be considered as issuing from the tomb where truth alone can be respected, and the happiness of man alone consulted. It will be entitled therefore to whatever weight can be derived from good intentions, and from the experience of one, who has served his country in various stations through a period of forty years, who espoused in his youth and adhered through his life to the cause of its liberty, and who has borne a part in most of the great transactions which will constitute epochs of its destiny."

The advice nearest to my heart and deepest in my convictions is that the Union of the States be cherished & perpetuated. Let the open enemy to it be regarded as a Pandora with her box opened; and the disguised one, as the Serpent creeping with his deadly wiles into Paradise.

James Madison, *Advice to my Country*, Orange, Virginia, 1834. James Madison Papers, Library of Congress.

Into that message Madison crowded his lifelong love of the United States of America.

Madison came to recognize that the search for American nationhood, which had consumed the energies of his life, was a dream beyond full realization. The nation was independent, and the people who made up that nation were free. All of the questions concerning man's ability to govern himself, his capacity for reaping the blessings of republican government, were still being raised. "If the earth be the gift of nature to the living their title can extend to the earth in its natural State only." Thus each generation of Americans would have to earn its title to freedom. And the Union Madison spoke of was not a geographic unit but rather a continental community of like-minded citizens carrying forward the commitment made by their forebears in 1776.

James Barton Longacre (1794–1869), *James Madison* (from life), oil on wood, 7⅛ in x 5⅞ in, Orange, July 1833. Collection of Mr. and Mrs. George Green Shackelford. Photograph courtesy of the American Institute of Architects Foundation/the Octagon, Washington, D.C.

As the days of summer turned humid in the Virginia Piedmont, Madison gently rebuffed those who reminded him that Adams, Jefferson, and Monroe had all died on July 4. Obviously his health was failing. Would he try to stay alive until the Glorious Fourth? Madison clearly explained he was not at all interested in adding to the national folklore. The Fourth of July as a date was meaningless. What it represented in the national mind was everything. This had been Madison's message from 1780 onward. Convinced that his countrymen were still listening, Madison died on June 28, 1836.

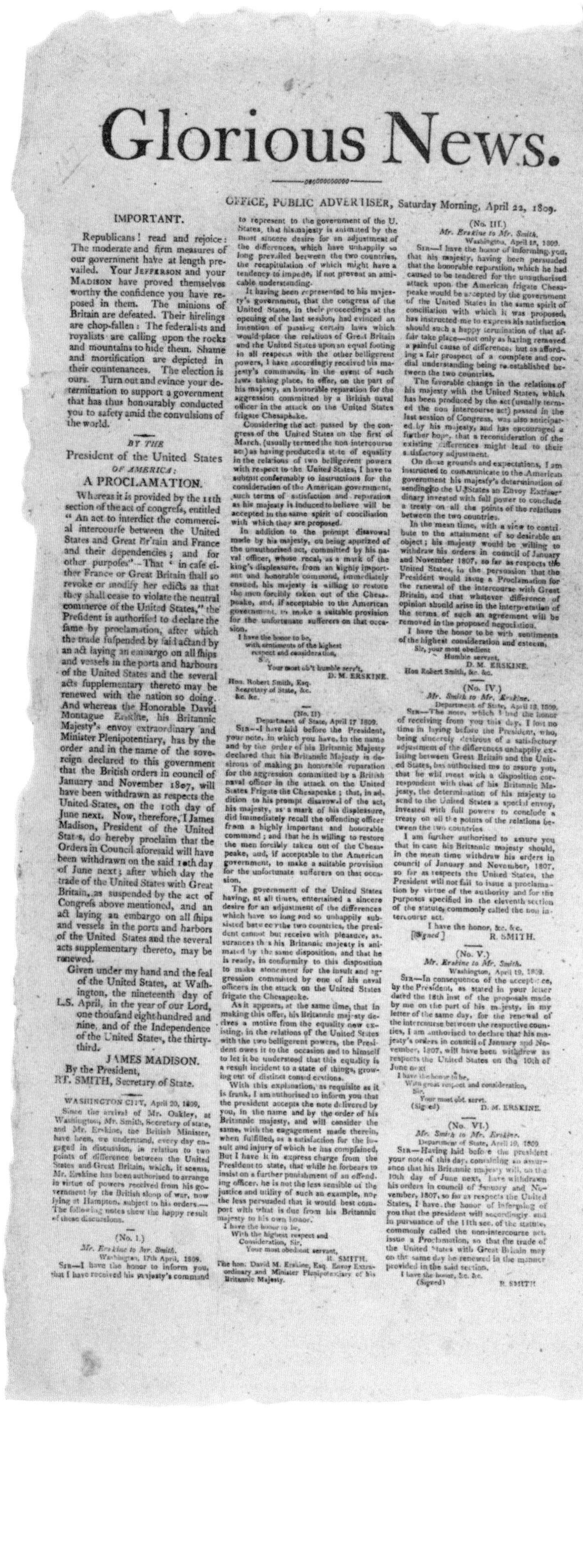

Glorious News.

OFFICE, PUBLIC ADVERTISER, Saturday Morning, April 22, 1809.

IMPORTANT.

Republicans! read and rejoice: The moderate and firm measures of our government have at length prevailed. Your JEFFERSON and your MADISON have proved themselves worthy the confidence you have reposed in them. The minions of Britain are defeated. Their hirelings are chop-fallen: The federalists and royalists are calling upon the rocks and mountains to hide them. Shame and mortification are depicted in their countenances. The election is ours. Turn out and evince your determination to support a government that has thus honourably conducted you to safety amid the convulsions of the world.

BY THE
President of the United States
OF AMERICA:
A PROCLAMATION.

Whereas it is provided by the 11th section of the act of congreſs, entitled "An act to interdict the commercial intercourſe between the United States and Great Britain and France and their dependencies; and for other purpoſes" – That "in caſe either France or Great Britain ſhall so revoke or modify her edicts as that they ſhall cease to violate the neutral commerce of the United States," the Preſident is authoriſed to declare the ſame by proclamation, after which the trade ſuſpended by ſaid act and by an act laying an embargo on all ſhips and vessels in the ports and harbours of the United States and the several acts ſupplementary thereto may be renewed with the nation so doing. And whereas the Honorable David Montague Erskine, his Britannic Majesty's envoy extraordinary and Minister Plenipotentiary, has by the order and in the name of the sovereign declared to this government that the British orders in council of January and November 1807, will have been withdrawn as respects the United States, on the 10th day of June next. Now, therefore, I James Madison, President of the United States, do hereby proclaim that the Orders in Council aforesaid will have been withdrawn on the said 10th day of June next; after which day the trade of the United States with Great Britain, as suspended by the act of Congreſs above mentioned, and an act laying an embargo on all ſhips and vessels in the ports and harbors of the United States and the several acts supplementary thereto, may be renewed.

Given under my hand and the ſeal of the United States, at Waſhington, the nineteenth day of April, in the year of our Lord, one thouſand eight hundred and nine, and of the Independence of the United States, the thirty-third.
L.S.

JAMES MADISON.
By the President,
RT. SMITH, Secretary of State.

WASHINGTON CITY, April 20, 1809.

Since the arrival of Mr. Oakley, at Washington, Mr. Smith, Secretary of state, and Mr. Erskine, the British Minister, have been, we understand, every day engaged in discussion, in relation to two points of difference between the United States and Great Britain, which, it seems, Mr. Erskine has been authorised to arrange in virtue of powers received from his government by the British sloop of war, now lying at Hampton, subject to his orders.—The following notes shew the happy result of these discussions.

(No. I.)
Mr. Erskine to Mr. Smith.
Washington, 17th April, 1809.

SIR—I have the honor to inform you, that I have received his majesty's command to represent to the government of the U. States, that his majesty is animated by the most sincere desire for an adjustment of the differences, which have unhappily so long prevailed between the two countries, the recapitulation of which might have a tendency to impede, if not prevent an amicable understanding.

It having been represented to his majesty's government, that the congress of the United States, in their proceedings at the opening of the last session, had evinced an intention of passing certain laws which would place the relations of Great Britain and the United States upon an equal footing in all respects with the other belligerent powers, I have accordingly received his majesty's commands, in the event of such laws taking place, to offer, on the part of his majesty, an honorable reparation for the aggression committed by a British naval officer in the attack on the United States frigate Chesapeake.

Considering the act passed by the congress of the United States on the first of March, (usually termed the non intercourse act) as having produced a state of equality in the relations of two belligerent powers with respect to the United States, I have to submit conformably to instructions for the consideration of the American government, such terms of satisfaction and reparation as his majesty is induced to believe will be accepted in the same spirit of conciliation with which they are proposed.

In addition to the prompt disavowal made by his majesty, on being apprized of the unauthorised act, committed by his naval officer, whose recal, as a mark of the king's displeasure, from an highly important and honorable command, immediately ensued, his majesty is willing to restore the men forcibly taken out of the Chesapeake, and, if acceptable to the American government, to make a suitable provision for the unfortunate sufferers on that occasion.

I have the honor to be,
with sentiments of the highest
respect and consideration,
Sir,
Your most ob't humble serv't,
D. M. ERSKINE.

Hon. Robert Smith, Esq.
Secretary of State, &c.
&c. &c.

(No. II)
Department of State, April 17 1809.

SIR—I have laid before the President, your note, in which you have, in the name and by the order of his Britannic Majesty declared that his Britannic Majesty is desirous of making an honorable reparation for the aggression committed by a British naval officer in the attack on the United States Frigate the Chesapeake; that, in addition to his prompt disavowal of the act, his majesty, as a mark of his displeasure, did immediately recall the offending officer from a highly important and honorable command; and that he is willing to restore the men forcibly taken out of the Chesapeake, and, if acceptable to the American government, to make a suitable provision for the unfortunate sufferers on that occasion.

The government of the United States having, at all times, entertained a sincere desire for an adjustment of the differences which have so long and so unhappily subsisted between the two countries, the president cannot but receive with pleasure, assurances that his Britannic majesty is animated by the same disposition, and that he is ready, in conformity to this disposition to make atonement for the insult and aggression committed by one of his naval officers in the attack on the United States frigate the Chesapeake.

As it appears, at the same time, that in making this offer, his Britannic majesty derives a motive from the equality now existing, in the relations of the United States with the two belligerent powers, the President owes it to the occasion and to himself to let it be understood that this equality is a result incident to a state of things, growing out of distinct considerations.

With this explanation, as requisite as it is frank, I am authorised to inform you that the president accepts the note delivered by you, in the name and by the order of his Britannic majesty, and will consider the same, with the engagement made therein, when fulfilled, as a satisfaction for the insult and injury of which he has complained. But I have it in express charge from the President to state, that while he forbears to insist on a further punishment of an offending officer, he is not the less sensible of the justice and utility of such an example, nor the less persuaded that it would best comport with what is due from his Britannic majesty to his own honor.

I have the honor to be,
With the highest respect and
Consideration, Sir,
Your most obedient servant,
R. SMITH.

The hon. David M. Erskine, Esq. Envoy Extraordinary and Minister Plenipotentiary of his Britannic Majesty.

(No. III.)
Mr. Erskine to Mr. Smith.
Washington, April 18, 1809.

SIR—I have the honor of informing you, that his majesty, having been persuaded that the honorable reparation, which he had caused to be tendered for the unauthorised attack upon the American frigate Chesapeake would be accepted by the government of the United States in the same spirit of conciliation with which it was proposed, has instructed me to express his satisfaction should such a happy termination of that affair take place—not only as having removed a painful cause of difference, but as affording a fair prospect of a complete and cordial understanding being re-established between the two countries.

The favorable change in the relations of his majesty with the United States, which has been produced by the act (usually termed the non intercourse act) passed in the last session of Congress, was also anticipated by his majesty, and has encouraged a further hope, that a reconsideration of the existing differences might lead to their satisfactory adjustment.

On these grounds and expectations, I am instructed to communicate to the American government his majesty's determination of sending to the U. States an Envoy Extraordinary invested with full power to conclude a treaty on all the points of the relations between the two countries.

In the mean time, with a view to contribute to the attainment of so desirable an object; his majesty would be willing to withdraw his orders in council of January and November 1807, so far as respects the United States, in the persuasion that the President would issue a Proclamation for the renewal of the intercourse with Great Britain, and that whatever difference of opinion should arise in the interpretation of the terms of such an agreement will be removed in the proposed negociation.

I have the honor to be with sentiments of the highest consideration and esteem,
Sir, your most obedient
Humble servant,
D. M. ERSKINE.

Hon Robert Smith, &c. &c.

(No. IV.)
Mr. Smith to Mr. Erskine.
Department of State, April 18, 1809.

SIR—The note, which I had the honor of receiving from you this day, I lost no time in laying before the President, who, being sincerely desirous of a satisfactory adjustment of the differences unhappily existing between Great Britain and the United States, has authorised me to assure you, that he will meet with a disposition correspondent with that of his Britannic Majesty, the determination of his majesty to send to the United States a special envoy, invested with full powers to conclude a treaty on all the points of the relations between the two countries.

I am further authorised to assure you that in case his Britannic majesty should, in the mean time withdraw his orders in council of January and November, 1807, so far as respects the United States, the President will not fail to issue a proclamation by virtue of the authority and for the purposes specified in the eleventh section of the statute, commonly called the non intercourse act.

I have the honor, &c. &c.
[Signed] R. SMITH.

(No. V.)
Mr. Erskine to Mr. Smith.
Washington, April 19, 1809.

SIR—In consequence of the acceptance, by the President, as stated in your letter dated the 18th inst of the proposals made by me on the part of his majesty, in my letter of the same day, for the renewal of the intercourse between the respective countries, I am authorised to declare that his majesty's orders in council of January and November, 1807, will have been withdrew as respects the United States on the 10th of June next.

I have the honor to be,
With great respect and consideration,
Sir,
Your most obt. servt.
(Signed) D. M. ERSKINE.

(No. VI.)
Mr. Smith to Mr. Erskine.
Department of State, April 19, 1809.

SIR—Having laid before the president your note of this day, containing an assurance that his Britannic majesty will, on the 10th day of June next, have withdrawn his orders in council of January and November, 1807, so far as respects the United States, I have the honor of informing you that the president will accordingly and in pursuance of the 11th sec. of the statute, commonly called the non-intercourse act, issue a Proclamation, so that the trade of the United States with Great Britain may on the same day be renewed in the manner provided in the said section.

I have the honor, &c. &c.
(Signed) R. SMITH.

Glorious News, broadside, 20¾ in x 9 in, New York, 1809. Rare Book and Special Collections Division, Library of Congress.

This broadside reproduces correspondence regarding the Nonintercourse Act and praises the "moderate and firm measures" of "your Jefferson and your Madison."

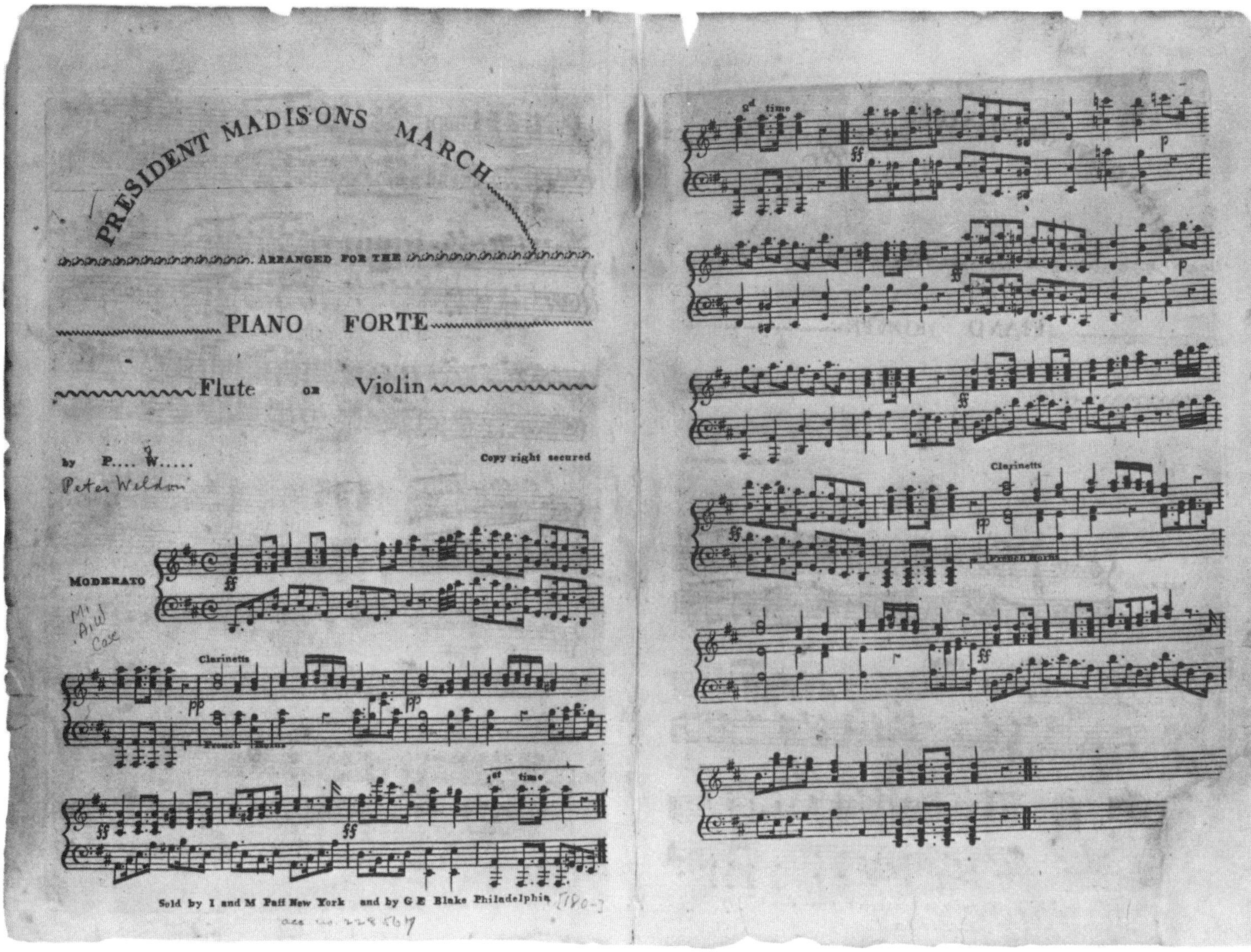

P(eter) W(eldon), *President Madisons March*, printed sheet music, 18½ in x 13 in, Philadelphia, 1809?. Music Division, Library of Congress.

Madison's inauguration in March 1809 prompted a suitable amount of ceremony and rejoicing. In the evening the new president was honored at the Federal City's first Inaugural Ball, held at Long's Hotel. The event was so crowded that the guests broke out the windows to get fresh air.

OPPOSITE:

Thomas Sully (1783–1872) after Gilbert Stuart (1755–1828), *James Madison*, oil on canvas, 27 in x 20 in, Washington, 1809. Courtesy Corcoran Gallery of Art, Washington, D.C., gift of Frederick Church.

A National Intelligencer *editorial praised Madison in 1809 as the man "best fitted to guide us through the impending storm," but his presidency was troubled from the beginning. Madison inherited all the unresolved problems of Jefferson's administration and was further plagued by a fractious Cabinet and an unfriendly Congress.*

Bass Otis (1784–1861), *Dolley Madison*, oil on canvas, 29 in x 24 in, America, ca. 1817. Courtesy New-York Historical Society, New York City, gift of Thomas J. Bryan.

The first lady's gracious style was an asset to Madison during his troubled administration.

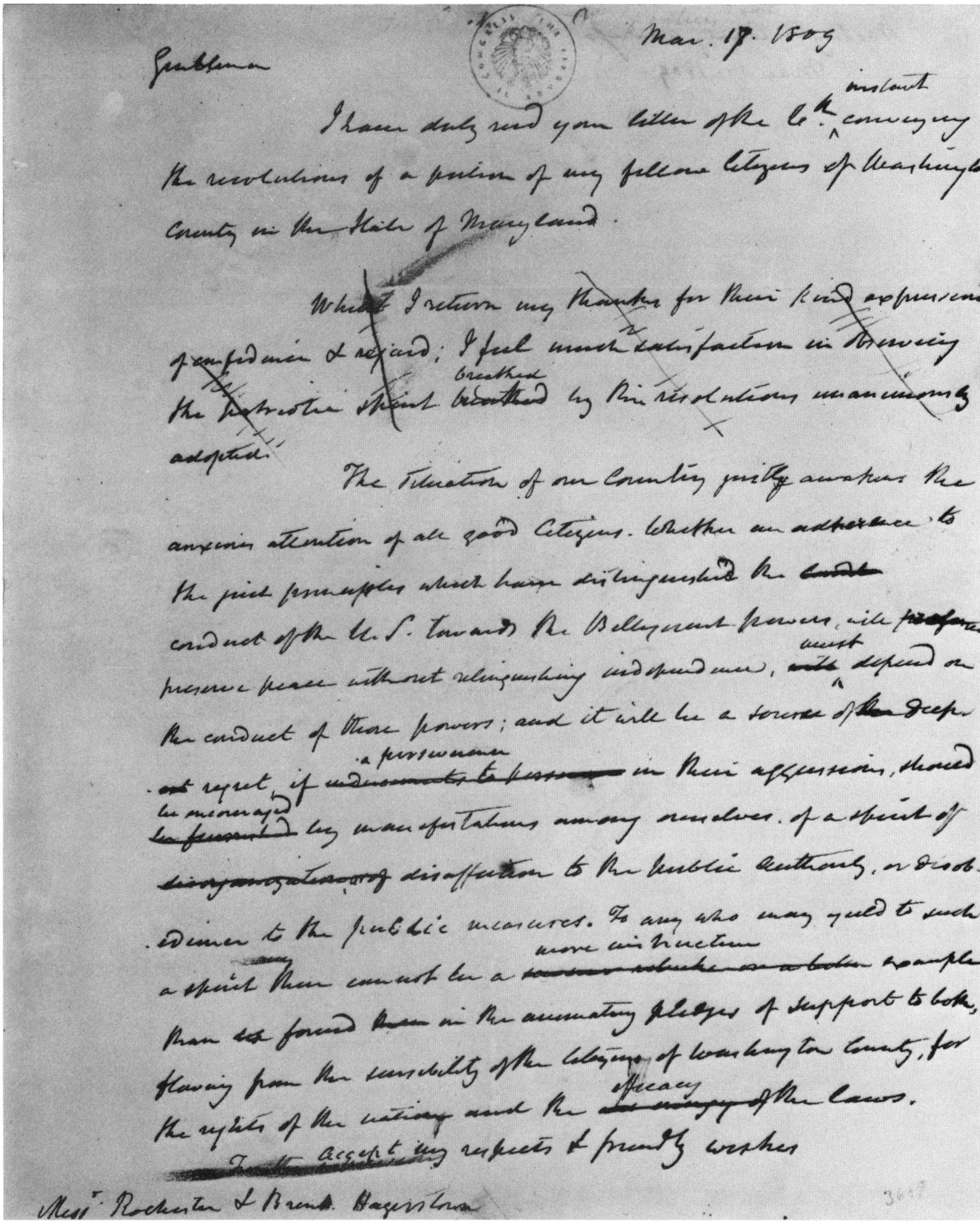

Mar. 17. 1809

Gentlemen

I have duly recd your letter of the 6th. instant conveying the resolutions of a portion of my fellow Citizens of Washington County in the State of Maryland.

While I return my thanks for their kind expressions of confidence & regard; I feel much satisfaction in observing the patriotic spirit breathed by the resolutions unanimously adopted.

The situation of our Country justly awakes the anxious attention of all good Citizens. Whether an adherence to the just principles which have distinguished the conduct of the U. S. towards the Belligerent powers, will preserve peace without relinquishing independence, must depend on the conduct of those powers; and it will be a source of deeper regret, if a perseverance in their aggressions, should be encouraged by manifestations among ourselves, of a spirit of disaffection to the public authority, or disobedience to the public measures. To any who may yield to such a spirit there cannot be a more instructive example than is found in the animating pledges of support to both, flowing from the sensibility of the Citizens of Washington County, for the rights of the nation and the efficacy of the Laws.

Accept my respects & friendly wishes

Messrs. Rochester & Brent. Hagerstown

OPPOSITE:

James Madison, *Letter to the Citizens of Hagerstown, Maryland* (excerpt, draft), March 17, 1809. James Madison Papers, Library of Congress.

Madison's presidential duties required him to respond personally to hundreds of letters from his constituents. Here he drafts a response acknowledging the receipt of a congratulatory letter from the citizens of a Maryland town.

Raphaelle Peale (1774–1825), *Benjamin Henry Latrobe* (1764–1820), watercolor on ivory, gold, 3⅛ in x 2⅞ in, America, ca. 1810. Maryland Historical Society, Baltimore. Photograph courtesy American Institute of Architects Foundation/ the Octagon, Washington, D.C.

Shortly after the election, Dolley Madison engaged the services of architect Benjamin Henry Latrobe to oversee the redecorating of the major public rooms in the White House.

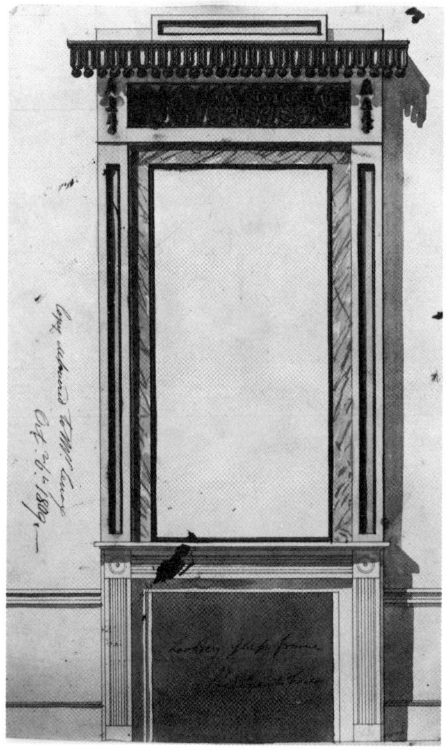

Benjamin Henry Latrobe (1764–1820), *Looking Glass Frame, President's House,* pencil, pen and ink, and watercolor on paper, 13⅝ in x 8$^{13}/_{16}$ in, Washington, October 6, 1809. Prints and Photographs Division, Library of Congress.

Between 1809 and 1811, Latrobe and the first lady spent nearly twenty thousand dollars redecorating the White House. This looking glass, designed by Latrobe in the latest style, was a focal point over the mantel in the Oval Room.

Benjamin Henry Latrobe (1764–1820), *View of the East front of the President's House,* pencil, pen and ink, watercolor on paper, 15⅜ in x 20 in, Washington, 1807. Prints and Photographs Division, Library of Congress.

Although still unfinished during Madison's administration, the White House in 1809 was one of the most elegant residences in the Federal City.

OPPOSITE:

Benjamin Henry Latrobe (1764–1820), *Plan of the principal Story,* the White House in 1803, pencil, pen and ink, and watercolor on paper, 19$^{15}/_{16}$ in x 15$^{3}/_{16}$ in, Washington, 1807. Prints and Photographs Division, Library of Congress.

Dolley Madison's weekly receptions were open to the public and social activities took place on the main floor of the unfinished mansion, in the large Oval Room.

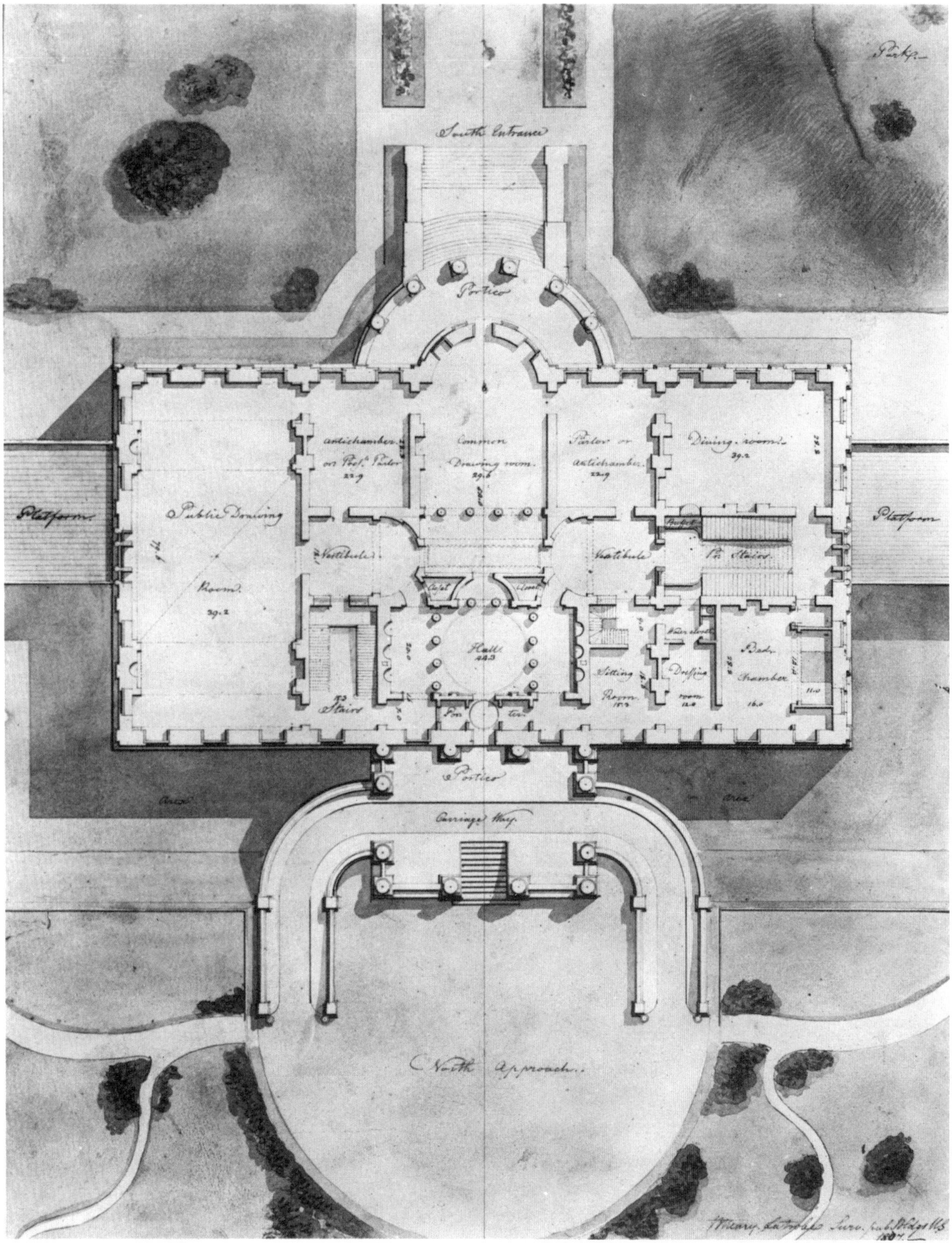
Park
South Entrance
Portico
Antichamber or Prest. Parlor
Common Drawing room
Parlor or antichamber
Dining room
Platform
Public Drawing Room
Vestibule
Pr. Stairs
Hall
Stairs
Sitting Room
Dressing room
Bed Chamber
Portico
Area
Carriage Way
North Approach

Late and Highly Important Intelligence from *FRANCE!!!*

☞ The French Decrees NOT repealed, on the 13th of March!!

☞ American Vessels AGAIN Sequestered!!

☞ No American Ship can leave France without FIRST obtaining a Special LICENSE!!

☞ Most all the American Masters will ABANDON their property, and return home in a CARTEL to New-York!!

☞ It is now ascertained, that the few American Vessels *released* from France, cost their owners, the *full amount of them!!*

From the Freeman's Journal.

1811. PHILADELPHIA, April 17.

Capt. *Cullen*, of the brig Fox, arrived yesterday, in 30 days from Bayonne, which place she left on the 13th March. The verbal and written news by this vessel are of such a nature as almost to extinguish hope. *Not only was the American property (which was faithfully promised to be restored on the 2d February,) not given up on the 13th March, but all American vessels arriving in France were refused an entry*, were put under sequestration, and their papers sent to Paris. On the 8th of March the Director General of the customs announced to the merchants of Bordeaux, that the emperor had adjourned the expression of his opinion respecting the admitting American vessels to an entry.—Another letter states that the Director General of the customs had declared that no more applications for admitting American vessels to an entry, would be received. Of course they will remain under sequestration. *The vessels which sailed from America under Napoleon's special licence, were equally sequestered with those which had none—no distinction being made.*

No American vessel is permitted to leave France, except under a special licence, which it is very difficult to procure, and costs a large sum.

"What the event will be (says a letter which we have seen) no one can tell—but beware, and advise your friends also to beware, of shipping any more property to this country."

From all we have been able to gather by this arrival, there appears not the least probability of Napoleon restoring American property, or rescinding his Berlin and Milan decrees, which are still in most rigorous operation.

From the Philadelphia Daily Advertiser.

By the Eagle and Fox, arrived here last evening from Bayonne, it appears that the Emperor had postponed the final decision of the question, "Shall the American vessels that have arrived in the ports of France since the repeal of the non-intercourse," be admitted to entry? and desired that no farther application should be made;—*thus are those vessels provisionally sequestered*, until his imperial majesty, (who loves the Americans,) shall have made up his royal mind!!!

In this situation of affairs, it was expected that many of the *masters and crews, would abandon the property and return home* in the brig Rose in Bloom, a cartel, preparing to leave Bayonne for N. York.

The Eagle has despatches for Government, and a file of French papers for Gen. Armstrong.

From the Philadelphia True American.

Yesterday arrived, brig Fox, Cullen, from Bayonne, in France. This is one of the vessels sequestered by Bonaparte, at St. Sebastians, in 1809, and was together with the Eagle, Hawk, and a number other American vessels carried to Bayonne, and as the captain informs all together with their cargoes, sold by order of the plunderer of the world.

After having purchased his vessel at the sale, he got a freight of brandy, wine and dry goods, when he got permission and left that port March 13, in co. with tho Eagle, Alfton, with passengers, for this port.

At the time of sailing, the 13th March, Capt. Cullen, says nothing that he heard, had been done in the repeal of the French decrees, or liberation of American trade, as the schr. Spencer, Moffat; schr. Purse, and brig Ann, all of whom had arrived at Bayonne from New York, were laying with their cargoes on board waiting the *ipse dixit* of Bonaparte from Paris.—The brig Meteor, Hauly, is said to be arrived at Bordeaux from this port and said to be in the same condition.

In the Fox came passenger, capt Chevers of Salem and 4 sailors who had been prisoners among the French for some time.

Extract of a letter from a gentleman who came passenger in the Fox, arrived at Philadelphia from France, to his friends in that city.

"The political disposition of the French government as respects this country, was, at the time of my departure as unpropitious as it has ever been, and there were no hopes entertained that there would be any relaxation of the system of spoliation that she has so long maintained.——If I except the actual and immediate confiscation, I may safely say that the same vexation to which our commerce was exposed prior to the 2d of November last exists at present. For those vessels which have arrived subsequent to that period, and upon the presumed faith of the repeal of the Milan, Berlin and other decrees, are still kept in a state of sequestration; or what is tantamount, no decision can be obtained as to what will be their fate. Such as arrived, were obliged to transmit their papers to Paris, to be submitted to the examination of the emperor, and I know of no instance wherein any notice has been taken of them, but in such as were provided with licences.——So far from there being any amelioration of our prospects the reverse was the fact, as I saw letters of good authority from Paris dated the 7th March, wherein it was said, that the Emperor had issued orders to all the custom houses, not to permit the admission of any American vessel and property, to seize such as should arrive, and not to report on the case of any whatsoever that had arrived."

Late and Highly Important Intelligence from France!!!, handbill, 10⅞ in x 9⅜ in, Philadelphia, April 17, 1811. Courtesy American Antiquarian Society, Worcester, Massachusetts.

Believing that Napoleon had repealed the Berlin and Milan decrees, Madison issued a proclamation on November 2, 1810, reopening trade with France and declaring nonintercourse with Great Britain as of March 2, 1811. As this handbill indicates, Napoleon deceived the Americans and the treachery was discovered in April of 1811.

DEMOCRATIC

Electoral Ticket.

This the *Standard* round which we rally,
This the *Motto* and we triumph.

Madison and Gerry.

"Free trade and Sailor's Rights."

No base Submission.

PEACE ON HONORABLE TERMS.

Charles Thompson
David Mitchell
Paul Cox
Isaac Worrell
Michael Baker
Joseph Engle
James Fulton
Isaiah Davis
John Whitehill
Edward Crouch
Hugh Glasgow
David Fullerton
Samuel Smith
Robert Smith
Nathaniel Michler
Charles Shoemaker
James Mitchell
John Murray
Clement Paine
Arthur Moore
Henry Allshouse
James Stephenson
Abia Minor
Adamson Tannehill
David Meade

Electoral Ticket, broadside, 21¼ in x 8⅜ in, America, 1812. Courtesy Rare Books and Manuscript Division, New York Public Library, New York City, Astor, Lenox and Tilden Foundation.

The war with Britain was the main issue during the presidential campaign of 1812. Preparations for war had begun in 1811 after Madison felt he had exhausted every diplomatic channel. The president hoped that war would illustrate to the world "the capacity and destiny of the United States to be a great, a flourishing, and a powerful nation, worthy of the friendship which it is disposed to cultivate with all others."

ginia, opposed the striking out. No question was taken.

TUESDAY, FEB. 19, 1811.

The debate on the motion to reject the U. States Bank Charter renewal bill, continued.—Mr. *Taylor* spoke against striking out the section; and Mr. *White-side*, of *Tennessee*, in favor of it. But no question was taken.

WEDNESDAY, FEB. 20, 1811.

THE QUESTION DECIDED!

The debate, as above, continued. Messrs. *Brent*, *Pickering*, and *Crawford*, opposed the striking out.—The debate continued until five o'clock, when the question was taken, and the votes stood as follow:—

AYES.—Messrs. Anderson, Campbell, Clay, Cutts, Franklin, Gaillard, Germain, Giles, Gregg, Lambert, Leib, Matthewson, Reed, Robinson, Smith, *Md.* Whiteside, Worthington—17.

NAYS.—Messrs. Bayard, Bradley, Brent, Champlin, Condit, Crawford, Dana, Gilman, Goodrich, Horsey, Lloyd, Pickering, Pope, Smith, *N. York*, Tait, Taylor, Turner—17.

The Secretary then declared the state of the votes, on which the Vice-President (Mr. *Clinton*) rose, and after reading a short discourse, which he had prepared for the occasion, very deliberately pronounced his decision in favor of rejecting the Bill—WHICH IS, THEREFORE, DEAD.

HOUSE OF REPRESENTATIVES, FEB. 18, 1811.

A resolution was moved by Mr. MILLER, and adopted, requesting the President of the United States to transmit any documents in his possession, respecting the repeal, modification, or practical operation of the French and English De-

"The Question Decided!" (excerpt) in the *Columbian Centinel*, Boston, February 27, 1811. Serial and Government Publications Division, Library of Congress.

Due to opposition in Congress, the Bank of the United States's petition for renewal of its charter was denied. Madison did not attempt to influence the vote; in fact, Vice President George Clinton cast the deciding negative ballot. The downfall of the bank further complicated the financing of the War of 1812.

William Russell Birch (1755–1834), *Bank of the United States, in Third Street, Philadelphia*, colored line engraving, 12¼ in x 15½ in, Philadelphia, William Birch & Son, 1798–99. Rare Book and Special Collections Division, Library of Congress.

Under the sponsorship of Secretary of the Treasury Alexander Hamilton, a national bank was established in 1791 with a twenty-year charter. Madison was opposed to the bank initially, arguing that its incorporation was not among the powers specifically delegated to Congress under the Constitution.

John Vanderlyn (1775–1852), *Elbridge Gerry* (1744–1814), black chalk on paper, 8¼ in x 6¾ in, Paris, 1798. Courtesy Fogg Art Museum, Harvard University, Cambridge, Massachusetts, Louise E. Bettens Fund.

A Republican caucus chose Massachusetts governor Elbridge Gerry as Madison's running mate for the election of 1812. Unfortunately, Gerry died two years later while serving as vice president.

OPPOSITE:

Amos Doolittle (1754–1832), *Splendid Victories gained by the United States Frigates*, colored line engraving, 9⅛ in x 14⅝ in, New Haven, March 20, 1813. Courtesy New-York Historical Society, New York City, Irving S. Olds Collection.

Although the United States Navy boasted only seventeen ships at the outbreak of the war, the inexperienced force won impressive victories on the water against the British. News of these triumphs was a great boost to American morale.

John Reich (1768–1833), *Indian Peace Medal*, silver, 2½ in, Philadelphia, ca. 1812. Courtesy Princeton University Library, New Jersey. Willard Starks photograph.

As a gesture of friendship, American presidents through Benjamin Harrison presented silver or bronze peace medals to native American chiefs. Madison posed for sculptor Giuseppe Franzoni in 1811 and the bust was shipped from Washington to the Mint in Philadelphia where the medals were struck. This example was reportedly given by the president to Chief Keokuk of the Sauk Tribe in 1812.

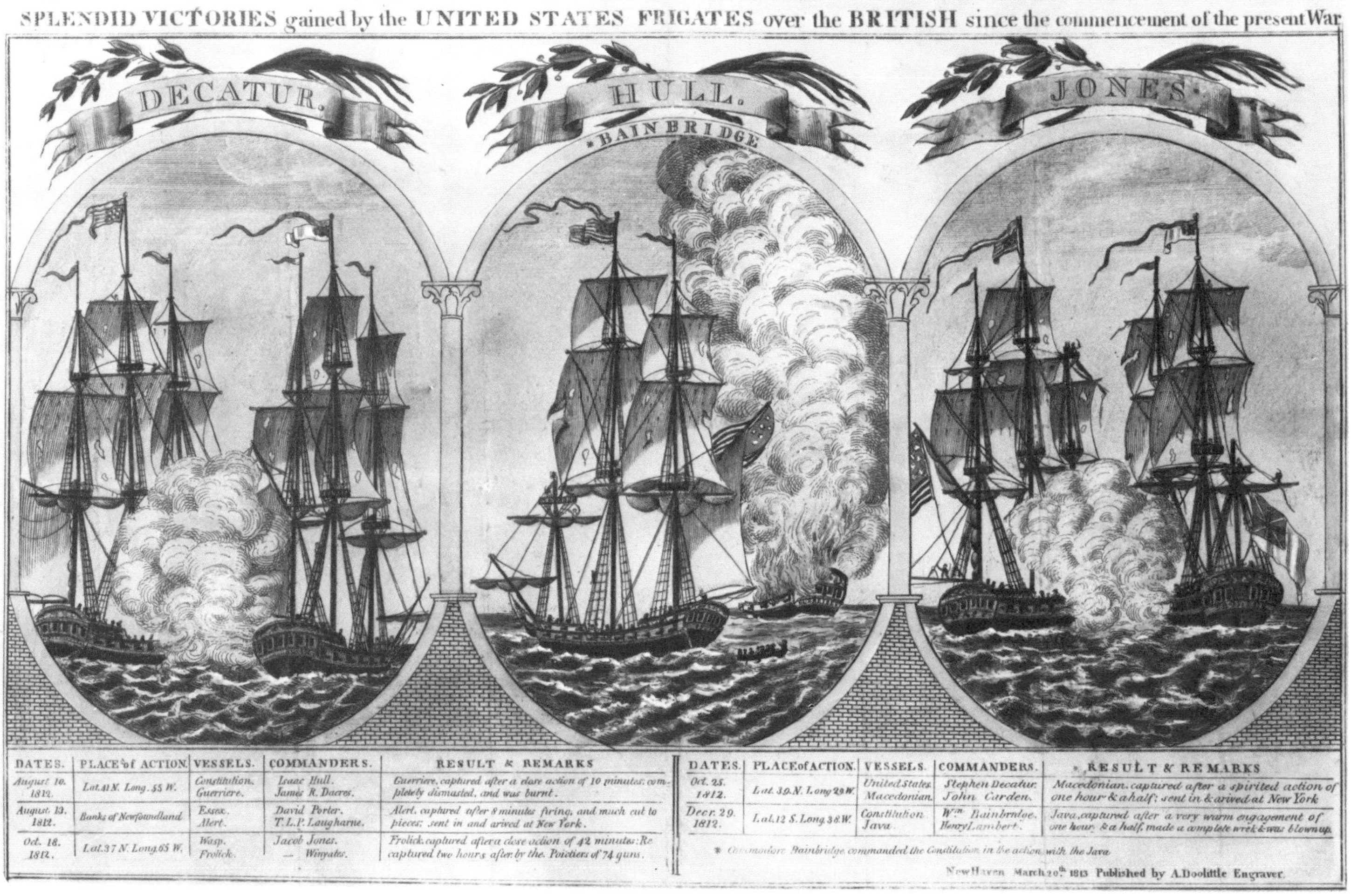

SPLENDID VICTORIES gained by the UNITED STATES FRIGATES over the BRITISH since the commencement of the present War
DECATUR.
HULL.
*BAINBRIDGE
JONES.
DATES. PLACE of ACTION. VESSELS. COMMANDERS. RESULT & REMARKS
August 10. 1812. Lat.41 N. Long. 55 W. Constitution. Guerriere. Isaac Hull. James R. Dacres. Guerriere, captured after a close action of 10 minutes: completely dismasted, and was burnt.
August 13. 1812. Banks of Newfoundland. Essex. Alert. David Porter. T.L.P. Laugharne. Alert, captured after 8 minutes firing, and much cut to pieces; sent in and arived at New York.
Oct. 18. 1812. Lat.37 N. Long.65 W. Wasp. Frolick. Jacob Jones. — Winyates. Frolick, captured after a close action of 42 minutes: Re captured two hours after by the Poictiers of 74 guns.
DATES. PLACE of ACTION. VESSELS. COMMANDERS. *RESULT & REMARKS
Oct. 25. 1812. Lat. 39 N. Long 29 W. United States. Macedonian. Stephen Decatur. John Carden. Macedonian, captured after a spirited action of one hour & a half; sent in & arived at New York
Decr. 29. 1812. Lat.12 S. Long 38 W. Constitution. Java. Wm. Bainbridge. Henry Lambert. Java, captured after a very warm engagement of one hour & a half, made a complete wrek & was blown up.
* Commodore Bainbridge commanded the Constitution in the action with the Java
New Haven March 20th 1813 Published by A. Doolittle Engraver.

William Charles (1776–1820), *A Boxing Match, or Another Bloody Nose for John Bull*, colored engraving, 10¼ in x 14¹⁄₁₆ in, New York?, 1813. Prints and Photographs Division, Library of Congress.

This cartoon illustrates a battle between the H.M.S. Boxer *and the U.S.S.* Enterprise *on September 5, 1813. In the foreground, Brother Jonathan (United States) is pummeling John Bull (Great Britain).*

George Cruikshank (1792–1878), *A sketch for the Regents speech on Mad-Ass-Son's insanity*, colored etching, $10^{13}/_{16}$ in x $15^{1}/_{8}$ in, London, Walker and Knight, December 1812. Prints and Photographs Division, Library of Congress.

On land, American military forces were less successful against the British. Madison was mortified when Gen. William Hull surrendered Detroit "without a shot" early in the war.

Ralph Rawdon (fl. 1813–1877), *The Battle fought near Moravian Town*, colored line engraving, 8 in x $12^{1}/_{2}$ in, Cheshire, Connecticut, Shelton & Kensett, December 6, 1813. Courtesy Anne S. K. Brown Military Collection, Brown University Library, Providence, Rhode Island.

This contemporary print depicts a rare victory for the Americans, the Battle of the Thames, which secured the United States military frontier in the Northwest.

Benjamin Tanner (1775–1848) after John James Barralet (ca. 1747–1815), *Perry's Victory on Lake Erie*, engraving, 28 in x 40$\frac{1}{16}$ in, Philadelphia, 1815. Prints and Photographs Division, Library of Congress.

Twenty-eight year old Commodore Oliver Hazard Perry led a small American fleet to victory in the most important naval engagement on the Great Lakes during the war. His report to his superiors describing the battle included the now-famous line, "We have met the enemy and they are ours."

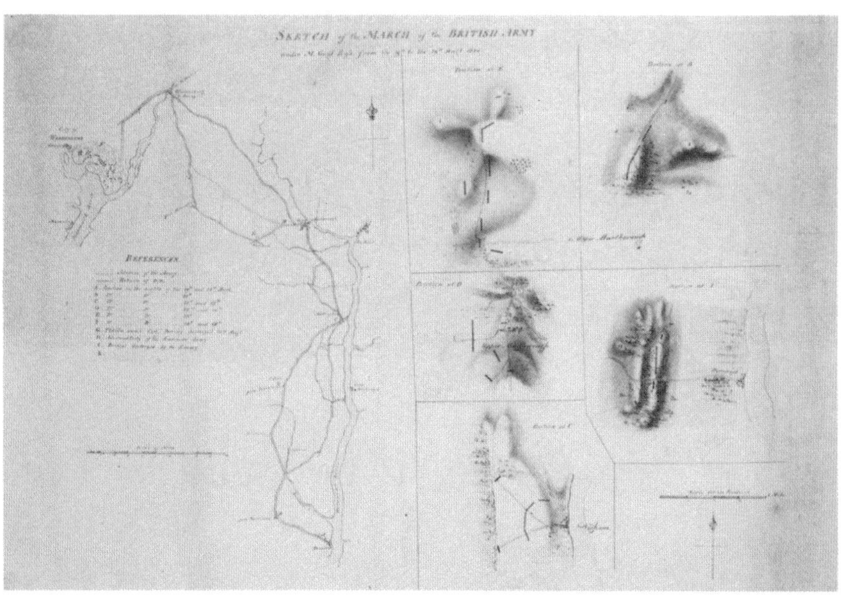

Lieut. Robert Smith, *Sketch of the March of the British Army under M. Genl. Ross*, pencil, pen and ink on paper, 17$\frac{15}{16}$ in x 24$\frac{1}{8}$ in, America?, August 19-29, 1814. Courtesy collection of Paul Mellon.

Plans for the defense of the Federal City were hampered by John Armstrong, Madison's incompetent secretary of war. Despite repeated warnings, Armstrong stubbornly maintained that local militia would be adequate to defend the Capital. A British fleet sailed up the Chesapeake Bay in mid-August, landed four thousand troops, and routed the inexperienced militia at Bladensburg, Maryland. Madison was present at the battle.

George Munger (1781–1825), *The President's House*, pen and ink, watercolor on paper, 23¼ in x 19½ in, America, ca. 1814. Courtesy collection of George H. Chittenden.

The British burned the White House and other public buildings during the August 24 attack. When the Madisons returned to Washington on August 27, they moved to rented quarters. The White House was rebuilt and reoccupied during James Monroe's administration.

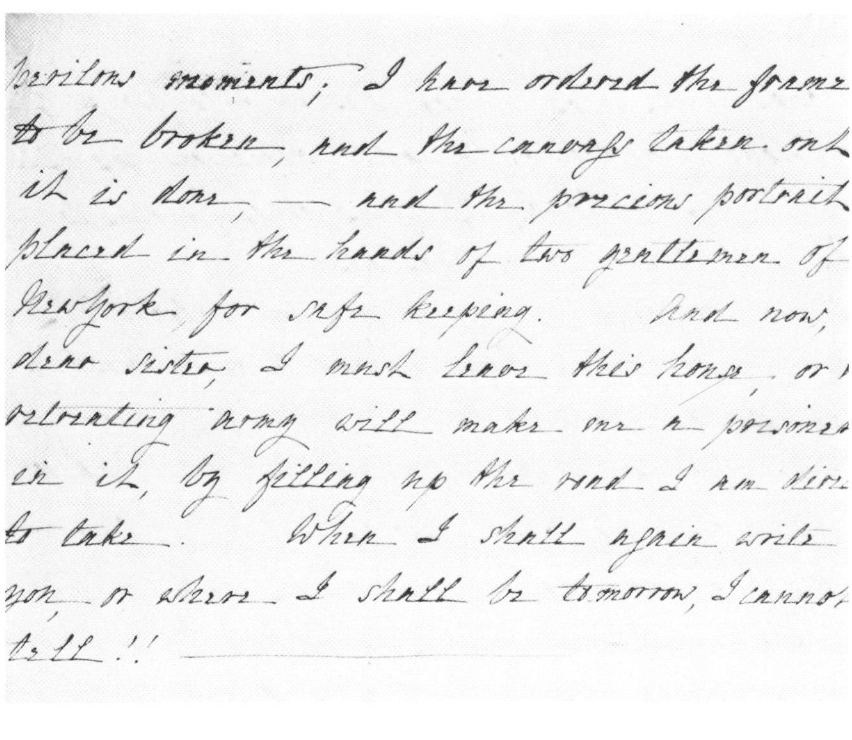

perilous moments; I have ordered the frame to be broken, and the canvass taken out it is done, — and the precious portrait placed in the hands of two gentlemen of New York for safe keeping. And now, dear sister, I must leave this house, or the retreating army will make me a prisoner in it, by filling up the road I am directed to take. When I shall again write you, or where I shall be tomorrow, I cannot tell!! ——

Dolley Madison, *Letter to Lucy Todd* (excerpt; copy of destroyed August 23–24, 1814, original), ca. 1830–36. Dolley Madison Papers, Library of Congress.

Hearing word of the American defeat at Bladensburg, the citizens of Washington panicked and fled the city. Dolley Madison remained at the White House until the last minute, and wrote this historic account of the final hours before the capital fell.

George Munger (1781–1825), *The Capitol*, pen and ink, watercolor on paper, 20 in x 25 in, America, ca. 1814. Courtesy collection of George H. Chittenden.

This rare watercolor records the extent of devastation to the Capitol after the fire. Damage to the City of Washington was estimated at more than $1.5 million.

William Charles (1776–1820), *Johnny Bull and the Alexandrians*, colored engraving, 11 in x 14 15/16 in, Philadelphia, 1814. Prints and Photographs Division, Library of Congress.

Four days after the attack on Washington, Adm. Alexander Cockburn advanced on nearby Alexandria, Virginia; the town capitulated immediately. Acting on a threat by Cockburn to demolish the city, the citizens agreed to turn over a quantity of provisions as ransom.

A VIEW of the BOMBARDMENT of Fort McHenry, near Baltimore, by the British fleet taken from the
Observatory under the Command of Admirals Cochrane & Cockburn on the morning of the 13th of Sepr 1814 which lasted 24 hours, &
thrown from 1500 to 1800 shells in the Night attempted to land by forcing a passage up the ferry branch but were repulsed with great loss.
References.
A. Fort McHenry
B. Lazaretto.
C. Salomons House
E. Ferry and Fort.

John Bower (fl. Philadelphia 1809–1819), *A View of the Bombardment of Fort McHenry near Baltimore,* colored aquatint, 10¾ in x 17¹⁄₁₆ in, Philadelphia, ca. 1815. Courtesy Chicago Historical Society, Illinois.

After capturing Alexandria the British advanced on Baltimore, a major port protected by Fort McHenry. The attack took place by night on September 13. Maj. George Armistead had ordered his troops to fly a giant flag from the fort, "so large that the British will have no difficulty seeing it at a distance." The fort withstood the attack.

OPPOSITE:

Francis Scott Key (1779–1843), *The Star-Spangled Banner,* draft, Baltimore, 1814. Courtesy Maryland Historical Society, Baltimore.

Francis Scott Key, a young lawyer, observed the bombardment of Fort McHenry from a ship in Baltimore harbor. At dawn he witnessed the American flag still "gallently streaming"; the event inspired him to write a verse that later became the National Anthem.

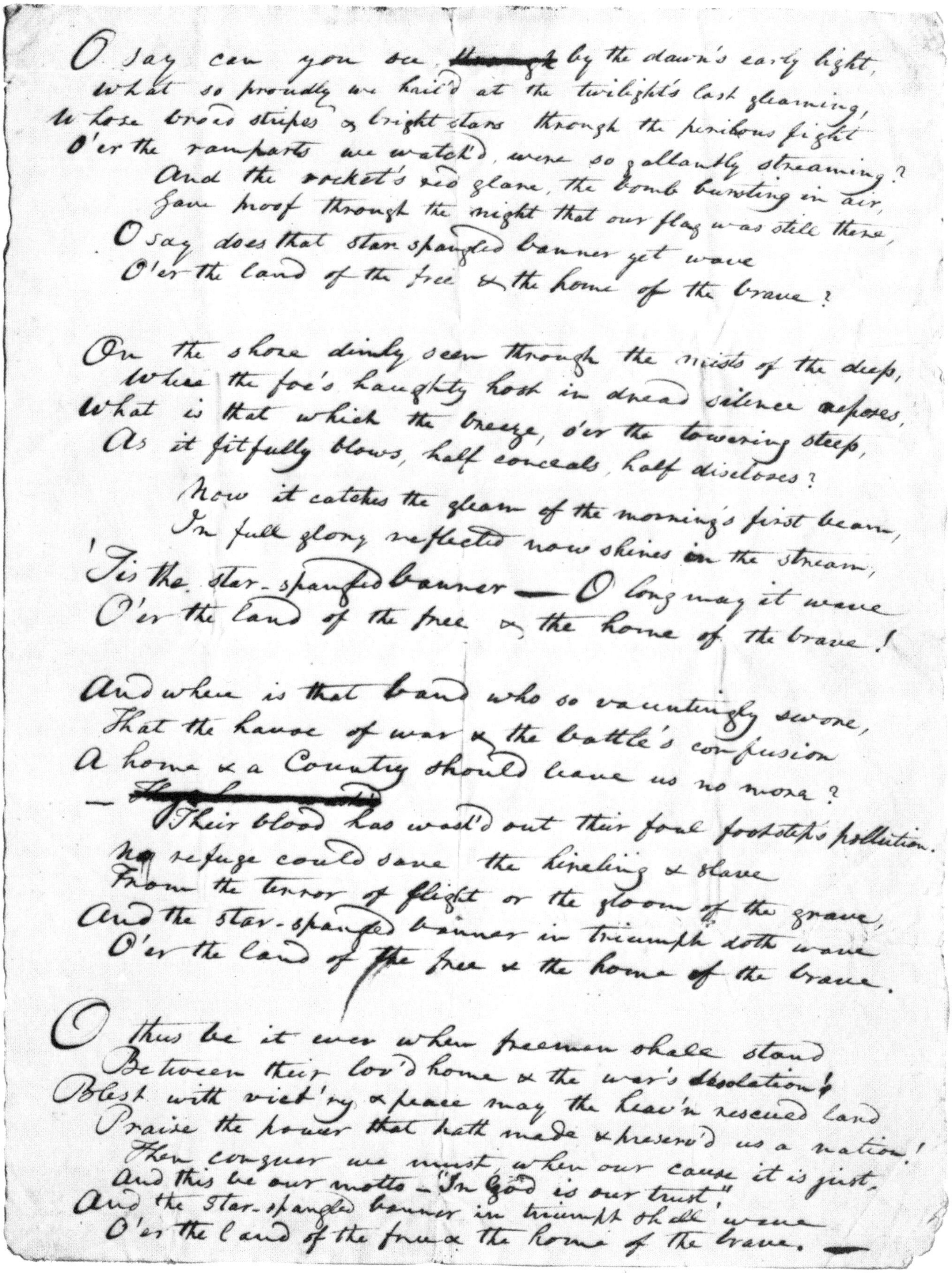
O say can you see ~~through~~ by the dawn's early light,
What so proudly we hail'd at the twilight's last gleaming,
Whose broad stripes & bright stars through the perilous fight
O'er the ramparts we watch'd, were so gallantly streaming?
And the rocket's red glare, the bomb bursting in air,
Gave proof through the night that our flag was still there,
O say does that star-spangled banner yet wave
O'er the land of the free & the home of the brave?

On the shore dimly seen through the mists of the deep,
Where the foe's haughty host in dread silence reposes,
What is that which the breeze, o'er the towering steep,
As it fitfully blows, half conceals, half discloses?
Now it catches the gleam of the morning's first beam,
In full glory reflected now shines in the stream,
'Tis the star-spangled banner — O long may it wave
O'er the land of the free & the home of the brave!

And where is that band who so vauntingly swore,
That the havoc of war & the battle's confusion
A home & a Country should leave us no more?
— ~~[illegible]~~
Their blood has wash'd out their foul footstep's pollution.
No refuge could save the hireling & slave
From the terror of flight or the gloom of the grave,
And the star-spangled banner in triumph doth wave
O'er the land of the free & the home of the brave.

O thus be it ever when freemen shall stand
Between their lov'd home & the war's desolation!
Blest with vict'ry & peace may the heav'n rescued land
Praise the power that hath made & preserv'd us a nation!
Then conquer we must, when our cause it is just,
And this be our motto — "In God is our trust,"
And the star-spangled banner in triumph shall wave
O'er the land of the free & the home of the brave. —

Pieter van Huffel (1769–1844), *John Quincy Adams* (1767–1848) (as Peace Commissioner), oil on canvas, 25 in x 20¾ in, Ghent, 1815. Courtesy National Portrait Gallery, Smithsonian Institution, Washington, D.C.

Negotiations to end the war with Great Britain took place in the Flemish town of Ghent, where Adams and four other American commissioners finally signed a peace treaty on Christmas Eve, 1814. Word of the agreement did not reach Washington until after Jackson's victory at New Orleans. Madison signed the document to end the war in his rented quarters at the Octagon House, and it was unanimously ratified by the Senate on February 17, 1815.

James W. Steel (1799–1879) after Samuel Seymour (fl. Philadelphia, 1797–1822), *Battle of New Orleans*, aquatint, 17⅝ in x 21½ in, Philadelphia, Wm. H. Morgan, ca. 1815. Prints and Photographs Division, Library of Congress.

The last major engagement of the war was fought two weeks after the signing of the peace treaty in Ghent. Gen. Andrew Jackson led his troops to a resounding victory over the British outside of New Orleans on January 8, 1815.

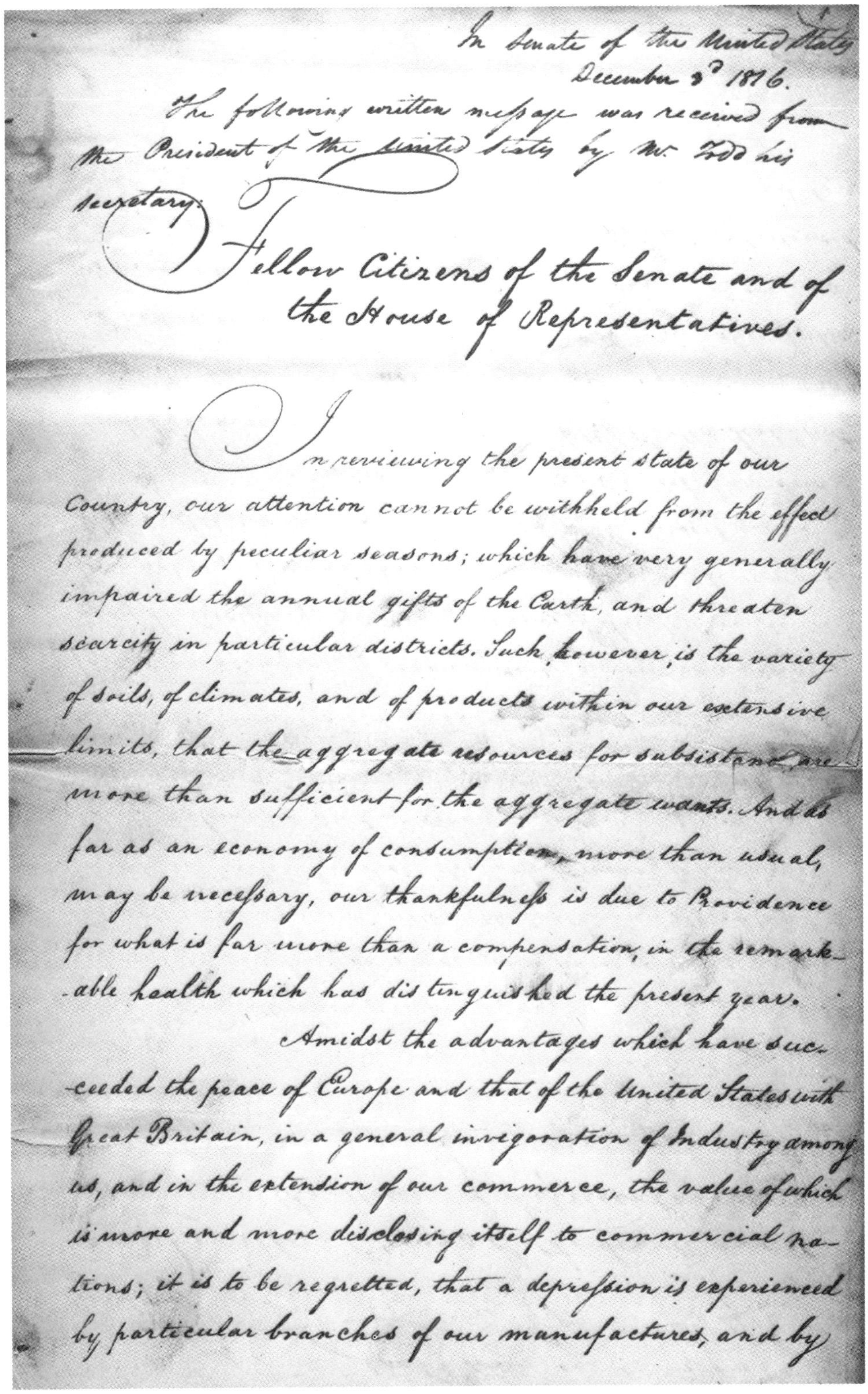

In Senate of the United States
December 3d 1816.

The following written message was received from the President of the United States by Mr. Todd his secretary.

Fellow Citizens of the Senate and of the House of Representatives.

In reviewing the present state of our Country, our attention cannot be withheld from the effect produced by peculiar seasons; which have very generally impaired the annual gifts of the Earth, and threaten scarcity in particular districts. Such, however, is the variety of soils, of climates, and of products within our extensive limits, that the aggregate resources for subsistance, are more than sufficient for the aggregate wants. And as far as an economy of consumption, more than usual, may be necessary, our thankfulness is due to Providence for what is far more than a compensation, in the remark-able health which has distinguished the present year.

Amidst the advantages which have succeeded the peace of Europe and that of the United States with Great Britain, in a general invigoration of Industry among us, and in the extension of our commerce, the value of which is more and more disclosing itself to commercial nations; it is to be regretted, that a depression is experienced by particular branches of our manufactures, and by

James Madison's *State of the Union Message* (excerpt), Washington, December 3, 1816. Records of the United States Senate. Photograph courtesy National Archives and Records Service, Washington, D.C.

Madison's popularity increased after the war. In his last speech to Congress before his retirement, the president noted "that the American people have reached in safety and success their fortieth year as an independent nation. . . ."

Montpelier, 1977. Courtesy American Institute of Architects Foundation/ the Octagon, Washington, D.C. William E. Barrett photograph.

When James Monroe was inaugurated as the fifth president, the Madisons retired to Orange.

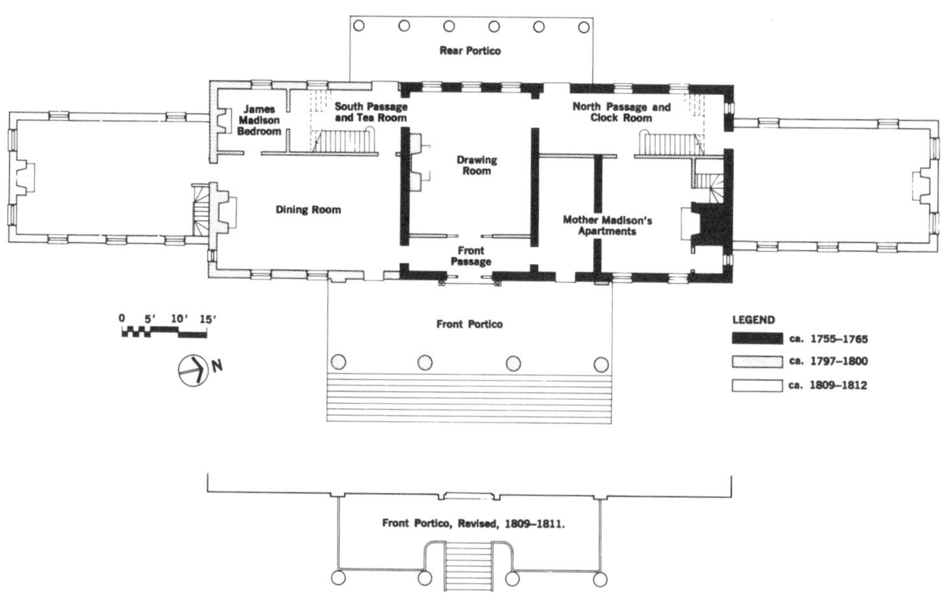

Nicholas A. Pappas, FAIA, *Plan of Montpelier*, 1809–36. Courtesy American Institute of Architects Foundation/the Octagon, Washington, D.C.

Since its original construction, Montpelier has grown through a series of additions. The Madisons doubled the size of the mansion house in the late 1790s and added one-story wings between 1809 and 1812. A second story was added to the wings early in this century.

Aerial View of Montpelier garden, 1978. Courtesy Virginia Museum of Fine Arts, Richmond, and the James Madison Museum, Orange, Virginia.

During Madison's lifetime the grounds at Montpelier were landscaped and cultivated with an exotic variety of plants and trees. The French-style horseshoe garden was laid out during the early nineteenth century.

John Gadsby Chapman (1808–1889), *Summer house at Mr. Madison's,* pencil on paper, 7¼ in x 13 in, Orange, ca. September 1833. Courtesy Valentine Museum, Richmond, Virginia.

This classical temple was constructed on the Montpelier grounds in 1811. It ranks among the finest examples of early garden architecture in America.

John Henri Browere (1790–1834), *Dolley Madison*, plaster, 22 in, America, 1825. Courtesy New York State Historical Association, Cooperstown.

John Henri Browere (1790–1834), *James Madison* (from life), plaster, 28½ in, America, 1825. Courtesy New York State Historical Association, Cooperstown.

The Madisons enjoyed the retirement years at Montpelier, which was the scene of relaxation and constant visitors. Browere traveled to Orange in 1825 and took life masks of both the Madisons.

Anonymous, *Amerigus Vespuccius* (ca. 1451–1512), oil on canvas, 28 in x 21¾ in, Italy?, early nineteenth century. Courtesy New-York Historical Society, New York City, gift of Mary Madison McGuire.

A visitor to Montpelier in 1828 was delighted to see that the Madison's home resembled "a museum of the arts." The Montpelier art collection, of which this is an example, included nearly seventy canvases, ranging in subject from Old Master religious and mythological scenes to portraits of early discoverers and American leaders.

Pietro Cardelli (?–ca. 1822), *James Madison* (from life), plaster, 20 in, Virginia, 1819. Courtesy Virginia Historical Society, Richmond.

Madison's sculpture collection at Montpelier numbered over twenty-five examples devoted primarily to portraits of early American leaders. This portrait of Madison was part of the collection.

Anonymous, *Armchair* (one of a pair), mahogany, 37 in x 23¾ in x 18 in, Paris, ca. 1805–15. Courtesy Virginia Historical Society, Richmond.

Many of the furnishings at Montpelier were French.

Anonymous, *Pier glass and table*, gilt, mahogany, marble, glass, 120 in x 56½ in x 20¼ in, France, early nineteenth century. Collection of Mrs. Joseph Prendergast. Courtesy of the American Institute of Architects Foundation/the Octagon, Washington, D.C. William E. Barrett photograph.

Charles-Honoré Lannuier (1779–1819), *Card Table,* mahogany and mahogany veneers, white pine, brass, 30 in x 35¼ in x 17½ in, New York City, ca. 1810. Courtesy Henry Francis du Pont Winterthur Museum, Delaware.

Anonymous, *Campeachy chair,* leather, mahogany, 39¾ in x 21½ in x 19¾ in, America?, ca. 1800–1820. James Madison Museum, Orange, Virginia, gift of Dorothy Madison Mulick Lyons. Photograph courtesy of the American Institute of Architects Foundation/the Octagon, Washington, D.C.

Describing the drawing room furnishings at Montpelier, one relative recalled that "Mr. Madison's favorite seat was a campeachy chair."

Michel Sokolnicki (1760–1816) after Tadeus Kosciusko (1746–1817), *Thomas Jefferson*, colored aquatint, 9⅞ in x 8$^{5}/_{16}$ in, Paris, ca. 1798. Courtesy National Portrait Gallery, Smithsonian Institution, Washington, D.C.

The Montpelier art collection boasted several likenesses of Thomas Jefferson, including a life portrait by Gilbert Stuart (page 37), a Houdon bust, an oil by "Peele," and a copy of the print shown here.

Cornelia Jefferson Randolph (1799–1871) (attrib.), *South Elevation of the Rotunda and Pavilions IX and X, University of Virginia*, ink and tinted washes on paper, 11 in x 17½ in, Charlottesville, ca. 1820. Jefferson Papers, University of Virginia Library, Charlottesville. Photograph courtesy American Institute of Architects Foundation/the Octagon, Washington, D.C.

Madison's final collaboration with his friend Thomas Jefferson was in organizing the University of Virginia, Jefferson's "academical village" in Charlottesville. Madison became rector of the university after Jefferson's death in 1826.

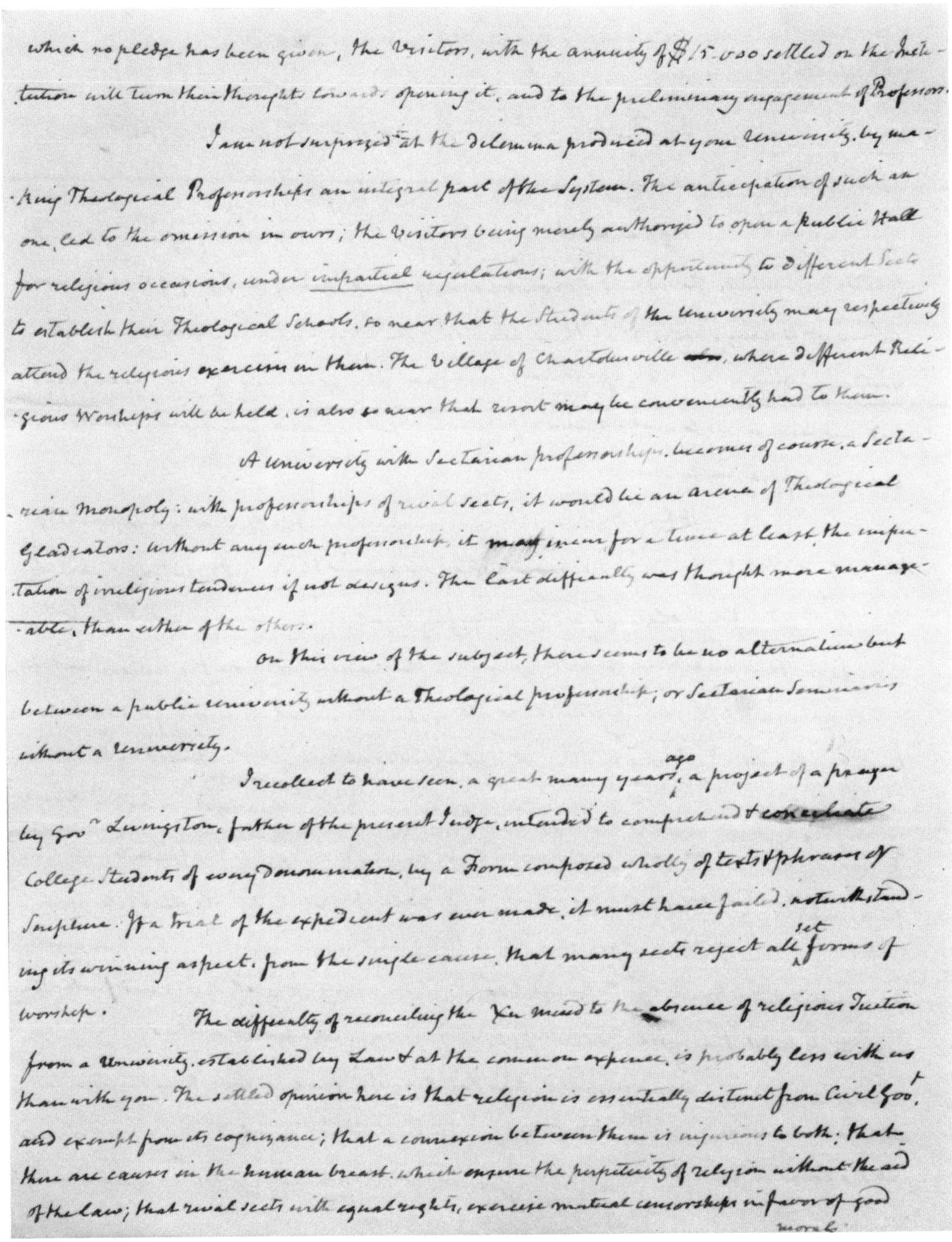
which no pledge has been given, the Visitors, with the annuity of $15,000 settled on the Institution will turn their thoughts towards opening it, and to the preliminary engagement of Professors.

I am not surprized at the dilemma produced at your University by making Theological Professorships an integral part of the System. The anticipation of such an one, led to the omission in ours; the Visitors being merely authorized to open a public Hall for religious occasions, under impartial regulations; with the opportunity to different Sects to establish their Theological Schools so near that the Students of the University may respectively attend the religious exercises in them. The Village of Charlottesville also, where different Religious Worships will be held, is also so near that resort may be conveniently had to them.

A University with Sectarian professorships, becomes of course, a Sectarian Monopoly: with professorships of rival sects, it would be an arena of Theological Gladiators: without any such professorship, it may incur for a time at least, the imputation of irreligious tendencies if not designs. The last difficulty was thought more manageable, than either of the others.

On this view of the subject, there seems to be no alternative but between a public University without a Theological professorship; or Sectarian Seminaries without a University.

I recollect to have seen, a great many years ago, a project of a prayer by Govr Livingston, father of the present Judge, intended to comprehend & conciliate College Students of every Denomination, by a Form composed wholly of texts & phrases of Scripture. If a trial of the expedient was ever made, it must have failed, notwithstanding its winning aspect, from the single cause, that many sects reject all set forms of worship.

The difficulty of reconciling the Xn mind to the absence of religious Tuition from a University established by Law & at the common expence, is probably less with us than with you. The settled opinion here is that religion is essentially distinct from Civil Govt, and exempt from its cognizance; that a connexion between them is injurious to both; that there are causes in the human breast, which ensure the perpetuity of religion without the aid of the law; that rival sects with equal rights, exercise mutual censorships in favor of good morals.

James Madison, *Letter to Edward Everett* (excerpt), Orange, March 19, 1823. Courtesy Massachusetts Historical Society, Boston. Stephen J. Kovacik photograph.

Both Madison and Jefferson were convinced that the new university in Charlottesville should be a secular institution. In his correspondence with future Harvard president Edward Everett, Madison restated his familiar theory of separation of church and state. Strong religious affiliation threatened to turn a university into either a "Sectarian Monopoly," argued Madison, or an "arena of Theological Gladiators."

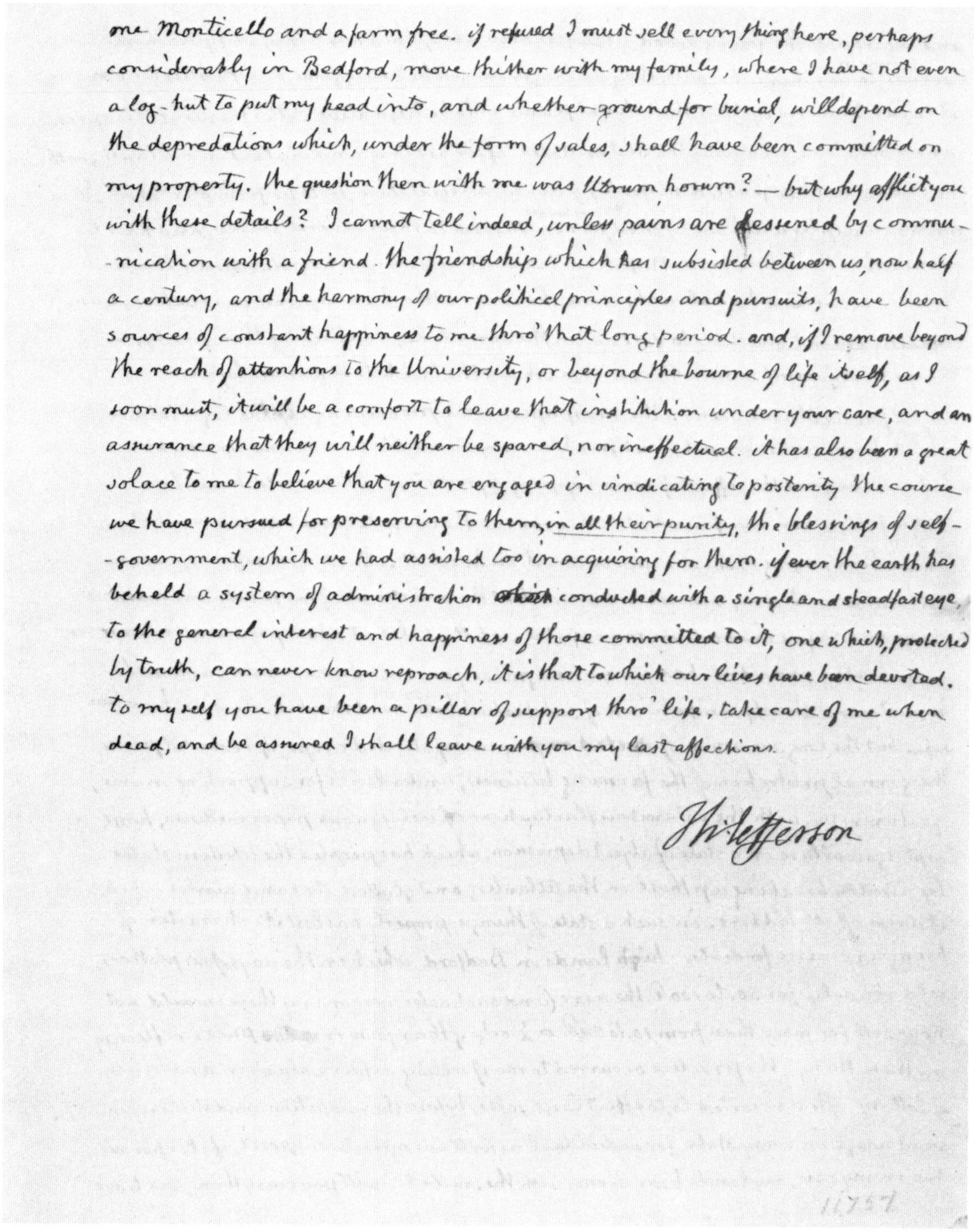
me Monticello and a farm free. if refused I must sell every thing here, perhaps
considerably in Bedford, move thither with my family, where I have not even
a log-hut to put my head into, and whether ground for burial, will depend on
the depredations which, under the form of sales, shall have been committed on
my property. the question then with me was Utrum horum? — but why afflict you
with these details? I cannot tell indeed, unless pains are lessened by commu-
-nication with a friend. the friendship which has subsisted between us, now half
a century, and the harmony of our political principles and pursuits, have been
sources of constant happiness to me thro' that long period. and, if I remove beyond
the reach of attentions to the University, or beyond the bourne of life itself, as I
soon must, it will be a comfort to leave that institution under your care, and an
assurance that they will neither be spared, nor ineffectual. it has also been a great
solace to me to believe that you are engaged in vindicating to posterity the course
we have pursued for preserving to them, in all their purity, the blessings of self-
-government, which we had assisted too in acquiring for them. if ever the earth has
beheld a system of administration ~~which~~ conducted with a single and steadfast eye,
to the general interest and happiness of those committed to it, one which, protected
by truth, can never know reproach, it is that to which our lives have been devoted.
to myself you have been a pillar of support thro' life, take care of me when
dead, and be assured I shall leave with you my last affections.

Th: Jefferson

11757

Thomas Jefferson, *Letter to James Madison* (excerpt), Monticello, February 17, 1826. James Madison Papers, Library of Congress.

Several months before his death on July 4, 1826, an ailing Jefferson wrote to his friend at Montpelier, "To my self you have been a pillar of support thro' life, take care of me when dead, and be assured I shall leave with you my last affections."

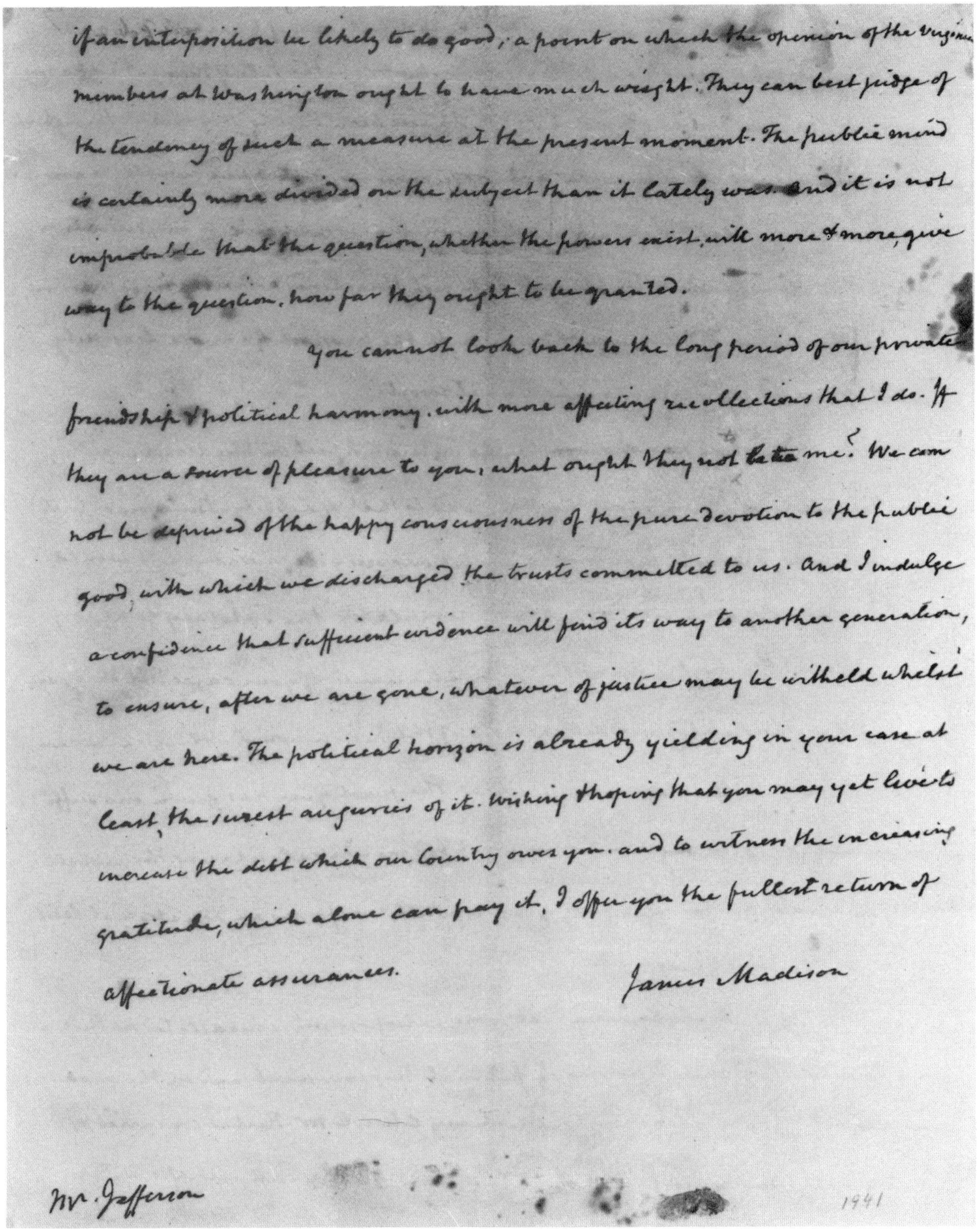

if an interposition be likely to do good; a point on which the opinion of the Virginia
members at Washington ought to have much weight. They can best judge of
the tendency of such a measure at the present moment. The public mind
is certainly more divided on the subject than it lately was. And it is not
improbable that the question, whether the powers exist, will more & more give
way to the question, how far they ought to be granted.

You cannot look back to the long period of our private
friendship & political harmony, with more affecting recollections than I do. If
they are a source of pleasure to you, what ought they not to be to me? We can
not be deprived of the happy consciousness of the pure devotion to the public
good, with which we discharged the trusts committed to us. And I indulge
a confidence that sufficient evidence will find its way to another generation,
to ensure, after we are gone, whatever of justice may be withheld whilst
we are here. The political horizon is already yielding in your case at
least, the surest auguries of it. Wishing & hoping that you may yet live to
increase the debt which our Country owes you, and to witness the increasing
gratitude, which alone can pay it, I offer you the fullest return of
affectionate assurances.

James Madison

Mr. Jefferson

1941

James Madison, *Letter to Thomas Jefferson* (excerpt), Orange, February 24, 1826. James Madison Papers, Library of Congress.

Madison replied, "You cannot look back to the long period of our private friendship and political harmony with more affecting recollections that I do. . . . I offer you the fullest return of affectionate assurances."

George Catlin (1796–1872), *The Virginia Constitutional Convention,* oil on wood, 24½ in x 36½ in, Richmond, Virginia, 1830. Courtesy Virginia Historical Society, Richmond.

James Madison returned briefly to politics in 1829. Madison, Monroe, and John Marshall were among the delegates who convened in Richmond to rewrite the Virginia Constitution of 1776. As the sole surviving member of the original convention, Madison held a unique status. He is shown here addressing the gathering.

George Catlin (1796–1872), *The Virginia Constitutional Convention*, pen and ink on paper, 33 in x 20 in, Richmond, 1829. Courtesy New-York Historical Society, New York City.

Artist George Catlin visited Richmond during the 1829 convention to record likenesses of the outstanding delegation. This key was drawn to identify the participants.

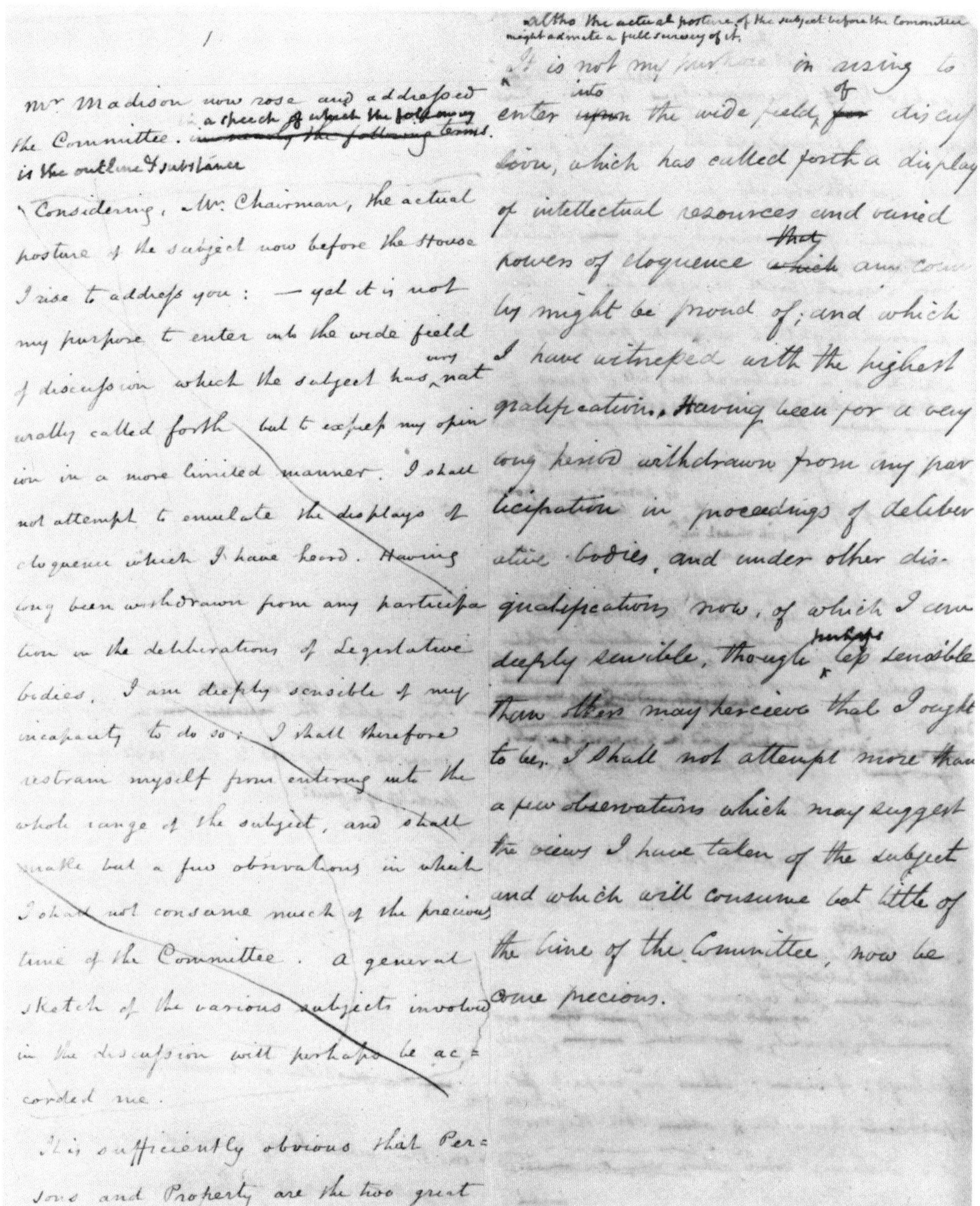

1

Mr. Madison now rose and addressed the Committee. ~~in nearly the following terms.~~ a speech of which the following is the outline & substance

Considering, Mr. Chairman, the actual posture of the subject now before the House I rise to address you: — yet it is not my purpose to enter into the wide field of discussion which the subject has very naturally called forth but to express my opinion in a more limited manner. I shall not attempt to emulate the displays of eloquence which I have heard. Having long been withdrawn from any participation in the deliberations of Legislative bodies, I am deeply sensible of my incapacity to do so: I shall therefore restrain myself from entering into the whole range of the subject, and shall make but a few observations in which I shall not consume much of the precious time of the Committee. A general sketch of the various subjects involved in the discussion will perhaps be accorded me.

It is sufficiently obvious that Persons and Property are the two great

altho the actual posture of the subject before the Committee might admit of a full survey of it,

It is not my purpose in rising to enter ~~upon~~ into the wide field of ~~for~~ discussion, which has called forth a display of intellectual resources and varied powers of eloquence ~~which~~ that any country might be proud of; and which I have witnessed with the highest gratification. Having been for a very long period withdrawn from any participation in proceedings of deliberative bodies, and under other disqualifications now, of which I am deeply sensible, though perhaps less sensible than others may perceive that I ought to be, I shall not attempt more than a few observations which may suggest the views I have taken of the subject and which will consume but little of the time of the Committee, now become precious.

A. J. Stansbury and James Madison, *Mr. Madison's First Speech in the Virginia Convention of 1829*, Richmond, 1829. James Madison Papers, Library of Congress.

Already recognized as the Father of the Constitution, Madison's unique knowledge of the nature of American government made him an important presence at the convention. Delegate Stansbury took careful notes on December 2, during Madison's only speech before the convention, and asked the aging statesman to correct these minutes to guarantee their accuracy.

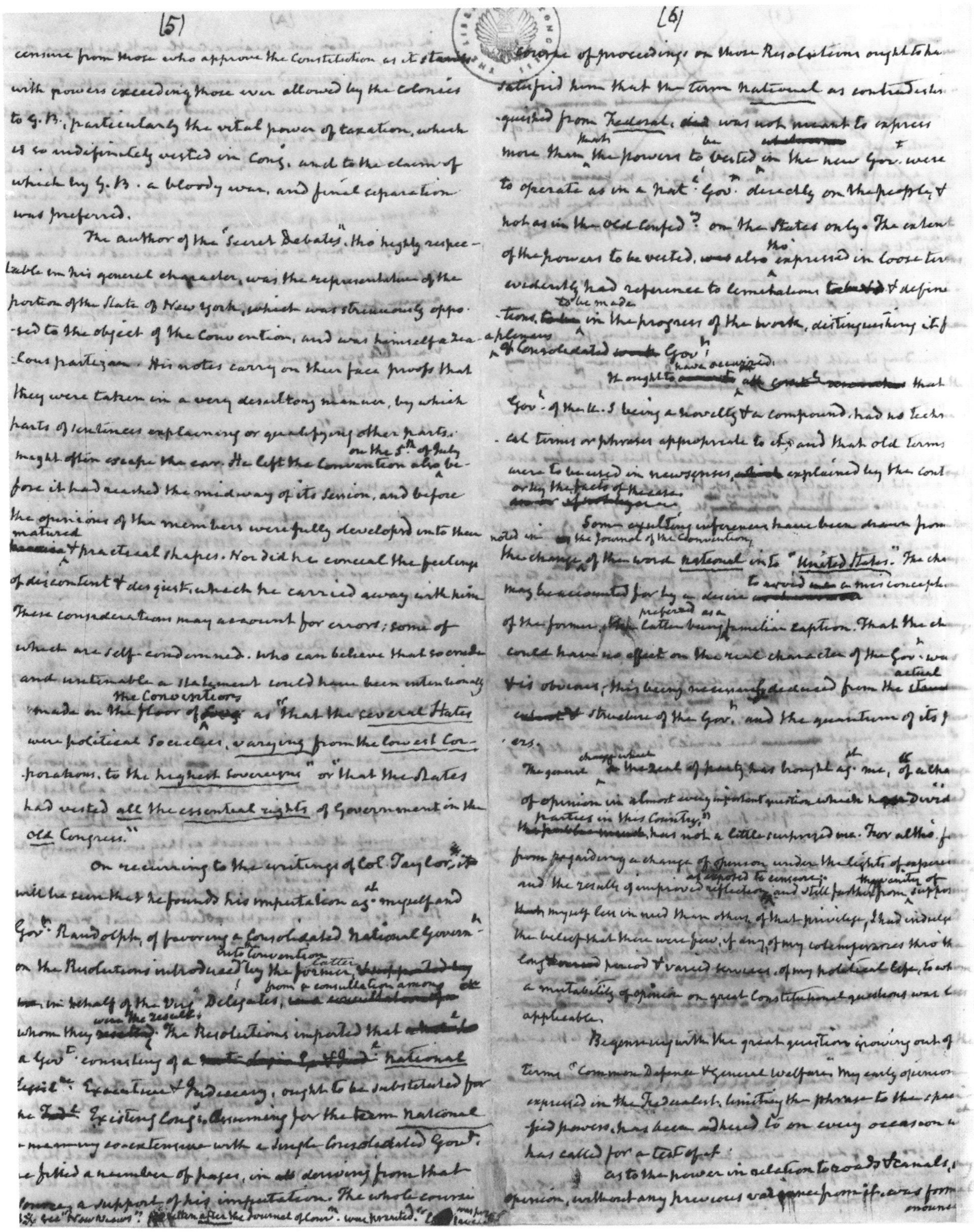
(5)

censure from those who approve the Constitution as it stands with powers exceeding those ever allowed by the colonies to G.B. particularly the vital power of taxation, which is so indefinitely vested in Cong. and to the claim of which by G.B. a bloody war, and final separation was preferred.

The author of the "Secret Debates" tho highly respectable in his general character, was the representative of the portion of the State of New York, which was strenuously opposed to the object of the Convention, and was himself a zealous partizan. His notes carry on their face proofs that they were taken in a very desultory manner, by which parts of sentences explaining or qualifying other parts, might often escape the ear. He left the Convention also on the 5th of July before it had reached the midway of its Session, and before the opinions of the members were fully developed into their matured & practical shapes. Nor did he conceal the feelings of discontent & disgust, which he carried away with him. These considerations may account for errors; some of which are self-condemned. Who can believe that so crude and untenable a statement could have been intentionally made on the floor of the Convention as "that the several States were political Societies, varying from the lowest Corporations, to the highest Sovereigns" or "that the States had vested all the essential rights of Government in the old Congress."

On recurring to the writings of Col. Taylor, it will be seen that he founds his imputation agst myself and Govr Randolph, of favoring a Consolidated National Government on the Resolutions introduced into Convention by the latter in behalf of the Virga Delegates, from a consultation among whom they were the result. The Resolutions imported that a Govt consisting of a National Legislre Executive & Judiciary, ought to be substituted for the Existing Cong. Assuming for the term National a meaning coextensive with a single Consolidated Govt. ...

(6)

... scope of proceedings on those Resolutions ought to have satisfied him that the term National as contradistinguished from Federal, was not meant to express more than that the powers to be vested in the new Govt were to operate as in a Natl Govt directly on the people, & not as in the Old Confedn on the States only. The extent of the powers to be vested, tho' also expressed in loose terms, evidently had reference to limitations & definitions to be made in the progress of the work, distinguishing it from a Consolidated Govt.

... Some exulting inferences have been drawn from the change noted in the Journal of the Convention of the word national into "United States." The change may be accounted for by a desire to avoid a misconception of the former, the latter being preferred as a familiar caption. That the change could have no effect on the real character of the Govt was & is obvious, this being necessarily deduced from the actual structure of the Govt and the quantum of its powers.

The general charge ... of a change of opinion in almost every important question which has divided parties in this Country, has not a little surprized me. For altho' far from regarding a change of opinion under the lights of experience and the results of improved reflection as exposed to censure ... I had indulged the belief that there were few, if any, of my contemporaries thro' the long & varied services of my political life, to whom a mutability of opinion on great Constitutional questions was less applicable.

Beginning with the great question growing out of the terms "Common Defence & General Welfare," my early opinion expressed in the Federalist, limiting the phrase to the specified powers, has been adhered to on every occasion which has called for a test of it.

As to the power in relation to roads & canals, my opinion, without any previous variance from it, was from ...

James Madison, *Letter to Nicholas Trist* (excerpt), Orange, December, 1831. James Madison Papers, Library of Congress.

Madison found himself in the middle of the nullification controversy of the early 1830s. Both states' rights advocates and opponents used Madison's early writings on the Virginia Resolutions of 1798-99 as the basis of their arguments for or against the powers of the national government under the Constitution. In this letter to Trist, Madison took the opportunity to refute "the right of a single state, as a party to the Constitution, to arrest the execution of a law of the United States."

PRES'T. MADISON'S LIBRARY, AT AUCTION.

AT Orange Court House Virginia, on Tuesday the 27th day of June, prox., being the day after the County Court of Orange in that month; I shall sell at public auction, to the highest bidder, that part of the Library of the late James Madison, which, in a recent division of his books with the University of Virginia, fell to the share of my testator; and at the same time I will sell other books, the property of my said testator. In all there are some

SEVEN OR EIGHT HUNDRED VOLUMES,

among which are many very rare and desirable works, some in Greek, some in Latin, numerous others in French, and yet more in English, in almost all the departments of Literature; not a few of them being in this manner exposed to sale only because the University possessed already copies of the same editions. The sale beginning on the day above mentioned, will be continued from day to day till all the books shall have been sold, on the following terms:

Cash will be required of each purchaser whose aggregate purchases shall amount to no more than Five dollars; those whose purchases shall exceed that amount, will have the privilege either to pay the cash or to give bond with approved security, bearing interest from the date, and payable six months thereafter.

ELHANON ROW, Administrator,
with the will annexed of John P. Todd, dec'd.

May 30, 1854.

Pres't. Madison's Library, At Auction, broadside, 10³/₈ in x 10³/₈ in, Orange, May 30, 1854. Rare Book and Special Collections Division, Library of Congress.

Madison's extensive Montpelier library was sold after his wife's death in 1849. The majority of the books in his collection have never been located.

to the intellectual and moral improvement of man, as they are conformable to his individual & social Rights. What spectacle can be more ~~instructive~~ edifying or more seasonable, than that of Liberty & Learning, each leaning on the other for their mutual & surest support?

The Committee, of which your name is the first, have taken a very judicious course in endeavouring to avail Kentucky of the experience of elder States, in modifying her Schools. I enclose extracts from the laws of Virginia on that subject; though I presume they will give ~~both~~ little aid; the less as they have as yet been imperfectly carried into execution. The States where such systems have ~~been completely organized and~~ been long in operation will furnish much better answers to many of the enquiries stated in your Circular. But after all, such is the diversity of local circumstances, more particularly as the population varies in density & sparseness, that the details suited to some may be little so to others. As the population however, is becoming ~~every where~~ less & less sparse, and it will be well in laying the foundation of a good System, to have a view to this progressive change, much attention seems due to examples in the Eastern States, where the people are most compact, & where ~~they has been~~ the longest experience in plans of popular education.

I know

James Madison, *Letter to William T. Barry* (excerpt), Orange, August 4, 1822. James Madison Papers, Library of Congress.

In this famous letter, Madison summarizes his philosophy about the importance of knowledge to the human spirit. "What spectacle can be more edifying or more seasonable," he wrote Barry, "than that of Liberty & Learning, each leaning on the other for their mutual and surest support?"

Asher B. Durand (1796–1886), *James Madison* (from life), oil on canvas, 32⁵⁄₁₆ in x 28½ in, America, ca. 1830. Century Club, New York City. Photograph courtesy of the American Institute of Architects Foundation/the Octagon, Washington, D.C.

Madison's retirement years were devoted to the management of his estate, arrangement of his papers, and correspondence on a wide variety of subjects with friends and strangers. His health gradually declined until he was virtually confined to a chair. Madison's mind remained lucid until the end of his life; he died at home on June 28, 1836 at the age of eighty-five.

"What spectacle can be more edifying or more seasonable, than that of Liberty & Learning, each leaning on the other for their mutual and surest support?"

JAMES MADISON

August 4, 1822

SELECTED READINGS

Madison was the last of the Founding Fathers fitted into those niches reserved for patriots whose careers provoked the fullest biographical treatment. The early collections of his papers concentrated on his experience at the Federal Convention of 1787 and tended to make light of his presidential tenure. The stiff, formal treatment of Madison came to an end when a newspaperman, Irving Brant, became interested in Madison during the sesquicentennial of the Constitution in 1937 and undertook the writing of a one-volume biography. The deeper he probed the more Brant realized he had set too limited a goal, and his labors did not cease until 1961, when the last of his six volumes, *James Madison: Commander in Chief, 1812-1836*, was published. The entire series (Bobbs-Merrill, 1941-61) is an overwhelming work, not critical enough for some trained historians, but a feast for those who consider Madison our most underrated president. Brant's summarization of these volumes appeared as a single book, *The Fourth President* (Bobbs-Merrill, 1970), to provide an easier reading if briefer review of Madison's life. Ralph Ketcham's *James Madison: A Biography* (Macmillan, 1971) is in the Brant tradition and generally follows Brant's friendly interpretation of Madison's career.

For readers seeking a more leisurely study of Madison's accomplishments, the *Quarterly Journal of the Library of Congress* (Spring 1980) offers a series of well-written estimates of Madison's contributions in a variety of fields. The overall effect is valuable, and the series can be read in a few sittings. The same laurels were earned by Harold S. Schultz when his *James Madison* (Twayne Publishers, 1971) appeared. Schultz's viewpoints are fresh, his insights are keen, and the small volume is probably the best brief biography of Madison ever written.

By far the most handsomely illustrated of all the Madison biographies is the edition prepared by Merrill Peterson, *James Madison: A Biography in His Own Words* (Newsweek Books, 1974). Peterson skillfully arranged Madison's writings and provided a rich interpretation that was enhanced by portraits, historical paintings, cartoons, and other illustrations bearing on the fourth president's long life.

For the specialists, nothing compares with two of Adrienne Koch's affectionate works, *Jefferson and Madison: The Great Collaboration* (Alfred Knopf, 1950), and *Madison's "Advice to My Country"* (Princeton University Press, 1966). A sound scholar and a delightful human being, Miss Koch brought a rare warmth and verve to her works, which she frankly admitted were written by a lady who was smitten. Her admiration for Madison, however, did not color her critical judgment of his public service, and these works are part of a large legacy left by this courageous lady.

Other scholarly works treating on the political-philosophy phases of Madison's life include Marvin Meyers, *The Mind of the Founder: Sources of the Political Thought of James Madison* (Bobbs-Merrill, 1973) and Neal Riemer, *James Madison* (Washington Square Press, 1968). Madison's key role in drafting *The Federalist Papers* is recognized in these books, of course, but there is no substitute for reading Madison's specific contributions to this classic statement of American constitutionalism. Clinton Rossiter's paperback edition (Mentor, 1961) identifies the authors of each essay and has a splendid index.

Scholars have reinterpreted the War of 1812 in the past two decades and are still hard at work. Harry Coles, *The War of 1812* (University of Chicago Press, 1965) is the best brief study of the military phases. For the diplomacy and the breakdown of negotiations which preceded the war, readers might consider Bradford Perkins, *The Causes of the War of 1812* (Krieger, 1976) or R. A. Rutland, *Madison's Alternatives: The Jeffersonian Republicans and the Coming of War, 1805-1812* (J. B. Lippincott, 1975). Roger H. Brown, *The Republic in Peril: 1812* (Columbia University Press, 1964) gives a full accounting of the route that led to our second war for independence. Bradford Perkins, *Prologue to War: England and the United States, 1805-1812* (University of California Press, 1961) is excellent in the way it unravels the diplomatic tangles preceding the war. In company with Henry Adams, *History of the United States during the Administrations of Jefferson and Madison* (9 vols.; Charles Scribner's Sons, 1889-91), Perkins indicates Madison was not an effective president. Both tend to overstate their case.

For the social scene in Madisonian Washington, the superb memoirs of Margaret B. Smith, *The First Forty Years of Washington Society*, ed. Gaillard Hunt (Charles Scribner's Sons, 1906) stand out, while Conover Hunt Jones, *Dolley and the Great Little Madison* (American Institute of Architects, 1977) is a work with many illustrations and much style. The social side is also emphasized in Virginia Moore, *The Madisons: A Biography* (McGraw-Hill, 1979), a loving, devoted portrait of the president and his wife—the very opposite of the "warts and all" school of biographical writing.

Specialists will find much attention paid to Madison in Drew R. McCoy, *The Elusive Republic: Political Economy in Jeffersonian America* (University of North Carolina Press, 1980) and Leonard D. White, *The Jeffersonians: A Study in Administrative History, 1801-1829* (Macmillan, 1951). Noteworthy articles in the *William and Mary Quarterly* and *Perspectives in American History* have appeared in recent years under the by-lines of Paul Bourke, Noble E. Cunningham, Jr., Charles F. Hobson, and J. C. A. Stagg. Finally, to read Madison's complete record it is necessary to look at the Gaillard Hunt edition of *The Writings of James Madison* (9 vols.; G. P. Putnam's Sons, 1900-1910) or, for more comprehensive coverage, *The Papers of James Madison* edited by William T. Hutchinson et al. (13 vols. to date; University of Chicago, University of Virginia, 1961-).

Little has been published on portraits of James Madison. Theodore Bolton's "The Life Portraits of James Madison," which appeared in the *William and Mary Quarterly* (January 1951), remains the most authoritative work to date. Ulysse Desportes' "Ceracchi's Medallion Portrait of James Madison," *Princeton University Library Quarterly* (Winter 1963), discusses one of these life portraits in greater depth. A number of portraits of Madison, his associates, and his family are reproduced in Conover Hunt Jones's *Dolley and the Great Little Madison* (AIA Foundation, 1977). Also included are original inventories and an analysis of the Madisons' art collection and personal tastes in the decorative arts. Martha Gandy Fales's "James Madison's Dining-room Prints, 1836," published in *Antiques* (August 1970), reproduces one such inventory. Changes Dolley Madison made in the presidential mansion are discussed in Margaret B. Klapthor's "Benjamin Latrobe and Dolley Madison Decorate the White House, 1809-1811," printed in the *United States National Museum Bulletin 241: Contributions from the Museum of History and Technology* (1965).

Portraits of Madison's many contemporaries are scattered throughout this country's major museums. Guides to pertinent collections include the National Portrait Gallery's *Permanent Collection Illustrated Checklist* (Smithsonian Institution Press, 1980), Donald Egbert's *Princeton Portraits* (Princeton University Press, 1947), New-York Historical Society's two-volume *Catalogue of American Portraits* (Yale University Press, 1974), and the National Gallery of Art's *American Paintings* (National Gallery of Art, 1980).

Albert Bush's classic study, *The Life Portraits of Thomas Jefferson* (University of Virginia Museum of Fine Arts, 1962), has been reprinted in *Jefferson and the Arts: An Extended View*, edited by William Howard Adams (National Gallery of Art, 1976). David Meschutt's "Gilbert Stuart's Portraits of Thomas Jefferson," which appeared in the *American Art Journal* (Winter 1981), offers new scholarly information on Jefferson portraits. William Howard Adams also edited the richly illustrated exhibition catalog *The Eye of Thomas Jefferson* (National Gallery of Art, 1976). Another exhibition, *The World of Franklin and Jefferson* (ARBA, 1976), more political in content, was sponsored by the American Revolution Bicentennial Administration. James Thomas Flexner's *The Face of Liberty* (Crown Publishers, 1975) includes major portraits of many of America's founders. Portraits of our first president may be found in Gustav Eisen's three-volume study, *Portraits of Washington* (R. Hamilton & Associates, 1932).

Among the excellent monographs describing the works of prominent artists illustrated in this publication are Theodore Sizer's *The Works of Colonel John Trumbull* (Yale University Press, 1950), Katharine McCook Knox's *The Sharples* (Yale University Press, 1930), Kenneth Lindsay's *The Works of John Vanderlyn* (Worldwide Books, Inc., 1970), Lawrence Park's four-volume *Gilbert Stuart* (W. E. Rudge, 1926), and Charles Coleman Sellers' *Portraits and Miniatures by Charles Willson Peale* (American Philosophical Society, 1952).

Brief biographies of many artists may be found in George C. Groce and David H. Wallace's *New-York Historical Society Dictionary of Artists in America, 1564-1860* (Yale

University Press, 1957). Mantle Fielding's *Dictionary of American Painters, Sculptors and Engravers* (reprint, James F. Carr, 1965) is also a useful reference.

A Cook's Tour of well-known engravings of the period has been compiled by the Smithsonian Institution in their *American Printmaking: The First 150 Years* (Smithsonian Institution Press, 1969) and the Free Library's *Made in America: Printmaking 1760-1860* (Free Library of Philadelphia, 1973). I. N. Phelps Stokes's *American Historical Prints* (New York Public Library, 1933) is an indispensible guide to the great collections of the New York Public Library.

The classic reference work on American printmakers remains David Stauffer's three-volume *American Engravers upon Copper and Steel* (Grolier Club, 1907).

Many contemporary magazines such as the *Columbian Magazine,* published in Philadelphia from 1787 to 1790, include engraved plates. Benjamin M. Lewis's *A Guide to Engravings in American Magazines 1741-1810* (New York Public Library, 1959) is a superb introduction to available materials. Sinclair Hamilton's two-volume *Early American Book Illustrators and Wood Engravers 1670-1870* (Princeton University Press, 1958) is based on the collections of the Princeton University Library.

For the best visual examples of political and social attitudes in the eighteenth and early nineteenth century, the reader should turn to the satirical print. M. D. George's multi-volume *Catalogue of Political and Personal Satires . . . in the British Museum* (Kegan Paul, 1883-1935) is a wonderful compendium of that vast collection. Colonial Williamsburg's smaller collection of English cartoons produced in the revolutionary era is illustrated and cataloged by Joan Dolmetsch in *Rebellion and Reconciliation* (University Press of Virginia, 1976).

Two exhibition catalogs, Ron Tyler's *The Image of America in Caricature and Cartoon* (Amon Carter Museum of Western Art, 1976) and Thomas Blaisdell and Peter Selz's *The American Presidency in Political Cartoons: 1776-1976* (University Art Museum, 1976), offer an excellent introduction to American satire. The interested reader may also want to consult Frank Weitenkampf's *Political Caricature in the United States* (New York Public Library, 1953) or his collaboration with Allan Nevins, *A Century of Political Cartoons* (Charles Scribner's Sons, 1944).

Donald Cresswell's *The American Revolution in Drawings and Prints* (Library of Congress, 1975) is a comprehensive survey of the graphics of that era. Similarly, an important effort by the Historical Society of Pennsylvania, the Library Company, and the American Philosophical Society produced *A Rising People* (HSP, LC, & APS, 1976), illustrating the founding of the United States, 1765-89.

The events of the War of 1812 fired the imagination of a number of American artists. One dedicated collector, Irving S. Olds, published *Bits and Pieces of American History* (Printed privately in New York, 1951) as a guide to his large collection, now in the New-York Historical Society. The Robinson Collection at the United States Naval Academy forms the basis for Roger B. Stein's *American Naval Prints* (International Exhibitions Foundation, 1976). Edgar Newbold Smith's *American Naval Broadsides* (Philadelphia Maritime Museum, 1974) is an equally attractive, informative source which may be supplemented by the Library of Congress's *An Album of American Battle Art 1775-1918* (U.S. Government Printing Office, 1947).

In recent years, a number of fine pictorial histories of American cities and states have been published. Among the best of these relating to James Madison are Lois B. McCauley's *Maryland Historical Prints: 1752-1889* (Maryland Historical Society, 1975), the Junior League of Washington's *An Illustrated History: the City of Washington* (Knopf, 1977), and Martin Snyder's Philadelphia, *City of Independence* (Praeger Publishers, 1975).

☆ U.S. GOVERNMENT PRINTING OFFICE: 1988 - 188 - 654

ce to m

As this advice, if it ever see the light w

as issuing from the tomb where truth alone c

It will be entitled therefore to whatever weig

-perience of one, who has served his country

espoused in his youth and adhered through his life to the cause of its liberty

-tions which will constitute ~~the~~ epochs of its d

The advice nearest to my heart

be cherished & perpetuated. Let ~~The~~ open enemy to it

-guised one, as the Serpent ~~& insinuating~~ creeping with his d